NINE IRISH LIVES

Written by Mark Bailey

Of All the Gin Joints
Hemingway & Bailey's Bartending Guide
to Great American Writers
American Hollow

BOOKS FOR CHILDREN
Tiny Pie

Edited by Mark Bailey
The Tibetans: A Struggle to Survive

NINE IRISH LIVES

The Thinkers, Fighters,
& Artists Who Helped
Build America

Edited by

MARK BAILEY

Illustrations by Edward Hemingway

ALGONQUIN BOOKS OF CHAPEL HILL 2018

Published by
Algonquin Books of Chapel Hill
Post Office Box 2225
Chapel Hill, North Carolina 27515-2225

a division of
Workman Publishing
225 Varick Street
New York, New York 10014

"Thousands Are Sailing" written by Philip Chevron / The Pogues.
Courtesy of Wardlaw Music.

A Cataloging-in-Publication record for this title is on file
with the Library of Congress.

ISBN 978-1-61620-517-1

10 9 8 7 6 5 4 3 2 1
First Edition

The island it is silent now,
But the ghosts still haunt the waves,
And the torch lights up a famished man,
Who fortune could not save.

Did you work upon the railroad,
Did you rid the streets of crime,
Were your dollars from the White House,
Were they from the five and dime?

Did the old songs taunt or cheer you,
And did they still make you cry,
Did you count the months and years,
Or did your teardrops quickly dry?

—"Thousands Are Sailing,"
by Philip Chevron, The Pogues

Contents

INTRODUCTION ix
by Mark Bailey

THE REVOLUTIONARY 1
Thomas Addis Emmet (1764–1827)
by Tom Hayden

THE CARETAKER 29
Margaret Haughery (1813–1882)
by Rosie O'Donnell

THE ORGANIZER 47
Mary "Mother" Jones (1837–1930)
by Terry Golway

THE SOLDIER 73
Albert D. J. Cashier (1843–1915)
by Jill McDonough

THE MUCKRAKER 99
Samuel S. McClure (1857–1949)
by Michael Moore

THE FATHER 121
Father Edward J. Flanagan (1886–1948)
by Mark K. Shriver

THE DIRECTOR 153
Rex Ingram (1893–1950)
by Pierce Brosnan

THE AUTHOR 181
Maeve Brennan (1917–1993)
by Kathleen Hill

THE PEACEMAKER 211
Niall O'Dowd (1953–)
by Mary Jordan and Kevin Sullivan

ACKNOWLEDGMENTS 241

BIBLIOGRAPHY 245

CONTRIBUTORS 255

Introduction

———◆———

BY MARK BAILEY

ABOUT THIRTY YEARS AGO, I came across a brief essay titled "Nine Famous Irishmen." I'd be hard pressed to say exactly where I found it; those were the days before Google, before the Internet really. But somehow, that essay reached the shores of my consciousness and then proceeded to quickly beat a path down to my heart—where it has remained. The essay reads as follows:

> In the Young Irish disorders, in Ireland in 1848, the following nine men were captured, tried, and convicted of treason against Her Majesty, the Queen, and were sentenced to death: John Mitchell, Morris Lyene, Pat Donahue, Thomas McGee, Charles Duffy, Thomas Meagher, Richard O'Gorman, Terrence McManus, Michael Ireland.
>
> Before passing sentence, the judge asked if there was anything that anyone wished to say. Meagher, speaking for all, said: "My lord, this is our first offense but not our last. If you will be easy with us this once, we promise, on our word as gentlemen, to try to do better next time. And next time—sure we won't be fools to get caught."
>
> Thereupon the indignant judge sentenced them all to be

hanged by the neck until dead and drawn and quartered. Passionate protest from all the world forced Queen Victoria to commute the sentence to transportation for life to far wild Australia.

In 1874, word reached the astounded Queen Victoria that the Sir Charles Duffy who had been elected Prime Minister of Australia was the same Charles Duffy who had been transported 25 years before. On the Queen's demand, the records of the rest of the transported men were revealed and this is what was uncovered:

THOMAS FRANCIS MEAGHER, Governor of Montana.

TERRENCE MCMANUS, Brigadier General, United States Army.

PATRICK DONAHUE, Brigadier General, United States Army.

RICHARD O'GORMAN, Governor General of Newfoundland.

MORRIS LYENE, Attorney General of Australia, in which office

MICHAEL IRELAND succeeded him.

THOMAS D'ARCY MCGEE, Member of Parliament, Montreal, Minister of Agriculture and President of Council Dominion of Canada.

JOHN MITCHELL, prominent New York politician. This man was the father of John Purroy Mitchell, Mayor of New York, at the outbreak of World War I.

To this day, the author of this essay remains unknown. As does its veracity. Is the story true? Most of it is, and some of it likely is not. Though to me that was never so important. "Nine Famous Irishmen" has persisted, a little nugget of Irish mythology, the very kind of historical gem found on posters, placemats, the backs of pub menus, a sheet of paper left in a drawer to be read over corned beef and cabbage around the dinner table on St. Patrick's Day.

So ignore the details; push whatever inaccuracies there might be aside. Stories like this persist not because they are necessarily true, but because they speak to a larger truth. And this truth we can probably all agree on: a large number of men, women, and children left Ireland, the country of their birth, and went out into the world to do great things. Whether it was political violence that drove them, whether it was hunger, oppression, or just the dream of a better life, off they went—first in ships, later in planes—into the unknown. This was the Irish Diaspora.

What I found meaningful, what I still find meaningful—why I carried this essay with me, a photocopy in a shoebox of letters carted around for three decades—is the idea that nine young men could have died quite brutal deaths, but instead, they left and went on to lead extraordinary lives, to achieve so much. All the energy, the brightness and daring, in those nine young men, it could so easily have been snuffed out. But that didn't happen. Instead that energy was released, sent out on a boat across the seas, where it would touch so many lives, light up a new world.

THERE IS NOTHING much any of us can do about the circumstances into which we are born—our parents, our class, our country—but these are the factors that by and large determine our lives, that most often shape who we are and what we are able accomplish. Yet since time immemorial, humans have struggled against this: whether they were forced to flee their homes or left of their own volition, they have chosen to believe in the possibility of a different life, a better future. Roughly fifty thousand years ago, our Afro-Asian ancestors built crude boats and headed across the waters to Australia. About fifteen thousand years ago, foragers in Northern Siberia made their way to Alaska pursuing better game, and then later, once the ice sheets had receded, pressed south further into North America. In a way, the journey of those nine famous Irishmen, along with the millions of other Irish immigrants, mirrors that movement, the movement of mankind itself—the perhaps uniquely human drive that has settled the planet and brought about civilization as we know it.

Certainly, no country in modern history has benefited from this drive more than the United States. Not just because we have been the recipients of so many Irish but because we have been (and still are) the recipients of so many other peoples too—immigrants from elsewhere fleeing hardship, fleeing pain and want. I was born here because my great grandparents, who were Jewish, put their belongings in a bag and boarded a ship. If maybe that sounds easy, it wasn't. Once here, they became storekeepers, seamstresses, traveling salesmen. My grandfather owned the Westville movie theater in New Haven, Connecticut; my grandmother was a schoolteacher; my other grandparents were lawyers in Knoxville, Tennessee. And I am now a part of that continuum, just as my children—whom I've moved out west to California—will be.

THIS BOOK EXISTS for a fairly simple reason. I wanted to share the stories of nine Irish lives. Not the famous Irishmen from the essay above, but nine other men and women who left Ireland and came to America. Spanning generations, from the dawn of our republic to today, their lives paint a particular portrait of our nation's rise. Through the battles they fought, the cases they argued, the words they wrote, the people they helped, these nine Irish men and women not only became American but also helped make America great.

The essays that follow were written by nine contemporary Irish Americans—journalists, actors, poets, politicians, novelists—themselves all links in the chain connecting past to present. Tom Hayden, activist, politician, and icon of the sixties cultural revolution, writes about his namesake, Thomas Addis Emmet, famed revolutionary leader of the 1798 Irish Rebellion. Rosie O'Donnell, mother of five adopted children, chose Margaret Haughery, the Mother of Orphans, who in antebellum New Orleans built four orphanages. Political journalist and historian Terry Golway profiles the labor firebrand Mary "Mother" Jones. Poet and LGBT rights advocate Jill McDonough chronicles the life of transgender Civil War soldier Albert Cashier; celebrated documentary filmmaker Michael Moore looks at celebrated news journalist Samuel S. McClure, founder of *McClure's Magazine*; and Mark Shriver, nonprofit executive for Save the Children, writes about Father Edward Flanagan of Boys Town. Renowned Irish-born actor Pierce Brosnan explores the famed silent-era director Rex Ingram, novelist Kathleen Hill examines short story and *New Yorker* writer Maeve Brennan, and Pulitzer Prize–winning journalists Mary Jordan and Kevin Sullivan write about Niall O'Dowd, journalist and legendary founder of the *Irish Voice* newspaper. It is a wide variety of writers whose voices are as rich and diverse as their subjects.

IN JANUARY 1892, a young woman named Annie Moore arrived in New York City. Irish, she had been born in what was then called Queenstown (now Cobh) in County Cork. She was the first immigrant to pass through Ellis Island. By then, many others—not just Irish, but Chinese, Italian, German, Polish—had already made their way to our shores. Over the next 125 years, many millions more would come. Just as today, Mexicans, Koreans, Syrians turn their eyes toward our country. And if the past is prologue, if this book serves as any evidence, we will be lucky to have them, blessed. This is, after all, the story of how our nation was built—and how it continues to evolve.

Thomas Addis Emmet (1764–1827)

BY TOM HAYDEN

IT WAS A BLEAK MOMENT for Thomas Addis Emmet.

The year was 1803 and the thirty-nine-year-old Irish exile had just served a four-year prison sentence for his political activity. He was released only on the condition that he never return to his native Ireland—the nation for which he and fellow members of the United Irishmen had planned a rebellion against British rule. Emmet, living in France, learned that his brother Robert and another band of rebels had once more taken up arms for Ireland, and that, again, the rebels were unsuccessful. Now, young Robert languished in a Dublin prison facing the executioner.

Thomas knew all too well the fate facing an Irishman who dared to challenge the Crown. In the wake of the 1798 rebellion, many of Ireland's brightest, most ambitious young men were killed—either on the battlefield or after swift legal proceedings. In this sense, Thomas had been one of the lucky ones. He had been arrested prior to the actual armed insurrection. He could never return home, but at least he was alive.

For some time Thomas had hoped to immigrate to America and perhaps put the events of 1798 behind him. America could provide him and his extended family with a fresh start. To Thomas's dismay, however, British officials persuaded anti-Irish elements in the U.S. government to block any emigration efforts on the Emmets' behalf. And so, Thomas and his parents had to watch as another family member was hauled off to prison, another victim of the intractable Anglo-Irish conflict.

On the night before his execution, Robert penned an emotional letter to his older brother.

> Dear Thomas. . . . I am just going to do my last duty to my country. It can be done as well on the scaffold as on the field. God bless you and the young hopes that are growing up about you. May they be more fortunate than their uncle; but may they preserve as pure an attachment to their country as he has done.

Thomas Addis Emmet never received this letter. British authorities confiscated it, scouring the words for intelligence as part of their centuries-old effort to suppress the forces of Irish liberation.

I ONCE ASKED my mother, just as my curiosity about my Irish heritage was peaking, why I was named Thomas Emmet Hayden "the fourth." Who were the other three that had come before me, and had the name originally been derived from Thomas Addis Emmet, when he was still a living legend? With a finger over her lips, as if to hide a family secret, the former Genevieve Garity said with a slight smile that it was because there was "the first, the second, and the third." My mother was a practicing Catholic assimilated into the suburbs of Michigan and Wisconsin and had no knowledge of who these other Thomas Emmets might have been. What she did know was the Irish tradition of passing the name Emmet down through the generations—she just did not know why. She had no knowledge of the actual Emmet brothers, the men whose exploits we Irish were so intent on honoring. I myself grew up an assimilated child of the Detroit suburbs who knew nothing about my Irish heritage. And then the sixties arrived—a decade that brought tumultuous civil rights movements not only in the United States but in Northern Ireland as well. It would be this upending of the established world view that plunged me into years of inquiry into my roots—and into my namesake.

Thomas Addis Emmet was a central nationalist figure between 1796 and 1803, a time of three attempted uprisings in Ireland. He would eventually immigrate to America and continue to advocate for Irish rights, becoming the "most respected Irish American of his generation," in the words of historian David Wilson

Just how much of this revolutionary legacy had I inherited? I do know that a Peter Hayden (in Irish, O Headon, O Eideain) of County Wicklow was "elected captain of the insurgents," only to be massacred along with thirty-five other United Irish prisoners during the failed uprising of 1798. Was he a distant blood relative? Unfortunately, meticulous as Irish researchers are, many family histories are incomplete, offering more questions than answers, stymied by the generations who died in famines or of typhoid fever, resting in mass graves covered in lime and mystery. Still, in my relationship to Thomas Addis Emmet, I tend to be less literal. I think this illustrates what the African scholar Clyde Forde was referring to when he wrote, "As long as the name of a departed ancestor can be called, that ancestor is not dead in some final sense of the word."

There are invisible ancestral influences we each inherit. And in my case, it was a powerful desire to question and challenge the status quo.

BY THE FINAL days of the sixties, my personal identity was in shambles. The Freedom Rides, the civil rights movement, and the Chicano Moratorium had me questioning my white racial identity; the women's liberation movement upended my male identity; the overall cascade of liberation movements left many of us wondering who we were, as individuals and as Americans. In short, as a certain Nobel laureate once put it, the times most definitely were a-changin'.

One of the deepest, most unexpected changes for me, at the time, was the uncovering of my Irish roots. After their assassinations, John and Robert Kennedy, who had previously symbolized the Irish dream of successful assimilation into the melting pot, now represented sudden martyrdom. Civil rights activists in Northern Ireland were marching from Belfast to Derry, singing "We Shall Overcome." Exhausted by a decade of imprisonment, beatings, tear-gassings, and fighting conscription for the war in Vietnam, I asked myself two simple questions: First, why had these Irish civil rights activists come to embrace an American anthem in their faraway struggle? And second, if they knew so much about us, why did I, as an Irish American, know so little about them? How had knowledge of them been excised so completely from my identity? True, there were millions of conscious Irish Americans, like the Kennedys themselves, who grew up knowing centuries of Irish history. But over time, as Jimmy Breslin wrote, "the blood lines were thinning." The past was being lost.

In the end, the sixties made me Irish—"Irish on the inside," as I titled my 2001 book. I sat on the sunny beaches of Venice, California, reading everything from Wolfe Tone and James Joyce to Republican histories of "the Troubles," a euphemism for the war that had inflamed the island. I listened to Irish ballads, drank at LA's Irish pubs, and eventually visited Dublin and Belfast in 1972. It was there I identified with the Irish cause then reemerging, at least partly inspired by the bubbling cauldron of the American protest movements of the time.

By 1992, when Bill Clinton allowed Sinn Féin leader Gerry Adams to enter the United States, I had already made twenty trips to Ireland as a witness to what became the historic Irish peace process. At one point, I was detained at the airport because of my involvement in the antiwar movement at home. The Irish attorney general even ordered me to be extradited. However, thanks to Senator Edward Kennedy, as well as New York City Council President Paul O'Dwyer and many others, that did not happen.

For a time, I was a counselor to assistant secretary for International Economic Policy Charles "Chuck" Meissner, who died in a tragic plane crash in the midst of frenzied diplomacy. I met with President Clinton and First Lady Hillary Clinton, the former U.S. senator and master peace negotiator George Mitchell, and Northern Ireland's secretary of state Marjorie "Mo" Mowlam. I sat down with Irish Republican leaders as well as Loyalist paramilitaries as they both made the risky transition from war to peace. All the while, I kept trying to untangle the history of the island itself, a place that had suffered centuries of brutal military occupations, land seizures, religious persecution, and violent sectarian divisions.

One thing was clear—the past was always present, and it always would be.

GIVEN THE LONG shadow cast by Irish history, I could easily begin Thomas Addis Emmet's story a thousand years ago. But I will begin in 1760, when Thomas's father, Robert, married the former Elizabeth Mason, from Cork. He had pursued a career in medicine and become one of Ireland's top doctors, running a facility for those who were then called "the insane." Dr. Emmet was eventually appointed Ireland's state physician, a position for which he had had to be approved by the Irish prime minister. Their first child, Christopher Temple, was born in 1761. Two years later, on April 24, 1763, Thomas was born.

An Irish revolutionary dynasty had arrived.

The Emmets were affluent, respectable Protestants. But they also knew hardship and heartache. "Eight more pregnancies followed over the next nine years, but none of the children survived," writes Trinity College Dublin professor Dr. Patrick M. Geoghegan, also the biographer of Thomas's younger brother Robert who was born in March 1778.

By this time, the Emmet family had moved to Dublin's Molesworth Street, near St. Stephen's Green.

And the world was changing rapidly.

The American colonies had declared their independence from

Britain in 1776. And though it would take seven more years before the Treaty of Paris officially established the United States of America, this revolt against British authority shed a particularly disturbing light on British rule in Ireland. Meanwhile, social and economic unrest in France erupted in July of 1789 with the storming of the Bastille and the subsequent French Revolution.

Though he held a government position, Dr. Robert Emmet sympathized with the American revolutionaries, as well as the Irish nationalists. Both were regular topics of discussion in the Emmet household. Indeed, Thomas would inherit many of his father's principles, with his brother-in-law Robert Holmes once commenting: "Those who came into contact with [Thomas] felt the presence of a man of . . . fixed, well considered opinions." True, Ireland did have its own parliament, but it mostly deferred to the British Parliament in London. And at the time, Catholics, as well as numerous non-Anglican Protestant denominations, were excluded from all of Ireland's political activity, including voting. The American colonists' war with Britain, challenging and preoccupying the empire, was seen as an opportunity by those seeking independence for Ireland. By the late 1770s, bands of militias—often with varying political agendas—took up arms: some to protest cruel landlords and high rents, others to defend Ireland from a possible French invasion, still others calling for greater Irish political power if not outright rebellion.

However, some nationalist reformers hoped to work with ballots rather than bullets. Henry Grattan was most prominent among them. A veteran of the Irish Volunteers movement, Grattan led the call for Catholic emancipation and the repeal of Poynings' Law, which subjugated Ireland's Parliament to London. "What was the case of Ireland, enslaved for a century, and withered and blasted with her Protestant ascendancy, like a shattered oak scathed on its hill by the fires of its own intolerance?" Grattan once proclaimed. "What lost England America, but such a policy, an attempt to bind men by a parliament wherein they are not represented, such an attempt as some would now continue to practice on the Catholics?"

Grattan and the forces of reform did win major concessions in 1782, though Catholics still could not vote, much less sit in Parliament. Still, it was a valuable lesson in protest and agitation for nationalist Irish reformers such as Thomas Addis Emmet.

DURING THE GRATTAN era, Thomas was finishing up his years as a student at Trinity College Dublin, where he was known for his sense of humor and sharp debating skills, not to mention a love of music. "I think those very lucky who can get through [life's] troubles by dancing and singing," he once said. After graduating in 1783, he moved to Edinburgh to follow in his father's footsteps and study medicine. Dr. Emmet, for his part, was proud of Thomas, as well as his eldest son, Christopher, known by his middle name, Temple. In the spring of 1785, Dr. Emmet noted that "few parents can look with the contented pride and satisfaction which I do on both my grown-up sons." His brother-in-law added that young Thomas "would not have committed a dishonourable act though secure of everlasting concealment."

Then tragedy struck. Temple, a dazzling student who seemed destined for great things, died after a short illness. The death would cast a long shadow over the entire family and, says Trinity College Dublin professor Dr. Patrick M. Geoghegan, "altered the destiny of Thomas Addis forever." First and foremost, Thomas abandoned medicine and gravitated toward Temple's field—law. Politics followed soon enough, as Thomas watched the revolutionary changes of the late eighteenth century sweep across the globe. One question haunted him: Would such a revolution ever reach Ireland's shores?

IN 1790, THOMAS joined a club dedicated to nationalist aims whose membership included a Dublin native by the name of Theobald Wolfe Tone, who would become one of Ireland's most revered revolutionaries. Tone later called Emmet "a man . . . completely after my own heart; of a great and comprehensive mind; of the warmest and sincerest affection for his friends; and of a firm and steady adherence to his principles, to which he has sacrificed much, as I know, and would, I am sure, if necessary, sacrifice his life."

In the wake of revolutionary movements in America and Europe, Thomas Paine published *Rights of Man* in 1791 to an immediate explosion of public interest, especially in Ireland. Paine's pamphlet "Common Sense" had already helped spark the American Revolution, and in 1787's "Prospects on the Rubicon," he'd written of "his suspicion that England governs Ireland for the purpose of keeping her low to prevent her from becoming her rival in trade and manufacturing." By some estimates, *Rights of Man* sold more than twice as many copies in Ireland as it did in England.

On Bastille Day in Dublin in 1791, public celebrations of Paine provoked a military response from outraged British authorities. That same year, the year Emmet would be admitted to the Dublin bar, Tone, though himself a Protestant, published a provocative essay titled "Argument on Behalf of the Catholics of Ireland." After directly acknowledging Paine's influence, Tone wrote, "If the odious distinction between Protestant, and Presbyterian, and Catholic were abolished, and the three great sects blended together, under the common and sacred title of Irishman, what interest could a Catholic member of Parliament have, distinct from his Protestant brother sitting on the same bench?"

It was in this revolutionary atmosphere that the Society of United Irishmen was born. Designed initially as a debating society of sorts, the United Irishmen had a strong presence in both Belfast and Dublin, and sought to bridge Ireland's numerous religious traditions. This was, of course, a daunting task—just as it was when many Americans of my generation were asked to reassess their racial identity in the face of the brutality that led to the civil rights movement. Some white Americans were willing to join a multiracial coalition in the name of social justice. Too many, though, were instead looking to exploit—rather than soothe—racial fears.

THOMAS JOINED THE United Irishmen in 1792, the same year he defended prominent Irish nationalist James Napper Tandy, the first of several treason cases Emmet took up during the 1790s. During the Tandy trial, Emmet sought not only to prove Tandy's innocence but also to undermine the concept of British rule in Ireland.

Thomas's increasing public radicalism was a boon to the nationalist movement, though some thought it was excessive. Henry Grattan, for one, commented that Thomas was a "very clever man" with a "powerful and logical mind, great talent and spirit." But he believed Emmet was drifting into dangerously radical territory.

The British authorities apparently agreed. In 1794, Thomas met with a former schoolmate of his late brother Temple's. The man was serving as an intermediary for the British government. Thomas was given an offer: abandon the United Irishmen and leave behind the rebel's life of persecution and hardship, and in exchange he would be guaranteed lucrative employment in his field, the law.

This must have been tempting. In many ways, Thomas had begun to build for himself a respectable middle-class life. Just three years earlier, he had married the former Jane Patten. They would go on to have ten children together. And as firm as his beliefs may have been, Thomas had already seen up close the price Irish nationalists were paying.

It must have been a tough decision. After all, isn't this a question all reformers must face, however dedicated? My own upbringing could certainly be characterized as at least modestly comfortable. That could make it difficult to do the necessary work of identifying with society's underdogs and demanding an end to oppression. When I was drafting *The Port Huron Statement* for Students for a Democratic Society, a central theme was the complacency that can manifest itself in a society where material comfort coexists alongside terrible injustice. The statement's very first line reads, "We are people of this generation bred in at least modest comfort, housed now in universities, looking uncomfortably to the world we inherit."

For all of his respectability, Thomas also looked with great discomfort on the world he and his children were inheriting, and in the end, he could not forsake his principles. "You said this was the crisis of my life," he wrote in response to the British offer. "I believe you said truly and therefore it is the moment in which I thought to adhere most directly to those principles of honor and morality which I have been taught to consider unerring guides. I believe this is the crisis of my life. God grant [that] I may have decided prudently. I feel I have decided honestly."

He had crossed a threshold. Within two years, blood, indeed, would be shed.

THE QUESTION INEVITABLY arises: Why did Thomas Addis Emmet commit himself so thoroughly to the cause of Irish freedom? What brought him out of his world of comfort? After all, as an Emmet family biographer, R. R. Madden, put it, "The charge of recklessness or unscrupulousness of conduct never has been brought against Emmet. . . . Under what circumstances or impelled by what motive, did such a person become a rebel?"

It was fairly simple, according to Madden: English treatment of the Irish, for so long, was simply too unjust to ignore.

Although the British had been gradually granting Catholics more rights through legislation such as the Catholic Relief Act of 1793, this was still a time of bitter religious division in general and virulent anti-Catholicism in particular. In September 1795 in Armagh, for example, a group of young Protestants known as the Peep o' Day Boys murdered dozens of Catholics who belonged to a faction known as the Defenders, a resistance group Napper Tandy and other Protestant nationalists sought to build alliances with. (The Peep o' Day Boys later evolved into the notorious Orange Order, an incendiary Protestant organization that began holding annual parades commemorating the 1690 defeat of Catholic King James II at the Battle of the Boyne—a provocative procession that still fans flames of hatred in Northern Ireland to this day.)

The United Irish viewpoint, it should be stressed, went beyond mere sectarian Catholic nationalism. Wolfe Tone and Emmet were Republican to the core, and the movement they were part of ultimately represented a populist outpouring of rage against centuries of injustice.

If the forces of revolution in America and Ireland had already been released, the forces of reaction were also already coalescing. In 1795, British authorities passed the Treasonable Practices Act as well as the Seditious Meetings Act. These were designed to clamp down on revolutionary activity in the British kingdom. Punishments for such activity not only included beheading but also required that the executioner raise the severed skull and pronounce, "This is the head of a traitor." Similarly, in the United States, Thomas Jefferson's political opponents, the Federalists, were not above exploiting fears of Irish revolutionary activity, not to mention old fashioned nativism and anti-Catholicism.

Within eighteen months, from December 1796 to the fateful summer of 1798, the United Irishmen would indeed put a scare into plenty of people on both sides of the Atlantic. Tone would be dead. And Thomas Addis Emmet would be in prison.

THEY KNEW THE weather might be bad. But they took a chance anyway.

In 1796, United Irish leaders decided a full-scale invasion of Ireland—with French support—would once and for all overthrow the British. In an effort to surprise the British, the invasion was to take place not in the summer, when the weather would be most favorable, but instead in December. A fleet of ships sailed from France, in the hopes that once the invasion of Ireland was underway, the British would be stunned. Thousands of Irish troops, rallied by the United Irishmen, would then rise up and overwhelm the colonial power.

Bantry Bay, Cork, was the designated landing spot. The mission, however, was doomed from the start. Many of the French ships got lost in the poor weather, while others, including the *Indomptable*—with Wolfe Tone aboard—were unable to land for days. Some of the vessels eventually headed back to France.

"England has had its luckiest escape since the Armada," Tone is said to have remarked.

The British were determined never to be caught off guard again. They proceeded to clamp down on all suspected revolutionary activity in Ireland. Members of the United Irishmen were driven underground as the British also set about establishing a network of spies and informers. In March 1798, British authorities received word of a United Irishmen meeting at the Dublin home of Oliver Bond. Over a dozen suspected rebels were arrested at the meeting, though not Thomas, who by then had been dubbed "the most dangerous man in Ireland" by one Crown informer.

Instead he was arrested the following morning. Brought before a committee at the House of Commons, he was asked directly, "Were you a United Irishman?"

Thomas's answer was also direct.

"I am one."

According to the Emmet family memoirs, Thomas initially endured terrible conditions in prison:

> He was confined for six weeks in total darkness, but in a fairly dry cell under the prison. The cell was about seven feet in length, with the walls within reach on each side, and the only ventilation was from a loop-hole above the door. He was

allowed no bed-clothing and lay on a stone shelf raised but a few inches from the floor. He had no change of underclothing during that time, and was deprived of every means of cleanliness, even of the facility for washing his hands and face. He was kept on bread and water, often insufficient in quantity to satisfy either his hunger or thirst. The bread was of the worst quality and the water always offensive both in taste and smell.

Even though the United Irish leadership was weakened significantly by this wave of arrests, Tone and others still wanted to move ahead with an uprising planned for 1798. Thomas would simply have to monitor events while imprisoned by the British.

REVOLUTIONS HAPPEN FOR three general reasons: first, a longstanding moral insult to dignity; second, a concrete material grievance that affects many people directly; and third, the rising of popular movements with visions of their own. With none of these issues having been addressed adequately by Great Britain, another Irish uprising was perhaps inevitable. The fighting began in late May 1798, mainly around Dublin. But rebel plans to seize the city were quickly dashed, and it seemed the rebels were drifting toward another swift defeat. Then on May 29 came a decisive rebel victory in Oulart, Wexford, with the locals passionately rallying alongside the rebels. The nationalist rebel forces were now fifteen thousand strong and next took Wexford town. This would turn out to be a high point of the 1798 rebellion. In the end, the rebels—poorly trained, with inferior weapons—faced too great a task. As many as thirty thousand of them lost their lives in the 1798 uprising, while those who were captured faced severe punishment clearly designed to exterminate once and for all the United Irish "threat."

Father John Murphy, a popular nationalist priest who fought in Wexford, was beaten, whipped, and then hanged before his lifeless body was decapitated and burned. To ensure that a clear message had been sent to the other rebels, Murphy's head was then impaled on a spike for all to see.

Wolfe Tone, meanwhile, was captured at sea coming from France. He might have been able to turn around and escape, but he refused. Instead he was taken to Dublin where he faced hanging.

In a letter from his Scottish jail cell, Thomas expressed concern for his friend and compatriot. "It is impossible for anyone to be more concerned or more anxious than we all are about the fate of Tone," he wrote to fellow United Irishman Thomas Russell. "There is not a thing that would appear to us to have any chance of saving his life that we would not gladly do."

Tone was put on trial November 10, 1798, and was unrepentant. "I have attempted to establish the independence of my country; I have failed in the attempt; my life is in consequence forfeited and I submit; the Court will do their duty and I shall endeavour to do mine."

Rather than be executed by the Crown in the gruesome manner dictated by the Treasonable Practices Act, Tone took his own life with a razor, saying on his deathbed a week later, "What should I wish to live for?"

In his 1966 poem "Requiem for the Croppies," Seamus Heaney wrote of what the rebels of 1798 had managed to accomplish, even in defeat. Seeds of liberation had been planted.

Until . . . on Vinegar Hill . . . the final conclave.
Terraced thousands died, shaking scythes at cannon.
The hillside blushed, soaked in our broken wave.

They buried us without shroud or coffin
And in August . . . the barley grew up out of our grave.

THE 1798 UPRISING in Ireland had consequences in the
United States as well.

Fear of Irish Catholics and other immigrants ran high in the
young nation during and immediately after the crisis in Ireland.
The Irish alliance with the French unnerved many in the dominant U.S. Federalist Party, whose membership included Washington, Adams, and even Alexander Hamilton. (Hamilton has come
to be associated with striving immigrants, thanks to Lin-Manuel
Miranda's Broadway hit, but Hamilton actually belonged to a political faction that feared immigrant influence.) One-time vice presi-
dential candidate Rufus King spoke for many Federalists when
he voiced his objection to settling United Irish exiles in America,
boasting that he had earned the "cordial and distinguished hatred"
of the United Irishmen —words that would rile the likes of Thomas
Addis Emmet, and later come back to haunt King.

These anti-immigrant sentiments produced the deeply sectarian, Federalist-sponsored Alien and Sedition Acts—not unlike this
century's Patriot Act and other anti-immigration laws—targeting
foreign-born "aliens" as well as political expression. The Natural-
ization Act of 1798, for example, extended the amount of time required to become a U.S. citizen from five to fourteen years. This
made it harder for immigrants to vote. The Alien Friend and (the
separate) Alien Enemies Acts made it easier for U.S authorities to
deport immigrants who could be deemed dangerous to the security of the United States, without the right of trial or appeal. Finally,
the Sedition Act called for imprisoning those seen as critics of the

federal government. One of the first public figures prosecuted under these laws, in 1800, was an Irish immigrant, Vermont congressman Matthew Lyon.

In this climate, Thomas's own future looked bleak. And so he
languished in a Scottish prison. He was able to visit with other Irish
prisoners, and his wife, Jane, relocated to a house nearby and even
became pregnant during these years. She gave birth to a daughter,
Jane Erin, in April 1802. Escape, however, seemed impossible. The
best Thomas could hope for, upon his eventual release, was a fresh
start in America, but even this hope was a complicated one. His
mother, still mourning her older son's death, was unsettled to hear
that Thomas was pondering a move to America. She feared she
might never see her son again, writing, "Between you and us there
will be a gulf over which we cannot pass."

Upon Thomas's 1802 release, with the condition that he not return to Ireland, he first went to Europe, in the summer, and was
joined there briefly by his brother Robert. Robert Emmet had not
given up on hopes for a successful Irish rebellion and had even been
meeting with Napoleon about yet another French invasion of Ireland. Thomas spoke to his younger brother about moving to the
United States, a desire he'd harbored since 1798, when U.S. and British officials had conspired to keep the Emmet family out of America.

Robert, though, seemed to feel something like destiny calling
him back to Ireland. "When I came to Ireland, I found the business ripe for execution," is how Robert put it later, describing his
willingness to participate in the 1803 rebellion. "I was asked to join
in it. I took time to consider and after mature deliberation I became
one of the provisional [United Irishmen] government."

The year 1802 ended on another sad note for the Emmet family.

December brought with it the death of Dr. Robert Emmet, the family patriarch, whose nationalist sympathies had so influenced his sons' thoughts and actions. Dr. Emmet was buried in St. Peter's churchyard on Aungier Street. He did not live to see the next attempt to liberate Ireland or the central role his son Robert played in that uprising—or the price Robert paid.

THE IRISH PROCLAMATION of Independence distributed just before the 1803 uprising was explicitly modeled on the American Declaration of Independence.

"You are now called on to show the world that you are competent to take your place among nations, that you have a right to claim their cognisance of you as an independent country, by the only satisfactory proof you can furnish of your capability of maintaining your independence by your wresting it from England with your hands," the proclamation reads. "[This] solemn declaration we now make. We war not against property. We war against no religious belief. . . . We war against English dominion. . . . If we are to fall, we will fall where we fight for our country."

In the end the proclamation "was nothing less than a complete programme for administering the country during and immediately after the rebellion. . . . And it had Robert Emmet's imprint all over it," Dr. Patrick M. Geoghegan has written.

Irish rebels attempted to seize control of Dublin Castle and other strategic symbols of British rule on July 23, 1803. The British were initially caught off guard, but a subsequent uprising in Wicklow failed to materialize, and then rumors—possibly started by the British or by Irish double agents—spread that the uprising was actually postponed. Robert fled to the mountains of Wicklow, where he was arrested in late August. He was brought to Dublin Castle, then Kilmainham prison, and charged with treason.

Executions of the rebels began on September 1. Before he was sentenced to death, Robert Emmet delivered a rousing speech that would go on to become a rallying cry for later generations of Irish rebels: "Let no man write my epitaph; for as no man who knows my motives dare now vindicate them, let not prejudice or ignorance, asperse them. Let them and me rest in obscurity and peace, and my tomb remain uninscribed, and my memory in oblivion, until other times and other men can do justice to my character. When my country takes her place among the nations of the earth, then and not till then, let my epitaph be written."

Here, then, is one description of Robert Emmet's subsequent execution, in language not unlike that which we hear coming out of the Middle East today.

> The punishment for treason was very specific. Emmet's body was taken down and placed on a table by the scaffold. The Executioner then removed a sharp blade from his tunic and cut the head from the corpse. Grabbing the head in his hand he carried it to the front of the Gallows and proclaimed in a loud voice: "This is the head of a traitor Robert Emmet." Emmet's blood seeped down from the table and ran onto the pavement. Some women came forward to dip their handkerchiefs in it and take them away as souvenirs. The Executioner's voice continued: "This is the head of a traitor Robert Emmet. This is the head of a traitor."

Elizabeth Emmet died later the same month. By 1804, then, Thomas had lost both of his parents as well as two brothers. Just as subsequent generations of Irish immigrants would, Thomas saw America as a place to start anew, and he set sail from Europe that very year, writing to a friend, "I wish most earnestly and anxiously to embrace you all again, but it must be on American ground; and if you wish to see me, come there."

IF REVOLUTION HAD been a primary motivation for Thomas when he was in Ireland, it seemed something shifted during his years in America. There, in this new nation based upon Republican principles, the nuts and bolts of politics, lawmaking, and building coalitions became increasingly central to his activism. He never lost his zeal for ending injustice and oppression, but more and more he did so from within the system. It was, in fact, men like Thomas who served as a clear and inspiring role model to me when I decided in the mid-1970s, after years of activism from the outside, to enter electoral politics.

Thomas had sailed for America with four of his children—the eldest, Robert, and three daughters, Margaret, Elizabeth, and Jane. Three younger sons remained in Dublin for several months before joining the rest of the family in March 1805. As soon as he arrived in America, Thomas had an opportunity to make a statement about racial equality, an issue that would eventually tear America apart.

Joseph McCormick, with whom Thomas had been imprisoned in Fort George, Scotland, tried to sell his friend on the benefits of living in the American south. But Thomas replied, "You know the insuperable objection I have always had to settling where I could not dispense with the use of slaves and that the more they abound, the stronger are my objections."

Indeed, once in America, not only did Thomas become a

prominent defender against the rise of anti-Catholic bigotry, but one of his first legal cases in the United States was the defense of a fugitive African American slave in New York. "Some supposed of the Irish what has been asserted of the Negro race, that the Irish were an inferior, semi-brutal people incapable of managing the affairs of their country," he once noted.

When Thomas arrived in New York, there was already a fledgling Irish American political network (albeit Protestant dominated) centered around the Clinton family. Charles Clinton came to the United States from Longford, serving as a colonel in the French and Indian War. His son George served as governor of New York and as Thomas Jefferson's vice president. His nephew DeWitt Clinton was mayor of New York City, where it so happened there was an opening at the bar, following the recent death of Alexander Hamilton at the hands of Aaron Burr. Controversy quickly ensued, however, when objections were raised about an "unnaturalized" citizen such as Thomas practicing law. This is more than a bit ironic, since Hamilton himself was an immigrant. But Thomas and his Irish American allies weathered the storm—and thus began his career in America, building up and channeling the growing political clout of the Irish American community.

Although the fury of the Alien and Sedition Acts had abated, it was still a toxic time for Irish Catholics and other immigrants. The city's first Catholic Church had been established fewer than two decades earlier in 1785. This was a time when people such as U.S. Congressman Harrison Gray Otis could openly worry over "hordes of wild Irishmen [and] the turbulent and disorderly of all parts of the world coming here with a view to disturb our tranquility."

Thomas himself "was viewed by the opponents of Mr. Jefferson's administration as a fugitive jacobin," according to a chronicle of his life written by Charles Glidden Haines. But he toiled mightily on behalf of New York's ethnic and religious minorities, a project that would eventually bear fruit as Irish Catholics in New York slowly but surely attained a political voice.

IN 1807 THOMAS at last had the opportunity to test the growing strength of the Irish American community, and get some political revenge as well. None other than Rufus King—who had once boasted of the hatred he'd earned among the Irish community— ran for governor of New York. This was the same Rufus King who'd blocked efforts by Thomas and his family to emigrate following Thomas's arrest in Ireland in 1798.

Thomas vigorously organized the Irish community and other elements of Jefferson's new coalition to defeat King, who blithely claimed that he was content to let the public decide between "me and these foreigners." Thomas wrote openly about King's role in blocking his family's emigration— which might very well have saved Robert Emmet's life. "The misfortunes which you brought upon the objects of your persecution are incalculable. . . . I should have brought along with me [to America] my father and his family, including a brother, whose name perhaps even you will not read without emotions of sympathy and respect," said Emmet. Indeed, as Robert Emmet's biographer contends, "If the entire Emmet family had emigrated to the United States in 1798, the history of Ireland would have been very different."

The story struck a chord with the public, and King lost the governor's race. But the past was still a source of great pain for Thomas. He confessed to a friend, Peter Burrowes, that he could not "bear to tread on Irish ground" and walk over "the graves of my nearest relatives and dearest friends." At another point he lamented that "there is not now in Ireland an individual that bears the name of Emmet"—though he would add prophetically that the family name would "perhaps be remembered in its history." In that he was right, both in history and in the given names of so many children of the diaspora, myself included.

Thomas went on to found a law firm, which to this day still practices under the name Emmet, Marvin & Martin. One contemporary witness described him in court as "a rollicking middle-aged Irish squire." He "had roguish Hibernian eyes, a very florid complexion, was of sound physical make. . . . and he used a musical, expressive and variable voice, pleasantly tinctured with a winning Corkonian brogue. He was persuasive and convincing, rather than strictly eloquent, but eminently graceful in gesture and pose." In 1809, Emmet served as executor of his much-admired old friend Thomas Paine's will. In 1812, he was appointed attorney general of New York State, though he only held the office for a year.

Thomas committed himself to the country he had adopted. He lamented the seemingly intractable divisions between Protestants, Catholics, and dissenters in Ireland, but affairs there eventually receded for him. As one friend, Samuel Mitchill, put it, Thomas "placed his pen in the inkhorn and never marked paper with it again on that subject."

As a lawyer, he proved he could be a man of government while remaining very much of a man of the people as well. He argued cases before the Supreme Court, commanding the attention of that august body, but in 1824, he also got involved in a legal clash between New York Irish Protestants and Catholics. On July 12, bands of Protestant Orangemen had marched through a heavily Catholic enclave in Greenwich Village, shouting and singing anti-Catholic songs such as "Croppies Lie Down."

The Orangemen "succeeded so well" in enraging the Catholics "that they received a most humiliating thrashing," Thomas noted. When it came time to sentence the Irish Catholic laborers, the judge seemed ready to rule in favor of the Orangemen, "not supposing apparently that there could be another side [and] was about to pass sentence." Even though he himself had long given up the bullet for the ballot, once he'd heard about the state of agitation to which the Catholic men had been pushed, Thomas spoke out in court "of the disgraceful state of intolerance which then existed in the city, and of the great injustice suffered in consequence." The presiding judge, "on hearing how matters stood, forthwith discharged the prisoners without even a reprimand being deemed necessary."

ACCORDING TO ONE biographical sketch, on November 12, 1827, Thomas "entered a New York court-room apparently in full health and spirits, to conduct a trial." He was suddenly struck ill and died the next day. He was sixty-three years old.

Thomas was buried at St. Mark's on the Bowery, and the city's Irish American community raised money to erect an impressive monument to his memory. But there is another monument to Emmet's memory that must be mentioned. Just two years after his death—following the 1820s campaign for Catholic emancipation led by Daniel O'Connell—the British Parliament, fearing another Catholic revolt, passed the Roman Catholic Relief Act in 1829, paving the way for full Catholic political participation in Irish life. It was a towering and momentous achievement and one the Emmet family had ultimately played a central role in achieving.

Over time, the act might gradually have led to a more just and prosperous way of life for Catholics, were it not for a black rot that mysteriously started appearing on the leaves of potato plants in Ireland in September of 1845.

WHEN LOOKED AT as a whole, Emmet's life—both the radical political activity in Ireland and the legal and electoral work in the United States—ultimately symbolizes the transatlantic Irish revolutionary movement. The Irish patriots who came after, from civil rights activist John Devoy right up to Sinn Féin's Gerry Adams, understood the importance of the Irish diaspora when it came to the movement for Irish freedom. Thomas, in the end, was a prophet of multicultural equality.

In 1903, exactly one hundred years after Robert Emmet's execution, several of Thomas Addis Emmet's direct descendants sat in a Brooklyn music hall and listed to the great Irish poet William Butler Yeats deliver a passionate speech about Thomas's life and revolutionary zeal. A decade later Patrick Pearse—a future martyr of 1916—visited the same music hall. Of Thomas Emmet, Pearse told the crowd, "There are in every generation those who shrink from the ultimate sacrifice but there are [also] in every generation those who make it with joy and laughter and these are the souls of the generations, the heroes who stand midway between God and Men."

In 1922, Thomas Addis Emmet's grandson, Thomas Addis Emmet III, organized his grandfather's reburial in Dublin's Glasnevin Cemetery, the final resting place of many of Ireland's most prominent patriots. And yet, given his influence, both in Ireland and in the United States, in our long march toward liberty and justice, it is clear that Thomas Addis Emmet is not dead in any final sense of the word.

———◆———

Thomas Emmet Hayden passed away on October 23, 2016. Like his namesake, Hayden was a once radical political activist who grew committed to electoral politics. Born almost two centuries after Emmet, he joined in that same long march, fighting for liberty and justice throughout his entire life. Like Emmet too, Tom Hayden is not dead in any final sense of the word.

At the request of Tom Hayden, this essay was completed posthumously by Tom Deignan.

THE CARETAKER

Margaret Haughery (1813–1882)

BY ROSIE O'DONNELL

TRAGEDIES. TRAUMAS. NATURAL DISASTERS. THERE are always far too many. Constant. Battering. So by the time Hurricane Katrina hit New Orleans in 2005, I had developed a new approach to surviving national emergencies—I would go there myself and personally help. Soon after the hurricane, I found myself in a place in Louisiana called Renaissance Village, full of survivors, most of them children, stranded with nothing.

I remember one night, while trying to clear my head, walking around New Orleans alone, I saw a statue of a woman—a monument in disrepair, the pedestal buried by weeds and surrounded by trash. I stepped closer, and the white, stained marble figure looked, well . . . familiar. She was stocky, maternal, her arm around a child.

She looked like my mother and my grandmother and my grandmother's mother all the way down the line. My line. She looked like
the people I saw in photos when I did *Who Do You Think You Are?*
for NBC, during which time I discovered the treacherous journey
from Ireland to America that my own family had taken.

The statue stayed with me long after I left. It was the familiarity
but also I think the sturdiness, the resolve. She looked like she had
been standing there for hundreds of years and damn well intended
to be there for hundreds more. A survivor here in a city that was
reeling, among poor and suffering people themselves all fighting
to survive.

I walked back to my hotel. Images from the morning scrolled
through my brain—a refugee camp in Baton Rouge; thousands of
people in beat-up trailers with swollen eyes and battered spirits;
little kids running around in the summer heat with nothing to do,
no toys to play with, no lemonade to drink—no relief. Those days
in Louisiana haunt my mind and my dreams. I will never shake it.
The hurricane had destroyed everything they'd known. The pain of
watching it all was enormous. Sadness swallows me still.

The statue had been labeled simply MARGARET. Hello, Google,
my digital disassociation addiction: #need2knowNOW.com. Margaret had lived almost two hundred years ago but was famous
enough to be remembered by her first name alone. What, I won-
dered, had this woman done to be so well known? I knew I had
to learn more about her. Maybe because she looked so much like
me. Maybe because she was a survivor, and I was working on, in,
and around survival. But what I didn't know was the many ways in
which her life would seem to mirror my own.

Margaret Haughery was born on Christmas Day, 1813, in Tully

South, in the parish of Carrigallen, Ireland. The world seems to stop on holidays, and it would be no different there in County Leitrim. The village was small and poor, with basic houses made of mud. Simple wreaths dotted the doorways, and candles lit each window. Because food was scarce in 1813, that Christmas would have been a lean one.

My son Blake was also born on Christmas Day, in 1999. I took a plane to sunny California, picked up my new baby boy, and brought him back home to Miami in time to watch the new millennium arrive. None of my children are Irish, but they have all been raised by an Irish mother—which I believe, in some significant way, must make them Irish too. My boy, Blake, turned out to be the one who looks like me. In reality, he's half Mexican and half German, but most people think we share DNA. When I am walking in the mall with him people say, "Oh, is *this* the one you had?" I answer, "Well, I didn't have any, but they are all mine."

No matter what challenges might lie ahead, the fact that Blake was born on Christmas makes him a little closer to God. Maybe that's just in my mind, but I don't care. And the fact that Margaret was also born on Christmas Day nearly two centuries before is no different. In her case, however, she was not lucky enough to be scooped up onto a plane and taken to a comfortable home. She was born into a country of famine and poverty and economic collapse. Still, she was a small miracle just like my son. All children are special, but some seem to come into this world full of light. Blake did. And I like to think Margaret did. I imagine her as bathed in yellow, with wide, luminous eyes.

Margaret was named after her mother—as I was named after mine. She would be called many things in her lifetime. Margaret was the Angel of the Delta; she was the Bread Lady of New Orleans, Margaret of Tully, and Mother Margaret. She was Margaret Friend of the Orphans, Lady Margaret, and, as on her statue, just Margaret.

She lived in the same Ireland my family emigrated from. By the time Margaret was two years old, a seemingly insignificant event changed the destiny of her generation. Mount Tambora erupted in the Dutch East Indies, eight thousand miles away. A thick layer of ash coated the skies in Europe and stole the summer and ruined all the crops. It was one of the wettest years on record, and it caused the potatoes to rot in the ground and the flour to harden in the barrels. People began to starve in Ireland long before the great potato famine. At two years old, Margaret already knew hardship and hunger.

In a country where suffering was the norm, life just kept getting harder. Things were breaking down. The banks were failing; farmers were leaving for the cities desperate to provide for their families. British rule oppressed the people more and more each day. The Anglicans and the Catholics were oil and water. The recipe was not good.

THE IRISH HAVE not cornered the market on suffering, although it can sometimes seem so. We are a vocal and a political people. And undoubtedly, politics was a topic in every household in Margaret's time too. Two centuries ago when Ireland struggled under British rule, the Gaffney family, along with so many others, were fed up. William Gaffney, Margaret's father, told his brother-in-law, Matthew O'Rourke, that he was leaving his homeland because he could no longer stand to live under English tyranny.

The Irish migration was just beginning. The people needed only to look out their window to see reasons to set sail. Every day villagers were dying. In a time when little was understood about disease, outbreaks of any kind were devastating. Typhus hit in 1817. Typhus is particularly brutal. It attacks the central nervous system, so people get delirious before they die. Myself, I don't think that there are any great ways to pass, but watching loved ones lose their sense of self on the way to death seems crushingly cruel.

Margaret's father, William, sold everything he owned and could still only afford passage for his wife and three of their six children. They made the gut-wrenching choice to leave the oldest three in Ireland. This is what happened to my father. He was one of eight children. He was sent over with my grandmother and the other three youngest. The rest of the children were left behind with his grandfather. Eventually they got all the kids to America and were reunited with the family, living in a tenement in New York City with rats running up the curtains, as my father loved to tell us. He wanted us to carry that with us—the identity of being an Irish family that "came over on the boat."

Margaret was five years old when she got on one of those horrible scows that were like prison ships: toxic vats of illness and starvation. The trip was hell. The conditions on board were unspeakable. The passenger decks were overcrowded, with half a dozen people jammed into a space six-feet square. The narrow bunks had only straw mattresses, the body fluids of the sick leaking down from the bunk above.

As it turns out, Margaret's family did not escape typhus at all. It was rampant on the ship, the screams of the dying mixed with the stench of illness: urine and feces and vomit and pain. Later these same vessels became known as coffin ships because so many people died during the crossings. But the dead were given no coffins. They were thrown overboard to the sharks that followed the boats waiting for a meal. Every day from morning until night, for six months of her life, Margaret faced a reality that would destroy most adults. What this child lived through, just on that ship, was enough to alter the course of her life. Does trauma make a tattoo on the heart, on the mind? And is it passed down, like emotional DNA, from generation to generation?

I TOO HAD trauma in early life. Not the same kind that Margaret had—illness, hunger, profound poverty—but trauma nonetheless. I see myself in her. I see myself from a very early age trying to survive against all odds. During an interview when I was at Renaissance Village after Katrina, the reporter kept focusing only on how difficult it was to navigate the red tape to deliver the kind of aid we were providing. I said, "I've lived impossible. I know impossible can be done." People often ask me, "How did you survive the loss of your mother at such a young age? How did you survive your father's drinking, his abuse?" I don't have any answer for why some pieces of coal turn into diamonds and others don't. I don't know. It's the combination of pressure and environment and timing. These all merge in a magical mix. This life of mine has been beyond anything I could have imagined.

And Margaret's surely was too. So many times she achieved the impossible. And it began so young, on that ship, finding life and not death—making her way to a new land. I have to believe it sparked inside her a glimpse of all that she would prove capable of. It awakened something in her.

The Gaffney family arrived in America with almost nothing. Their trunk, along with the rest of the passengers' luggage, was lost during the storms. But they found comfort and support in the Irish community. As poor as they were, they still had more than what they'd left behind. William sent "glowing accounts" of their new life in America back to his brother-in-law Matthew in Ireland.

While he had been a farmer and sometimes a tailor back in Tully, in Baltimore William would take whatever work he could get. Irishmen and black men competed for the lowest-paying jobs. William landed employment as a carter on the docks, hauling heavy loads of cargo from the ships in wheeled wagons, pulling and pushing like a draft animal. It was backbreaking labor, but he would have been happy to have it.

Meanwhile, Matthew, William's brother-in-law, was still caring for his sister's three oldest children. By 1822 William had saved almost enough to send for them. Things seemed to be looking up for the Gaffneys. But yellow fever changed all that. The fever took both of Margaret's parents and her baby sister, Kathleen, most likely within a short time of each other. She would have seen them suffering with chills, nausea, and jaundice. Then the bleeding began. During that same time, her brother Kevin disappeared. Margaret was nine years old—a lone survivor.

She had met a Welsh woman, Helen Richards, on the ship coming over. Helen's husband also died of yellow fever. When she learned of Margaret's predicament, Helen took her in. I like to think that Helen was a loving maternal figure. No one can know for sure, as the records are hazy, but I hope Margaret found another mother in this woman.

I too was orphaned at that same age when my mother died.

Even though my father was alive, he was not present, and I felt very much alone. The amount of terror is hard to articulate when you're a child and your ballasts are removed. You can float away to somewhere in your own mind and never return.

In Margaret's day and age, it was a common practice to take in orphans and turn them into unpaid help, but I believe Helen Richards must have loved Margaret in some way. What happened later in Margaret's life tells me that somewhere she had been cherished, and that she had learned to cherish others. Margaret devoted her life to the health and the love of all orphans, thereby taking care of the child she once was.

MARGARET LIVED WITH Helen Richards and, when she was old enough, went into domestic service, as so many young Irish women did. We don't know how she met Charles Haughery, but we do know that she married him on October 10, 1835, when she was twenty-two years old. Certainly, Margaret would have known the ache of intense longing for a family. Her marriage made her a family of two. She was no longer alone.

However, Charles was not a well man and would have already been sick at the time of their wedding. It was probably tuberculosis, called consumption in those days, growing progressively and inexorably worse, the cough, the blood bright on the handkerchief. Tuberculosis was a slow killer, and back then there were few treatments. Doctors recommended a change of climate, so only about ten days after their wedding, the newlyweds locked arms, and again Margaret walked up the gangplank of a ship. They arrived in New Orleans on the *Hyperion* about six weeks later.

Her husband got a little better for a time, and Margaret became pregnant. However, soon Charles's health started sliding back downhill. This time the doctors suggested a sea voyage. He decided to go back to Ireland to visit his family, but he delayed his travels until after the birth of their child, a daughter, Frances. He set sail around 1837.

A few months after Charles arrived in Ireland, Margaret received a letter. She would have taken it to her priest, Father Mullen, for him to read. Margaret was illiterate, as so many immigrants were. The letter was a blow. Charles was dead. She must have mourned for him. But was there even time for grief? Margaret was now forced to find a way to care for herself and her child.

Within a few months of her husband's death, baby Frances got sick. By some accounts, it was yellow fever. Not even one year old, Frances died in Margaret's arms. Margaret wrapped her in a little blanket and carried her to the Catholic church. She asked Father Mullen to arrange the funeral.

Strangely, after losing her husband and daughter, it was then that Margaret came into her power. As quoted in her biography, compiled by an unknown family friend, Margaret said, "My God, thou hast broken every tie. Thou hast stripped me of all. Again, I am all alone." Her words, both haunting and resonant.

Margaret got a job as a laundress at the St. Charles Hotel. Every day while she was on break she saw all these orphans walking with the Sisters of Charity. She was captivated by them. Again I see myself in her. My kids call me a "creeper" because when I see a bunch of kids playing in the park or at the mall, I am like, "Oh my god, look!" I am drawn to children like a magnet to metal. I find myself filled with joy just from watching kids play. Margaret was also a creeper.

While today's foster kids are largely the children of living

parents, in the early 1800s the young were forced to fend for themselves when their parents died. There were no laws protecting
them. They were often left uneducated and put to work for minimal wages. Churches and wealthy philanthropists did their best,
but many, many children fell through the cracks.

I WISH I could hear Margaret talking, expressing her
thoughts and revealing her feelings, but since Margaret could neither read nor write, most of her words did not survive her. What
does live on in the archives of the Williams Research Center on
Chartres Street in New Orleans is a lean collection from which I
have been able to learn about this extraordinary woman. When she
was around twenty-five years old, Margaret got to know the Sisters
of Charity, who ran the Poydras Orphan Asylum. She quit her job
at the laundry and applied to work with the orphans. Margaret
talked about her strong passion and desire to work with children.
The Mother Superior, Sister Frances Regis, looked into this young
woman's eager face and replied, "There is no future here. Only a
constant struggle."

I remember when I was getting my communion, right before
my mother died. We were walking through Christ the King Catholic Church, where my mother was on the parish council. She was
wearing her claddagh ring and had her five Irish Catholic kids in
tow. I said, "Mommy, when I grow up I want to be a nun." And she
said, "Don't do it, honey. The pay is really bad." Margaret's story
reminds me of that day. "There's no future here, only a constant
struggle." Or to put it another way, the pay was really bad. But Margaret knew what she wanted and shortly thereafter she was working and living at the orphanage.

I believe this is how Margaret began to save herself. I think that the orphanage filled her heart with something that she really needed. When a car runs out of oil it seizes and never works again. With so much death, damage, and abandonment in her life, Margaret was low on oil. So she immersed herself in the blindingly pure love of children.

There's a story about her that I think really defines who she was at this point in her life. Her first job at the orphanage, in addition to taking care of the children, was to find enough food to feed them. One day she went to a greengrocer and asked if there were any extra vegetables. She told him that she was working at the orphanage and that the kids were hungry. She was still in her twenties and looked quite young. The grocer was not terribly nice. He knew the orphanage was far away. He had a wheelbarrow, and he filled it. He piled on everything that he could, but the vegetables he chose would have been a little old and wilted—items he couldn't sell anymore. He said to her, "Okay kid, if you can push that wheelbarrow home, you can have it all for free."

Margaret hoisted the load onto the front wheel and put her weight behind it. After this skinny young woman had gotten it a couple hundred feet, defying all the laws of physics, the man could see her dedication. He was so impressed, he told her, "I'll do it for you. You've proven you'd do it." But, "No," Margaret responded, "I always keep my bargains." And she pushed it all the way home.

Quickly, Margaret saw that the orphanage needed a reliable source of milk, and so she bought two cows, either with savings or borrowed money. In this way, she was able to have not just milk but cheese and butter too. She even had enough left over to sell some, thereby bringing in much needed cash.

It started with two cows, but Margaret would eventually have a dairy of forty head. The larger her herd grew, the more customers she had. She talked to every single one of them about her orphans. She used most of the profits from her dairy for the kids—for maintaining the orphanage and building new ones.

Although run by Catholic nuns, the Poydras Orphan Asylum was owned by the city and administered by a committee of Protestant ladies. One day they told the nuns that they were going to have to include Presbyterian teachers for the children, in addition to the Sisters of Charity. The nuns, wanting autonomy, felt they had to move. Who did they turn to but Margaret. Not only did Margaret help them do it, she involved the orphans themselves. She had the kids, two at a time, out canvassing the neighborhoods, looking for a suitable property. I think Margaret wanted to give them a sense of control, a feeling that however young, they could help shape their own fate. I also think she knew a twenty-odd-year-old Irishwoman doesn't pull on the heartstrings quite like young orphans.

Margaret eventually found a dilapidated house on New Levee Street. The story goes that she saw old Judge Kennedy on the porch. When she asked him if it was he who owned the house, the old man groused back about women who start asking him questions before he's had his morning coffee. Margaret heard opportunity knocking. Before uttering another word, she walked right on inside and made him a pot.

As soon as Judge Kennedy had had a few sips, she started in again. The kitchen was almost bare. What was he even doing there? As it turned out, the judge had recently moved with his son uptown. "A new house?" Well, Margaret didn't see what use he could have for the broken-down old one they were standing in. Might he let the orphans stay in it for a while? She told the judge they would fix it up and live there just until they had raised enough money to build a brand-new orphanage for the Sisters of Charity. By the time he got the house back, she promised, it would be fully repaired and worth much more. Judge Kennedy agreed, asking only that every time he visited, Margaret make him another pot of coffee.

MARGARET'S COMPASSION AND caring was not limited to orphans, and she became known throughout the city as someone you could count on. During the Mexican-American War, when General Winfield Scott attacked Mexico City, in 1847, five nuns belonging to the Sisters of Charity were imprisoned. The order went to Margaret. She was sick in bed, but they went into her room and woke her up anyway. "Help us," they said. And that was all Margaret needed to hear. She rose up, got dressed, and went immediately to the docks. She hired a ship to rescue the nuns, giving the captain half of his payment upfront, the other half to be delivered when the task was completed. Then, while the ship was en route, she negotiated with the government and General Scott for the nuns to be released.

In 1853, the yellow fever epidemic took an enormous toll on the city of New Orleans. Port cities have many advantages, but they also sometimes receive unwanted cargo. This time the ship *Augusta*, from Jamaica, brought in mosquitoes that would change the city's destiny. Salt marshes and drenching heat created a perfect breeding ground. Two hundred people a day were dying. Yellow jack, as it was called, took lives, while the treatments—bleeding and purging—did nothing but weaken the patients.

Margaret risked her life at the bedsides of the dying, helping when she could and taking in the orphaned children when she couldn't. At least five nursing sisters died. Bodies were lying in the open streets. The smell of death was everywhere. One tenth of the population succumbed that season, leaving more and more children orphaned.

Margaret and her lifelong friend Sister Regis came up with a new dream out of the epidemic: to build an infant asylum. Margaret called it a "baby house." She had already completed St. Teresa's, as the new Sisters of Charity orphanage was named. Now she turned her energy to this new venture. She just leapt in. "Build the asylum," she said, "and God will pay for it."

I'm with Margaret. That's the only way to get things done: Leap in. Believe. Because if you are all too aware of how impossible the challenge actually is, you'll never even try. I was a kid who, from a very young age, had to run my own life. So was she. In 1862, the St. Vincent de Paul Infant Asylum would open its doors. And Margaret still wasn't done.

A woman who clearly had a head for business, she had loaned so much money to a bakery that over time she'd become the major shareholder. When the bakery went bankrupt, Margaret was faced with the choice of losing her sizable investment or running the business herself. Once again, she just leapt in. She sold her dairy and used the money to update the baking equipment. The bakery would become known simply as Margaret's—the first steam bakery of its kind in the country. It was an instant hit; people supported the bakery because Margaret made the best bread in New Orleans. Driven to succeed, Margaret soon realized she would have to sacrifice one of her greatest joys: living with the children.

And so it was that Margaret moved out of her room with the nuns at St. Theresa's and moved into an apartment above Margaret's bakery. She would rise before dawn to bake her loaves, basting them with butter in the early light. She made crackers and cakes, cookies and macaroni, her hands dusted with fine powder. The smell—it must have been its own kind of heaven.

And certainly it fell like manna to New Orleans' poor and hungry, for Margaret never turned anyone away. She cut her loaves in half so the recipients couldn't sell them off for liquor, but she happily fed everyone. All were served: white, black, Catholic, Protestant, Jewish, and soon enough blue and gray.

THERE HAD BEEN rumblings of war in New Orleans for a long time. Lincoln was elected in 1860. Louisiana seceded from the Union the next year, and shortly after, war became a reality. A port city is a valuable asset and therefore a high-value target. The Union navy blockaded the docks, and the city's booming economy went bust.

New Orleans was not decimated, but it was occupied by a sometimes-brutal Union army. General Benjamin Butler was put in charge of the city. Butler was a former criminal lawyer who knew nothing about being a soldier. One of his first official acts was to condemn a man to death for flying a Confederate flag. The general soon became known as "Beast Butler." After a woman spat on him in the street, he passed what was known as the Woman Order. It relegated any woman found alone on public walkways to prostitute status for the pleasure of Union soldiers. It was to this man Margaret had to appeal when the blockade threatened the supply line for her bakery. The port of New Orleans was closed, but there was flour in nearby states, and Margaret desperately needed it.

We know Margaret was of strong, broad Irish stock. She gave everything she had to others and counted herself happier for having done so. By her own grit and fierce determination, she had been able to cross the state line more or less at will. That is, until she was caught smuggling. She was brought before Beast Butler. Her friend Father Mullen came with her. Against the backdrop of the Woman Order, Margaret held firm. She had defied the rules that she thought ridiculous. In doing so she had risked rape, murder, and arrest. Now, to Beast Butler, she said,

> I understand you have threatened to hang me if I continue sending food to starving people. I've come to tell you that I will not be stopped by your threats. I will continue until you hang me. I wonder if you feel it is Mr. Lincoln's opinion that there is a military advantage in starving helpless people to death and am I wondering now if you have any reverence for God? If so, you will not hang me for I am needed here.

The general was reportedly amused by her courage and provided her with signed papers allowing her to travel as needed.

IN MARGARET'S LIFETIME, she donated at a minimum $600,000, the equivalent of over $16 million today. And before she was done, she opened four orphanages: St. Teresa's Orphan Asylum on Camp Street, the Louise Home for Working Girls on Clio Street, St. Elizabeth's House of Industry on Napoleon Street, and the St. Vincent de Paul Infant Asylum at Race and Magazine Streets. She would contribute to countless others. She had built up an empire, an orphanage empire.

As generous as she was with others, she was parsimonious with herself. She owned only two dresses: an everyday dress for the orphanage and the bakery and a black silk dress for Sundays and special occasions. She wore a Quaker bonnet, her signature. And she was, like me, plump, what we call plus-size. For some reason, I like this fact.

She devoted herself, body and soul, to her work, but although she never remarried, she did have some sort of personal life. Margaret found her two closest friends among the Sisters of Charity: Sister Regis, the Mother Superior who first hired her, and Sister Irene. Although little has been written about anything other than Margaret's good works, her personality shows through in what sources we do have. In one instance the *Daily Picayune* called her "the kind, good natured dame who drives the milk cart of the Orphans' Asylum" and reported that Margaret had quietly gone to court to speak to the magistrate on behalf of a black woman, a servant at the asylum, who had been arrested for getting drunk. With Margaret's support the woman was let go with a warning.

In 1853 her friend Sister Irene became ill—with what, we do not know, but it was significant enough that she left the convent and resumed using her given name, Louise Catherine Jarboe. Louise became Margaret's personal assistant, most likely managing private and business correspondence. This would have been of great value for the illiterate Margaret, who appears to have been embroiled in a handful of lawsuits stemming from her inability to understand contracts she had signed with an *X*.

At the age of sixty-eight Margaret suddenly fell ill. The sisters took her to their private hospital, but though Margaret spent many months there, she never recovered. Pope Pius IX sent his blessing and a crucifix. The nuns prayed at her bedside. It may have been a brain tumor, although we'll never know for sure. She died on February 9, 1882, and the entire city went into in mourning. It was an abrupt ending to an extraordinary life. The newspapers of the day were edged in black. This illiterate Irish immigrant received a state funeral.

If you go to New Orleans today you can visit Margaret Place.

The statue, now restored, sits in a small park between wide, empty streets underneath an interstate overpass. It is only the second statue in the United States to have honored a woman and the first in a public square.

It has been a while since I have visited the monument, though I have been back to New Orleans a number of times since Katrina. Still, I think about Margaret often. If you don't see yourself reflected in history, then you can't adequately define yourself. When, that day years ago, I first looked into Margaret's eyes of stone—there I was. I discovered in her my archetype, my ego ideal, something, or rather someone, to stretch for, to be like. I am a mother who has adopted five children. Children born of other women, but whom I am loving and raising—who are now my own. But it is a peculiar exchange, this giving, because I am getting so much back—I am saving myself. And I feel it must have been this way for Margaret. Two hundred years ago or right now, we are here to help each other along, and we do it for each other, as well as for ourselves.

I sometimes dream of Margaret, her fine-as-flour hands, her butter-basted breads, her vermillion heart with flower chambers just like mine and yours, yet larger in some admittedly mysterious way than all of ours. Margaret gives to me across the centuries, and I like to think, in this telling, that maybe I am giving a little back. So that some circle is closed, some salve applied, for the both of us—as it always is.

There at Margaret Place in New Orleans, the stone softens and a living, breathing being steps before me. I don't believe in ghosts, but this I know: Margaret is always near.

THE ORGANIZER

Mary "Mother" Jones (1837–1930)

BY TERRY GOLWAY

DISCONTENT IN THE COAL MINES of Colorado, fall of 1913. The miners are poorly paid and working in horrendous conditions. Immigrants, most of them, from places like Greece and Italy, they left their homes filled with visions of the great American dream. And here they are, living in squalor in the great American West, digging for riches inside the earth for the benefit of companies controlled by the Rockefeller family.

But if they believed that nobody outside of their miserable little towns knew of their plight, they were wrong. That fall, an aging Irishwoman would come to live and agitate with them, and regardless of their command of English, the miners soon would understand that here was a person with the courage to speak out. She addressed meetings and rallies in the mining towns of southeastern Colorado, urging the workers to walk off their jobs until the Rockefellers and their managers gave them what they wanted: better pay, safer working conditions, and simple dignity. Her words, delivered in the cadence of County Cork, were direct and forceful, and that they were coming from an elderly woman only added to their power.

"Don't be afraid, boys," she said. "Fear is the greatest curse we have. I never was anywhere yet that I feared anybody. I do what I think is right and when I die I will render an account of it. . . . You are the biggest part of the population in the state. You create its wealth, so I say let the fight go on; if nobody else will keep on, I will."

The woman was called Mother Jones, and she stirred the miners like no other. In short order, they voted to strike and so set in motion a series of events leading to the infamous Ludlow Massacre of April 1914, when National Guard troops and security guards opened fire on a mine encampment, killing some two dozen, with women and children among the dead.

Ludlow was a turning point for the U.S. labor movement, and it placed a nearly eighty-year-old Irish immigrant at the center of the nation's suddenly urgent conversation about the lives of those who worked in dark, dangerous mines, who trudged dreary factory floors, who picked vegetables and fruit in the searing heat, all for the benefit of gigantic corporations controlled by families who possessed riches beyond description.

Mary "Mother" Jones became the voice of American labor in the early twentieth century by transforming her own life, her own immigrant story, and, perhaps, if subconsciously, her own personal tragedies into a passionate campaign for justice and democracy during a dangerous time in American history. She was unafraid to enrage her foes with incendiary language—"I'm a Bolshevist from the bottom of my feet to the top of my head," she would say in late 1919, as Attorney General Mitchell Palmer scoured the countryside in search of Communists. Around the same time, she told striking steelworkers in Indiana how they ought to deal with scabs: "I'll be ninety years old the first of May, but by God if I have to, I'll take ninety guns and shoot the hell out of them."

Her unapologetic hell-raising and core beliefs reflected the injustice she saw in the streets, tenements, factories, and mines of America. But to hear her tell it, the passion she brought to the picket line could be traced not to her own hard luck but to her family's experience in Ireland. As she later told a congressional committee, "I belong to a class which has been robbed, exploited, and plundered through many long centuries. And because I belong to that class, I have an impulse to go and help break the chains."

Not all immigrants, from Ireland or from elsewhere for that matter, took such a path. A penniless Andrew Carnegie arrived in the United States from Scotland in 1848 and chose to identify not with the poor in his adopted country but with the industrialists. Carnegie did not break chains; his companies imposed them—he himself literally wrote the book on the "Gospel of Wealth." And although the vast bulk of immigrants obviously did not become fabulously wealthy, many aspired to create their own immigrant success story, identifying more with the perceived champions of the Gilded Age than its victims. Here was a place where the penniless could become rich, a place where the heroes of Horatio Alger's yarns pulled themselves up by their bootstraps and lived happily ever after.

But Mother Jones was different. She saw the creators of the industrial age in much the same way as her Irish ancestors saw their British overlords. They were not figures to be emulated but the enforcers of an oppressive and inequitable system. She saw opportunities in her new country, all right—the opportunity to create a fairer, more democratic society, a place where lives could be improved not through riches but through justice. That was her American dream.

And so by the early twentieth century, she became a familiar presence on picket lines, at union rallies, and at government inquiries. Workers, journalists, public officials, and even the occasional capitalist—like John D. Rockefeller Jr., with whom, oddly, she was quite friendly—called her Mother and thought they knew her. And in a way they did. They knew a person named Mother Jones, a name she adopted for herself as her fame grew. She was, in fact, not the first labor agitator to adopt the name—an English immigrant in Indiana, married to a coal miner, served as editor of a journal for railroad workers in the 1880s and signed her poetry and writing Mother Jones. But that other Mother Jones's fame was short-lived, and she stopped writing by 1889. Soon after that, Mary Jones began referring to herself as Mother Jones. Did she know about the poet and coal miner's wife from Indiana? Maybe. More important, though, she saw something in this name—recycled, perhaps, but new for her—that represented the person she had become.

MOTHER JONES WAS born Mary Harris in Cork, most likely in 1837. Some historians have argued that she was born several years later, but historian Elliott J. Gorn seems to have settled the debate, noting that she was baptized in St. Mary's Cathedral on August 1, 1837. "I was born in revolution," Mary later wrote. And indeed, there had been a political revolution that shook the British ruling establishment to its core in the years just before her birth. In 1828, a middle-class barrister from County Clare named Daniel O'Connell became the first Catholic elected to the House of Commons since Britain had imposed a religious test for elected officials in the late 1600s, a test that effectively barred Catholics from power. When O'Connell took his seat in the Commons, after years of peaceful agitation and political organizing among Ireland's poor, authorities in London predicted civil war. After all, was not the British ruling structure built on the ideology of Protestant supremacy?

No such strife broke out, at least not on the scale authorities feared. But in places like Cork, landless peasants banded together in secret societies to carry out limited, though often brutal, acts of violence against the propertied class. Some accounts describe the rural violence of the early nineteenth century as defensive and conservative, a reaction to enclosure movements, falling prices, and other developments that did nothing to lift the burdens of poor tenant farmers. Other accounts portray the secret societies, with names like Rockites, Terry Alts, Threshers, and Whiteboys, as virtual guerrilla armies seeking to exact revenge against landlords and their agents, who, in their view, had stolen the soil of Ireland from its native Gaelic inhabitants.

O'Connell was the uncrowned king of Ireland when Mary Harris was born, and he and his allies used their considerable leverage to negotiate for reform in Ireland. But some in Ireland, like members of the Harris family, were not content with the actions of middle-class reformers or the political jockeying in the Palace of Westminster. They lived on the brink, subject to the whims of landlords, nature, and free-market dogma. And they fought back against those forces with clandestine, late-night raids against livestock, property, and, sometimes, those who represented the landlord class.

Mary's grandfather was among those who joined in the struggle. There is no indication that, aside from their poverty, he had experienced a tenant farmer's worst nightmare—abrupt eviction. But others did, and once thrown off the land they tilled but did not own, they were homeless and hungry, with few alternatives save emigration. Grandfather Harris often slipped away at night to join other landless farmers as they sought to instill fear in those whom they believed were terrorizing them with uncertainty and injustice.

He was arrested and hanged when Mary was about two years old.

According to one of Mary's biographers, her father, Richard Harris, also became involved in secret society violence and was a wanted man. In this account, which has more than a dash of melodrama, soldiers came to the Harris cottage and searched the house for Richard, even checking the chimney, while little Mary and her mother looked on. But Richard was gone. He left abruptly and was on his way across the Atlantic. Soon, he had told his family, he would send for them, and they would be together again.

In her autobiography, written 1925, Mother Jones devoted four sentences—the first four—to the Irish childhood of her former self. Biographers and historians have pieced together other details about her life from various sources, but there is a great deal we do not know. It is safe to say, however, that the trauma of her early childhood—her grandfather hanged, her father forced to flee, the spectacle of soldiers in her house, looking for her father—influenced how she thought about resistance and power. Mary witnessed first-hand the kind of power the state can bring to bear against those who threaten it. She saw in Ireland what happens to rebels and revolutionaries more often than not.

But despite the value of these early lessons, Mother Jones was always reticent to reflect on her formative years and that distant person named Mary Harris. Rather, as historian Gorn has pointed out, she seemed far more intent on focusing on the character she had created.

She insisted, for example, that she was born in 1830—and, a century later, her friends and allies celebrated her hundredth birthday with a five-layer cake. An early newsreel camera was on hand to record the images and capture her voice. Workers should "stick together and be loyal to each other," she said, before cutting her enormous birthday cake.

But that wasn't so much Mary Harris speaking as Mother Jones, the wonderful character that Mary had created years earlier. Not a hundred years old, she was in her early nineties. She insisted that her father left Ireland in 1835, a decade before the famine, and that he sent for his family "as soon as he became an American citizen." But most historians believe she actually left a bit later—after the potatoes turned black and failed, and failed again, year after year.

Growing up in the city, rather than in the countryside, Mary may not have seen the rotting fields or heard the moans and weeping from rural cottages. But all of that took place not far from her home. Famine Ireland was a dreadful place. Eyewitnesses wrote of corpses lying in fields and along roadways, of rats gnawing on the remains of children, of hollow-eyed men, women, and children in the final stages of fever and disease. The British administrator who presided over relief efforts, Charles Trevelyan, complained that the "great evil with which we have to contend is not the physical evil of the famine, but the moral evil of the selfish, perverse and turbulent character of the [Irish] people." Indeed, Ireland actually had no shortage of food, but as the immigrant Roman Catholic bishop of New York, John Hughes, noted, the poor simply could not "pay for the harvest of their own labor." Crops were exported while the Irish starved to death because political and economic dogma insisted that the government ought not to interfere with the marketplace.

The potato would return to health in 1852. But by then, so many were gone from places like Cork and the western province of Connaught, where the Irish language and Gaelic customs and traditions had been so strong. A million people were dead. Another two million had emigrated to somewhere else. The population of Ireland had been eight million in 1840, five years before the hunger began. It was five million in 1880. The famine had changed Ireland—and the United States—utterly.

How did it change Mary Harris and her family? Mary is silent on the topic. It is a puzzling silence. Perhaps it's no wonder so many have accepted the narrative that she created, concluding that she must have left before the hunger and the dying began. Why else would she say nothing about it?

Perhaps she simply chose not to remember; perhaps she felt guilty, having fled her home as others starved. But as Mary transformed herself into Mother Jones, she pushed aside her childhood memories of hunger and death, as others did too. For silence followed the famine wherever the starving survivors settled, so much so that its centennial in the late 1940s and early 1950s passed almost without notice on both sides of the Atlantic. Irish American children two generations removed from the experience knew little or nothing about what it was like to see neighbors, friends, loved ones reduced to starvation. Had they asked, they likely would have been told that it is better not to speak of such things. Certainly Mother Jones did not.

Historians believe that the Harris family had to separate, in about 1847, when Mary was ten. Her father and her twelve-year-old brother left Ireland for work in North America. It seems likely that she and her other siblings and their mother followed about five years later. We know nothing of what she saw or how she felt as she left behind her native land, nothing about the journey across the Atlantic. Most likely it was uncomfortable at best, terrifying at worst. The emigrant ships were packed with the starving and the sick in appalling conditions. One passenger described the sight of hundreds of people "huddled together without light, without air" below decks, "wallowing in filth and breathing a fetid atmosphere, sick in body, dispirited in heart." Many did not survive, dying of starvation or disease en route or drowning when rickety, unseaworthy ships sank to the bottom of the Atlantic.

The Harris family was reunited in the New World, not in the United States but in Toronto, where her father had found work after first living in Vermont. There the family began to build a new life three thousand miles from the land they thought of as home. It was, and remains, no easy task, but at least they had the comfort of each other.

Mary attended school in Toronto, learned the art of dressmaking, and was considered promising enough to earn a recommendation from a priest for admission to a normal school, a type of college that specialized in the training of teachers. While it seems she attended only the first year of a two-year program, she considered herself qualified to teach, having had a good deal more education than most people in either Canada or the United States. But she faced an obstacle: it was hard, if not impossible, for Catholics to obtain teaching jobs in Toronto's public schools. Things were little better in America at the time: in many cities with large Irish Catholic populations, a nativist movement supported overtly anti-Catholic curricula in public schools, leading to the expansion of a separate Catholic school system.

Still, Mary left Canada for the United States in search of a teaching position. It is not clear whether she ever saw or spoke with her parents and siblings again. Like her memories of Ireland, her family is mentioned only in the first paragraph of her autobiography.

She found a teaching job eventually, but perhaps that second year in normal school would have served her, because she quickly learned that teaching was not what she hoped it would be. She moved to Chicago and opened a dressmaking shop. "I preferred sewing to bossing little children," she wrote.

Her skepticism of bosses, authority figures—even of herself as an authority figure—was understandable. Authority figures in her native country were the very people against whom her father and grandfather rebelled. They were the people who enforced a skewed system of justice. They were not empowered to protect the likes of her or her family. Their job was to keep people like her in their place.

Nevertheless, she found herself back in the classroom, back to bossing little children, when she moved down to Memphis, Tennessee, in 1860, just as her adopted country was being torn apart.

There, for what might have been the first time, she found happiness. George Jones was his name, an iron molder active in the National Union of Iron Molders. The two met in the fall and married soon thereafter, as Southern states, including Tennessee, came to terms with the election of Abraham Lincoln. Tennessee became the eleventh and last state to secede from the Union, in June 1861, about two months after South Carolina forces fired on Fort Sumter, marking the beginning of the Civil War. Mary Harris Jones, who left privation and rural violence in Ireland, now found herself living in a strategically important city in what was to become the nineteenth century's bloodiest conflict, a war in which her neighbors and fellow Tennessee residents fought to preserve their ability to own and sell human beings.

Precisely how Mary reconciled herself to living in a Confederate state, in a nation whose founding principles supported the degradation of men, women, and children with black skin, is another mystery. To be sure, she had little time for reflection, for she became, in short order, the mother of three small children all under the age of five. The woman who had no taste for "bossing little children" found herself doing precisely that, twenty-four hours a day, seven days a week.

The war in Memphis was blessedly short, but the city was not immune to the tensions that accompanied peace and the beginning of a new era in U.S. history. Black people, now free from the shackles of the slave owner, left the countryside in search of work, as so many white people had been doing since the beginning of the Industrial Revolution. But white residents, including Irish members of the city's police department, were not prepared to surrender the privileges of white supremacy. Nearly fifty blacks were murdered and dozens of homes burned during a three-day race riot in the city from May 1 to May 3, 1866. The violence ended only when federal troops arrived to restore order.

Through all of this, Mary tended to the needs of her growing family while her husband labored at the foundry and devoted some of his spare time to his union. Iron molders like George Harris were in demand, and he and his fellow workers used their leverage to increase union membership throughout the region and the nation itself. The iron molders' chief organizer, William Sylvis, declared that "all wealth and all power centers in the hands of the few, and the many are their victims and their bondsmen."

She gave birth to her fourth child, Mary, in 1867. But in late summer of that same year, reports of a yellow fever epidemic in the Deep South began to trickle into Memphis. The disease was a frightening killer of people who lived in close quarters in humid locales (its association with mosquitoes was unknown at the time). The disease struck Memphis in mid-September, and before long, the epidemic crossed the threshold of the Jones home, sickening the children. One by one they showed the symptoms: aches, intestinal pain, vomiting. One by one they died, all of them— Catherine, the eldest, born in 1862; Elizabeth, born in 1863; Terence, born in 1865; and baby Mary, just a few months old. And then the disease carried away George. His union brothers raised money to bury him.

Mary was quite suddenly alone again and in every way imaginable. No one dared even venture into her home to comfort her for fear of contracting the disease. She lay awake at night, listening to the sounds of carts as they moved through the stricken streets, collecting the bodies of the dead. After a while, she received permission from the city to tend to the sick and dying, putting her own health and life in jeopardy to try to save or at least comfort others.

But she could not remain in Memphis, not after this. Memphis held the graves of her children and her husband and her memories. She had to move away and move on.

She went back to Chicago, where she had lived briefly before the Civil War, and returned to running a dressmaking business with a partner she chose not to identify in her autobiography. Her description of this time in her life is almost as sparse as that of her childhood, and with good reason. Her children and her husband were dead and buried, but the memories of their suffering were fresh. She very likely was in a daze. If she chose not to dwell on this pain, she could hardly be blamed.

In these bitter years following her heartbreak, Mary developed a keen awareness of the injustices of the fledging Gilded Age. She sewed dresses for the wealthy, who lived in splendor on Lake Shore Drive along Lake Michigan, but often found herself looking out from her shop and seeing "the poor, shivering wretches, jobless and hungry, walking along the frozen lake front" in the winter or sleeping in parks to escape the heat of their tenement apartments in the summer.

On the night of October 8, 1871, a small fire broke out near the home of Patrick and Catherine O'Leary on DeKoven Street (named for the founder of the banking giant Northern Trust Company). The neighborhood's wooden cottages were quickly turned to cinders, and within hours, the entire city seemed to be in flames. The great Chicago fire left one hundred thousand people homeless and destroyed nearly 17,500 buildings. One of them was Mary's dress shop. She lost everything she had. She joined thousands of other residents on the lakefront, watching the city burn, watching her life take another tragic turn.

Decades later, Mother Jones would write that her devotion to the cause of labor and workers' rights rose from the ashes of the Great Chicago Fire. But her sense of empathy and capacity for outrage already had been formed by all that she had seen and experienced, both in Ireland and in the United States. If anything, the fire in Chicago brought to an end her time of grieving and reflection after the trauma of Memphis. Her days on the sidelines were over.

But her transformation was not entirely complete. She still was Mary Harris Jones, Irish immigrant, widow, childless mother. She had not yet reinvented herself into the character that would make her famous.

How and where she spent the years immediately following the Chicago fire is another mystery. Many accounts have Mary on the barricades as early as 1877, when one hundred thousand rail workers went on strike to protest their second pay cut in a year. She said her friends in the labor movement asked her to stand with them in Pittsburgh, where workers were demonstrating against the Pennsylvania Railroad. The state militia was called in, shots were fired, and nearly two dozen people were killed.

But again her most careful biographer, Elliott J. Gorn, makes a persuasive argument that this account is very likely not true, that it was another instance of Mother Jones creating a narrative for her character. She was not well known in 1877 and certainly was not as active in the union movement as she would later be. But she was living in Chicago, in the right place to observe the inequities of the age with the eyes of the newcomer, the immigrant, and the natural-born skeptic. While so many others dreamed of trading their rags for riches—the great American saga—she would seek to create a system in which fewer wore rags, because riches were more justly distributed.

Chicago was the home of men who were making great fortunes—Marshall Field, founder of the department store chain; Cyrus McCormick, founder of the company that became International Harvester; and George Pullman, who invented the sleeper railroad car. Along Lake Michigan's shoreline, the wealthy built replicas of European villas where they entertained each other in grand style while sharing their anxieties about the dangerous ideas circulating among the city's workers and jobless—the desperately poor families who sent their children into the factories so as to keep a leaky roof over their heads and stale bread on their table.

The city was restive and tense, alive with ideas that ran counter to the transatlantic dogma of free and unregulated markets and the unfettered pursuit of private profit. Mary may not have been a part of this conversation, at least not yet, but she surely was an eager listener. Almost fifty, she joined the nation's dominant labor union, the Knights of Labor, in the 1880s, after it began admitting women. The union's leader (with the title of "grand master workman") was Terence V. Powderly, the son of Irish immigrants, mayor of Scranton, Pennsylvania, and a member of the secretive Irish nationalist organization Clan na Gael. She and Powderly became friends and allies; in fact, the bond between them was so strong that Mary addressed Powderly as "my own dear son" in a letter in the early twentieth century. Powderly's involvement in Clan na Gael, a group that did not flinch from supporting violent revolution in Ireland, faded over time as he devoted most of his energy to improving the plight of American workers—regardless of their hyphen. Irish immigrants like the famous Fenian agitator Jeremiah O'Donovan Rossa, who saw his father die of starvation in Cork, raised money to send men with dynamite to blow up targets in London in the 1880s. But Mary, like Powderly, was more intent on winning justice for American workers than she was on winning freedom for her native land.

The Knights were the most formidable challenge to capital in the 1880s. They were a million strong, they admitted women and African Americans as equals, and they recruited skilled and non-skilled workers alike. The Knights and Powderly played a key role in providing support, education, and a platform for Mary's final transformation into Mother Jones.

While so much of Mother Jones's youth and early middle age is shrouded in mystery and half-truths, there is little question that May 4, 1886, truly was a pivotal date for her. It might be said that it was the day her new persona became complete. On that day in Chicago's Haymarket Square, somebody threw an improvised bomb loaded with dynamite at police officers as they were about to break up a pro-labor demonstration. Seven officers died. Shots then rang out, and civilians fell, although the precise number of civilian deaths remains uncertain. The deadly violence came three days after May Day, when workers in Chicago and across the country had gone on strike, demanding an eight-hour workday.

The city reacted as though a revolution were imminent. Radicals, or people thought to be radicals, were rounded up. The press stoked fears that Chicago would soon fall into the hands of anarchists. Eight activists were arrested and convicted in short order, and four were hanged six months later. Another committed suicide before he could be brought to the gallows. The others received life sentences. Business exploited fears by lashing back at unions, and membership in the Knights of Labor began to fall precipitously, from a million to about a hundred thousand in just three years.

While Mary said she did not agree with the anarchists, she had attended meetings they organized and listened "to what these teachers of a new order had to say to the workers." The Haymarket violence did not turn her into an agitator overnight. That part of her life was still to come. What it did do was remind Mary that the goals she sought—justice and equality—required disruption, and disruption could and often did lead to violence. It happened in the darkened fields of County Cork. It happened in the streets of Chicago. It seemed, at times, inevitable—and yet was it necessarily so? Could it be avoided? This was an issue she seemed to struggle with during her many decades of hell-raising.

No longer young, indeed, verging on elderly, Mother Jones began her public career in the mining regions of West Virginia, Pennsylvania, and elsewhere in the 1890s, delivering speeches of encouragement to strikers. If she was, in fact, born in 1837, she would have turned sixty during the last decade of the nineteenth century. But her new cause and her new life seemed to invigorate rather than exhaust her.

She first came to public notice after the terrible economic depression following the Panic of 1893, when she joined forces with Coxey's Army, named for a businessman from Ohio, Jacob Coxey, who aimed to bring thousands of unemployed men to Washington, DC, to demand a government jobs program. Mother Jones visited a platoon of Coxey's Army near Kansas City, Missouri, raised money for them, and delivered fiery speeches, including one that encouraged the men to help themselves to food stored at a nearby army outpost. After all, she said, they had helped produce the food—it belonged to them as much as to the real soldiers for whom it was intended. One can only imagine how these militant words, coming from a little gray-haired Irishwoman who hardly looked a radical, must have lifted the spirits of these destitute men.

Mother Jones was a fervent supporter of the broader union movement and the still broader struggle of workers seeking to win a measure of dignity for themselves and ownership of the products they created, but over time she developed a special place in her heart and in her activism for mine workers and their union, the United Mine Workers. In an era when factories and slaughterhouses were virtually unregulated, at a time when workers were considered disposable commodities, few if any workers endured the conditions and dangers that mine workers experienced on a daily basis.

Every morning, often before the sun came up, they were transported into darkness, into the very bowels of the earth, where they breathed in foul gases and poisonous dust as they collected the fuel that powered the nation's industrial might. When their workday was done, they retreated from the mine and returned to the surface, returned to homes the company owned in a town the company ran. They rarely saw the light of day. They died terrible deaths, being buried alive when things went wrong, as they often did, or wasting away before their time of lung diseases.

In the late 1890s, Mother Jones traveled primitive country roads to support striking members of the United Mine Workers in West Virginia. Although she was a woman, although she was older, and although she lived much of her life in cities, she instantly connected with the young, male, rural miners. One union official recalled that she "would take a drink with the boys and spoke their idiom, including some pretty rough language when she was talking about the bosses. This might have been considered a little fast in ordinary women, but the miners knew and respected her." They knew and appreciated that she had made a conscious decision to side with them, to see in their struggles a variation of her own family's history in Ireland. She sought not to escape from her class and background but to defend it.

Mother Jones immersed herself into the work of organizing the miners and railing against the injustices of the mines and company towns of Pennsylvania, West Virginia, Virginia, and other coal-rich areas. And the men who ran the unions and worked the mines did more than simply welcome her help; they made her a leader. She was put in charge of organizing miners in parts of West Virginia in 1902 and was arrested and jailed for her activities. Her autobiography is filled with colorful anecdotes about this formative decade in her career, although it's hard to know how many of the stories are true. But even if she exaggerated by half, her work and energy were remarkable all the same. She told of traveling to support a mine workers' strike in Virginia and being greeted by a "terribly frightened" miner who said that her life was in danger. "The superintendent told me that if you came down here he would blow out your brains," the miner warned. "He said he didn't want to see you 'round these parts."

Ah, but Mother Jones had the perfectly defiant response: "You tell the superintendent that I am not coming to see him anyway. I am coming to see the miners."

Too melodramatic to be true? Perhaps, but there's no question that mine owners and managers would not have wanted to see this eloquent and passionate Irishwoman anywhere near a picket line. And while they probably wouldn't have threatened the life of a gray-haired woman, they had few qualms about brutalizing their young, male workers, or summoning state power on behalf of the company's interests. In a dramatic turning point for the mine workers' union, law-enforcement officers shot and killed nineteen miners during a peaceful demonstration near a mine in Lattimer, Pennsylvania, in 1897.

While women throughout the nation were stepping up their demands for a greater role in civic and public life, Mother Jones remained exceptional because of the world in which she chose to live (with and among miners), the leadership role she attained, and her unapologetic embrace of radical economic change. She was not satisfied with demanding higher wages, although she agitated for them, or a limit on the workday, although she supported such measures. She wanted to change the system top to bottom. And she recognized that oppression wore many faces—it divided not only classes but races as well. Her radicalism included challenges to white supremacy as well as to capitalist plutocracy. "The enemy seeks to conquer you by dividing your ranks, by making distinctions between North and South, between American and foreign," she told a group of miners in Colorado in 1903. "You are all miners, fighting a common cause, a common master. . . . I know of no East or West, North or South, when it comes to my class fighting the battle for justice. If it is my fortune to live to see the industrial chain broken from every workingman's child in America, if then there is one black child in Africa in bondage, there I shall go."

As her fame spread, so did her commitments. She spoke out

on behalf of Mexican revolutionaries who opposed the dictatorial regime of General Porfirio Díaz; she traveled to New York to encourage a strike by garment workers (whose plight would become a rallying cry for change when more than 140 workers died in the Triangle Shirtwaist Company factory fire in New York in 1911); and she organized a parade of children to march against the horrors of child labor.

Wherever she was, whatever the cause, Mother Jones left little doubt what she believed and how she felt about the injustices of industrial America. And she clearly relished her role as a provocateur extraordinaire. "Some people call us Bolsheviks . . . some call us Reds," she told a labor conference in Mexico City. "Well, what of it! If we are Red, then Jefferson was Red, and a whole lot of those people that have turned the world upside down were Red."

Her rhetoric was provocative and inspired great outrage in the press, which was probably the point. But without taking away from Jones's steadfast principles, it is also true that she understood the theater of politics and of protest, as perhaps only she could. For she was, after all, playing a role she invented, a character who provided emotional distance from the realities of her own tragic story.

Behind the scenes, Mother Jones was not quite as incendiary. She often tried to find a middle course between more conservative union leaders and the radicals of the Industrial Workers of the World, better known as the Wobblies. As time wore on, this would become more difficult. The tensions between labor and capital seemed only to worsen, not improve, after the progressive administration of Theodore Roosevelt. In the fall of 1910, a homemade bomb planted near the Los Angeles Times building, which housed a newspaper known for its anti-union positions, killed twenty workers and injured more than one hundred. The bomb, made up of more than a dozen sticks of dynamite, was on a timer and designed to explode at four o'clock in the morning, when few people, if any, would be in the building. Instead, it went off about three hours early, when late-night workers were finishing up their shifts. Two brothers, John and James McNamara, who were active in the ironworkers' union, were arrested for the sensational crime. James McNamara eventually pled guilty to the Times bombing, while John pled guilty to another bombing, this one at the Llewellyn Iron Works on Christmas Day, 1910. Both were sentenced to prison at San Quentin.

Mother Jones took part in a labor-backed campaign to win pardons for the two brothers, whose actions may well have reminded her of those of the secret societies her grandfather joined in early nineteenth-century Ireland. The effort on behalf of the bombers failed, and James McNamara died in prison in 1941, while his brother, who pled guilty to the less destructive ironworks bombing, was released and returned to organizing, dying the same year as his brother.

The Times bombing led President Woodrow Wilson to appoint a commission, headed by labor lawyer Frank Walsh, to investigate the very conditions that Mother Jones had been agitating against for decades. She traveled to New York to answer the commission's questions, including Chairman Walsh's formulaic question about her place of residence. She told him that she resided "wherever the workers are fighting the robbers."

It was a very Irish moment in American labor history, as Chairman Walsh, an ardent Irish nationalist and renowned union activist, guided Mother Jones, a native of Cork, through two days of extraordinary testimony about her career as one of the nation's most prominent voices for workers. She told of the hazards of organizing unions and strikes in the face of state and private power. She condemned the press for not reporting on industrial abuses. And she recounted her attempt to organize a march by children to the Long Island home of President Theodore Roosevelt to protest the use of child labor. The march, she said, never got close to the president's Oyster Bay residence because of security guards. Roosevelt, she said, "had a lot of secret service men watching an old women and an army of children. You fellows do elect some wonderful presidents. The best thing you can do is to put a woman in the next time."

The *New York Times*, which was not especially friendly to union organizers, described Mother Jones as "one of the most entertaining witnesses" the commission had heard. The paper noted that the commissioners had allowed her to speak virtually without interruption, so she "proceeded in her quaint way without being tied down to geography or continuity of events."

It is hard not to notice the condescension in the *Times's* description, but there was a bit of truth in what the paper said. Mother Jones certainly was entertaining, not only in front of the commission but on the picket line and on her soapbox. She understood the importance of theatrics and drama—even her physical presence was a performance, dressed as she invariably was in a flamboyant hat, and she delighted in shaking her fist at the imagined presence of bosses and capitalists.

The stories she told Walsh and his colleagues were filled with dramatic—and, as the *Times* suggested, mostly unverifiable—tales from the picket lines, where the workers were always heroic and the bosses always villainous. Nobody asked for details, perhaps because they understood that beneath the theatrics and the tall tales, Mother Jones truly did speak truth to power. American industrial workers in the late nineteenth and early twentieth centuries had no safety net—they and their families were on their own. Meanwhile, the great industrialists of the age built fabulous fortunes, controlled politicians, manipulated supply and demand, and entertained each other with tall tales of their own, often ending with the moral that those who work hard will grow rich, while those who remained at the bottom were lazy and worthless. Many embraced social Darwinism and eugenics, which argued that success was a sign of fitness, and failure could be ascribed to genetics.

Mother Jones remained a voice for labor through the 1920s, a time associated with superficial prosperity and frivolity. She would have none of it. Despite failing health, she worked on her autobiography, visited with striking dressmakers in Chicago in 1924, and fretted over what she saw as "a peculiar apathy" among workers during the Roaring Twenties.

She picked out her final resting place—Mount Olive, Illinois, where seven mine workers and four security guards were killed during a strike in 1898.

She declared that May 1, 1930, was her one hundredth birthday. It wasn't, but no matter—few would argue with her at that point in her life. Among those who sent good wishes was John D. Rockefeller Jr., whose anti-union sentiment was as profound as her loathing of capitalists. Somehow, the titan of corporate America and the Joan of Arc of the labor movement managed to get along, no doubt to the chagrin of their friends. "He's a damn good sport,"

Mother Jones said of Rockefeller. "I've licked him many times, but we've made peace."

She refused to wear a corsage for the occasion, but she summoned the energy to smile and greet hundreds of admirers who had gathered for the party. On hand to record the event was the latest marvel of the age, a moving-picture camera that recorded sound. Her friends hushed as Mother Jones took a sip of water and then talked directly into that camera. "America," she said, "was not founded on dollars but on the blood of men who gave their lives for your benefit. Power lies in the hands of labor to retain American liberty, but labor has not yet learned how to use that power."

It was her last hurrah. She died several months later, on November 30. American workers, reeling from the effects of the stock market crash, mourned one of their greatest champions. She had been "in the forefront of labor struggles, cheering and inspiring men and women to fight for the cause of organized labor," said William Green, head of the American Federation of Labor.

She had lived through hell on both sides of the Atlantic—from Mary Harris, child of Cork, to Mother Jones, voice of American labor. A member of an exploited class, she knew how those with power treated those without it. And as a witness to tragedy, she became even more so a participant in resistance. Mother Jones carried unexpressed sadness and loneliness wherever her activism brought her, but she refused to be defeated and would not allow those who called her "mother" to surrender to hopelessness or to resign themselves to the status quo. Rather than submit to heartbreak and tragedy, she chose to raise hell at a time when hell needed raising.

Albert D. J. Cashier (1843–1915)

BY JILL MCDONOUGH

PRIVATE ALBERT D. J. CASHIER was the smallest recruit in the Illinois 95th Volunteer Infantry Regiment, just nineteen when he joined the Union Army in 1862. It was August, after Shiloh, and little guys were welcome; there were plenty of boys lying about their ages and names, signing up for the cause, or to prove how tough they were, or to get the forty-dollar advance, or all of the above. The boy they called Al or Chub was only five feet tall and didn't shave yet. He couldn't read or write. But he had worked on a farm and as a shepherd; he was strong, and he seemed willing enough. At the end of his life he shrugged off enlisting, telling the newspapers, "They needed men and I needed excitement."

He got it: Al served three years, leaving the army only when the war was over. Decades later, at his pension hearing, fellow soldiers remembered he was "selected whenever dependable men were absolutely needed." They described the nearly ten thousand miles they marched, and how he good-naturedly posed for pictures with the tallest soldier in the regiment, using their contrasting five-foot and six-foot bodies to show how the pup tents were okay for Al but pretty much everybody else needed either more tent or less body. In photographs, he's serious, gazing straight at the camera, a boyish face on a soft-looking body in a rumpled uniform.

A few of Al's comrades also remembered a day they were outnumbered, cut off from the rest of the troops by sudden rebel gunfire. The line in front of them ran on ahead, marching double time. But they dove for cover behind some fallen trees, a lucky natural barricade. Bullets zinged around them, hitting branches, ticking into the bark. Splinters rained down while they peered out, trying to see what the enemy was up to, where they were shooting from. It was tense, and the men of the 95th were tired and hungry, frustrated and afraid, in their dirty wool uniforms. No one knew how long they'd be stuck there, how many outnumbered them, how far ahead the rest of the column was getting. Al waited for a while before he'd had enough. He scrambled up on top of the barricade and hollered, "Hey! You darn rebels, why don't you get up where we can see you?"

His fellow soldiers loved him. He was old when he died, but his comrades still regretted his death, the year he spent in decline in the Watertown, Illinois, state mental hospital, committed there for being "loud" and "distracted." Long after his death they were still writing to each other about Al, still putting it all together, remembering the time he climbed a tall tree to tie the Union flag back onto a branch after it was shot down by rebels, remembering how he kept to himself, didn't play poker, baseball, or dominoes like everybody else.

His commanding officer told the *Omaha Bee*, years later, "I left Cashier, the fearless boy of 22, at the end of the Vicksburg campaign." The next time that officer would see him, almost five decades had passed, and Albert looked very different. It wasn't so much the wrinkles or missing teeth, the liver spots and thinning hair, all the inescapable signs of aging. Albert was now a woman, a frail old woman of seventy.

It turned out Private Albert D. J. Cashier was born Jennie Irene Hodgers in County Louth, Ireland, in 1843.

SO. THERE'S A lot to say about that. There is naturally the *how* of it all: how did he manage to fool so many people for so many years? Then there is the *why* of it—what did he do it for? Specific to Al's story—as opposed to our more contemporary understanding of transgenderism and cross-dressing—the circumstances here include not just what gender looked like in the nineteenth century but what the Great Hunger felt like to the Irish poor, what a new country offered up to fleeing immigrants, and what the Civil War meant to the soldiers who fought in it.

I love Jennie/Albert's crazy, brave story. I'm Irish, and I'm a homo. Jennie Hodgers looks like every girl I wanted to sleep with in college. I can't believe people thought she was a man: I see breasts and a woman's face in those few surviving photos. As for the how and the why? I can only speculate, against the backdrop of a particular time and place. But I will say, for the purposes of this essay, I have chosen to refer to Albert as "he" throughout. I realize there's a lot of thinking and conversation surrounding gender pronouns these days, but to me this seems most likely to be what Albert would have wanted. And even his Civil War comrades who fought alongside him in the early 1860s allowed him the dignity of his chosen pronoun. As one of his fellow soldiers wrote in a letter after Albert's sex was discovered, "they found out he was a woman."

LET'S SAY ALBERT CASHIER grew up in County Louth, from 1843 to 1856, as he offered in one version of his past. This gave him an unenviable view of the famine that killed a fifth of the people around him. Primary sources from those years include stories of whole fields gone so rotten the stench drove people away. Sheriffs report on the number of corpses found on the side of the road. Newspapers describe a family found living with bodies stacked around their shack like sandbags against a flood. Accounts from that place, that time, read like *The Walking Dead*, some zombie apocalypse from our nightmares. The word *unspeakable* gets used a lot.

In County Louth in the 1840s and 1850s, when you lost your home and had nowhere else to go, you could go to the workhouse. These were like big dorms where you were able to trade work for food and a place to sleep. Men spent their days breaking rocks for roads, women and kids walked in a circle together pushing a huge wheel to grind corn, old people picked apart old ropes to make them into new ones. But the workhouses were quickly patched together and were just as quickly overwhelmed, and soon they had to turn people away. So you'd walk to the nearest one, hear it was full, and walk on to the next. Help was there, you heard, you hoped, if you could keep walking.

If Albert Cashier ever spoke of these scenes, it was never recorded. Maybe for him it was unspeakable to survive when so
many around him had died. Though surviving was certainly better
than falling down dead by a turf rick, or of famine fever, or having
pigs eat your legs while you were maybe dead or maybe still working on dying. Is it any wonder he set off for America? After all, how
scary could America be? Even for a young girl, a teenager more or
less, alone in the world. How scary could it be?

So maybe Jennie's passing as a man isn't the most remarkable
thing here. Maybe it's his coming from open trenches filled with
victims of the great hunger and cholera and all the other diseases
that came with it. Stowing away on a ship likely filled with immigrants—your great-great-great-grandmother, my grandfather's
grandfather—whose landlords found it was cheaper to book passage for their tenants than to keep them alive in Ireland. A million
Irish poured off the island in droves, heading into the unknown,
leaving behind everything familiar, their families, their loved
ones, living and dead. They left their homes, their language. They
ran away from death and into a new world, a new life. It's getting
from there, from all that, to a time and place so safe and tame that
gender, something so frivolous, can become the most remarkable
thing about your safe, well-fed, miraculous life.

AMERICA WAS A clean slate, a do-over, a place to become
a new person. America, for Jennie Hodgers and for so many others,
was a land of reinvention. And Jennie made the most of it. We don't
know when Jennie used the name Albert for the first time, when
he cut his hair and put on pants instead of skirts, petticoats, bod-
ices, those shoes that called for a buttonhook. Illinois was still the

frontier when Albert went west from New York; jobs there offered higher wages to bring people out to help, and back then, like now, men made more money than women. Irish immigrants went there in waves, looking for a safe and fertile place to use their hands, to do the kind of work they knew how to do—often the only kind of work they knew how to do. So Albert Cashier ended up in Illinois, working as a farmhand for a year.

Rolling fields green as those in Ireland. Planting corn and to-matoes, weeding, feeding chickens, milking cows. Birdsong, wind brushing across meadows, a richly bruised sunrise, day after day after day. I think of this as a sort of recovery period from the hor-rors of the famine and the uncertainty of immigration. A quiet routine on a farm, regular meals, a safe place to sleep. Waking up before dawn to plant or weed a patch before the sun got up too high in summer. Chopping wood to warm yourself twice in win-ter. A lot of solitude, plenty of food, sleeping safe and alone in a bed. With enough time and quiet it might occur to you that you're pretty lucky, getting away with this whole dressing-up-like-a-man thing. But by then you're already in it, and you see that even if you had some desire to go back to being a woman, you'd be crazy to give up the higher wages and other perks. Would you rather work as a farmhand, be outside all day, or start up with the laundering, work just as hard for a lot less money, with the ever-present risk of people messing with you. *No way. You've got ladies doing your laundry, man!*

AS FOR THE army—there were lots of good reasons to sign up for the army: adventure, patriotism, money. Perhaps the most likely reason Albert enlisted is that it is just what men did.

He signed up on August 6, 1862, in Belvidere, Boone County, Illinois. On the records, someone wrote "Albert D. J. Cashier" in nice, big handwriting. Description: nineteen years old, five feet three inches, light complexion, blue eyes, auburn hair. Where born? New York City. Look at him, reinventing himself! Adding a couple inches, using the name that's been working for him for a while, making himself not just an American but a New Yorker.

So he signed up for a training camp on how to be an American man. All the guys were doing it. And some of those people ended up nicknaming Albert "Chub." His fellow soldiers saw that smooth round face, those soft breasts, but they couldn't see them for what they were. To them, Albert's body read as fat, not female. Chub! Not bad for someone who lived through the famine.

WHEN YOU READ about the hundreds—hundreds!—of women who have disguised themselves as men and become soldiers, every author eventually gets to the wonder of how they hid their breasts and dealt with their periods. The books on lady soldiers spend more time on this than on the military physicals that these recruits apparently passed without revealing their sex. Mostly, it seems like all they had to do was show their working hands and feet; if you could march and pull a trigger, you were good to go. Also, no one would ever have suspected it—why on earth would a lady sign up for that? Anyone who wanted to be a soldier must be a man, at least according to the definitions of gender they were working with.

Wartime was probably an easier than usual time to deal with your period on the road: throwing bloody rags on the fire was part of the routine, and everybody's clothes were wrecked. Everyone was also starving and overworked, walking hundreds of miles, experiencing the kinds of conditions that stop menstruation anyway, that make you skinny and muscled, that make your breasts shrink.

The volunteers cobbled together what military experience they had, looking at the books they were given on how to be a soldier. They read "Revised Army Regulations" and "Tactics" and tried that stuff out. They stuck around Illinois drilling and prepping for two and a half months, learning how to march in formation, how to load and fire their muskets, where to stick a rebel with a bayonet. Then they took off for Kentucky to join the Army of the Tennessee under Ulysses S. Grant. It was a great time to fake being a man. How does a man march fifteen miles with a heavy knapsack in new country? How did he crowd into a freight car or board a steamer in the middle of the night with his new friends? None of the men had done anything like this before. There wasn't ever anything like this to do. Like Al, they came forward when Lincoln called for more troops. They got cash money, new uniforms, knapsacks full of coffee and hardtack, and a musket. They also got a chance to learn from each other, to meet other soldiers from other states, other countries. Not just to study how to be an American man but to define what American manhood was going to be going forward.

AS FOR THE 95th Regiment, the men spent a lot of time on steamers, positioning themselves up and down the Mississippi. Steamers moved troops to wherever they were needed throughout the war. They'd spend whole days standing around waiting to board these cavernous, wooden riverboats. Or they'd rush the dock late at night, trying to keep rebel spies in the dark about troop movements. They'd fill the underdecks with horses and mules and wagons and artillery, then fill in the top with themselves, often with just enough room to stand. The regimental history recalled one late-night boarding like this: "Everything was in an uproar, everybody was mad, and *somebody* must have been drunk." This may be my favorite observation on the Civil War.

During Al's three years of fighting, passing through dangerous country on steamers with names like *Universe, Meteor, Dacotah,* or *White Cloud,* the men of the 95th would line the decks with hay bales and crates of hardtack to protect themselves from Confederate musket fire. The sharpshooters in the 95th, the snipers, scanned the banks and picked off rebels with "admirable coolness," often so near to the enemy that Confederate shots and shells went over the boat. It was too close to get hit.

Of the 983 men who signed up with Al in Illinois in 1862, only about half made it to the end of their three-year tour, mustering out together in Mississippi: 190 were discharged early for disability and disease; 83 died from wounds received in action; and 177 died of disease. So these men needed to be brave, needed to cultivate fearlessness. Good hygiene would have been a plus, but they didn't often have the information or means to make that a reality. Maybe Al's need for privacy kept him cleaner, exposed him to fewer germs and risks than those unlucky 190, 83, and 177.

The ones who made it through needed loyalty, connection, things to fight for. They loved most of their leaders and told and retold stories about why: when rebels suggested Major McKee surrender, he replied, "I don't scare worth a damn. We are ready for you." They loved General Smith for drawing his saber on men from another regiment when they cut in line at a pontoon bridge.

They loved him for drinking and swearing, getting his men on the steamers by arguing "in his effective, though profane phraseology, that 'These boats, sir, by G-d, sir, can carry these troops, sir, and five thousand more, by G-d, sir.'"

These men needed a sense of humor. When the 95th gathered for reunions later, they'd pass around that photo of Cashier, the littlest man in the regiment, under a pup tent with Gleason, the tallest. Men gave each other shit and didn't grumble.

In Mobile once, the Union commanders tried using the regimental bands to trick the Confederates. The plan was for the bands to play three different reveilles each, so they sounded like twelve regiments coming rather than four. But one band was so famously crappy, a last-minute band of guys who couldn't actually play, that they couldn't pull it off. After three other bands played nine distinct versions of reveille, the drum corps from the Missouri 44th produced their usual discordant, horrible effort. And then they tried to do another version, and it came out the same pathetic way. All of the men, thousands, spread out camping in the woods for miles around, cracked up at once with "irrepressible laughter, making the woods ring for a long distance around. Thus this event, which furnished the men with so much merriment, may possibly have disclosed to the rebels the real character of the present expedition." They didn't care.

They made fun of themselves, of their troubles. And they loved making fun of soft people, civilians who couldn't hack it. Outside Nashville, needing some defensive structures built in a hurry, the general conscripted locals to pitch in. "To see the clerks and city dandies, and other non-combatants, provided with haversacks well filled with hard bread, and marched out to the front where an

opportunity was afforded of developing their soft muscles by work
upon the forts and other defenses, was the cause of much merriment among the boys in blue." Being an American man, a soldier,
was better than being a city-dandy civilian. You belonged. Imagine
how much better that was than being a *lady* civilian—a poor lady
civilian, no less! Albert was not some loser Irish immigrant girl. He
was a fighting infantryman who was proud of his service.

OF COURSE, STAYING strong and healthy was crucial.
They came to see the constant marching as a sort of tonic rather
than a chore; stuck in camp, disease was a killer. More men died
of dysentery, typhoid, pneumonia, measles, TB, and malaria than
the minié balls. Al had only one bout of dysentery bad enough
to put him in the hospital—he was there less than a day. He was
part of a group prized for its snipers and known for its bravery
and over-the-top attention to detail with dress parades. He seemed
to specialize in the new American manhood they were inventing
together: staying alive and healthy while messing stuff up for your
enemies. American ingenuity and flexibility, an early draft of "by
any means necessary."

Being a man in the Union Army meant doing the things that
needed doing, starting with Vicksburg, which Lincoln called the
"key": "The war can never be brought to a close until that key is
in our pocket." It took forever, but the Union finally did it. Grant's
plan meant dredging canals through the swamp around the city,
making it possible for big boats full of soldiers to slip quietly behind rebel lines. Al's battalion provided details of men day and
night to do that sloppy, swampy digging and clearing—horrible
work. And they MacGyvered their way through the muck, coming

up with new steam-driven underwater saws to cut cypress trees at the base, going through whatever they couldn't go around.

On May 22, 1863, moving on Vicksburg, they slithered through their network of ravines filled with logs and branches while their snipers covered them, or tried: most casualties occurred within those first hours. Driven back to just outside the city, they waited for more than a month while the citizens of Vicksburg dug caves, starved, ended up eating even their mules. One time, doing a little recon in the area, Albert got captured. But don't worry: he grabbed a guard's gun, knocked him down, got away. No problem. How cool is that?

On the day of Vicksburg's surrender, July 4, 1863, Al's regiment was one of the first to go in. "With the victorious stars and stripes unfurled, and with music playing the national airs, these dusty, scarred, and war-worn battalions, keeping step to the music of the Union, marched through the streets of Vicksburg."

But ultimately, the history of the 95th Regiment speaks less about glory like that and a lot more about drinking, carousing, and pillaging. Early on, they were encouraged to "supply the men" using those very skills. They got started with Grant's notion of feeding his army on the fly, taking hams and chickens and pickled vegetables and whatever else they could carry from the plantations they passed. These enemy plantations, they discovered, were surprisingly well stocked, which gave Grant the idea to keep going with the steal-the-food plan. Grant was making it up as he went along too.

When winter supplies dwindled, and they had to eat the horses' corn, they made corncakes and popcorn, joked that next they'd get harnessed and eat rations of hay. In April 1865, on the two-hundred-mile march from Mobile to Montgomery, a lot of them ended up barefoot, the hard road having worn right through their soles. So they cheered each other on with joking signs posted on trees en route: "To Selma, one hundred and fifty miles, sore feet or no sore feet." "To good living, one hundred and ten miles."

They had gotten so accustomed to "gleaning" meals from Confederate homes that when they came across some unoccupied country, where they couldn't easily rustle up supper, they remarked on it. On the way to Montgomery they caught and ate a snake: "a monstrous reptile, fat, sleek, and scaly, and its appearance demonstrated fully that if human beings could not find enough in that barren country to grow fat on, rattlesnakes could." It was delicious, but they didn't often need to resort to snake-tasting. They usually had better luck, though by the end of the war they were boasting about their abilities as scroungers, not giving credit just to luck. Both armies were depending on stolen civilian supplies at that point, but the Union soldiers of the 95th prided themselves on being better. "Though the rebel army had been through this section twice within a short time, and nearly drained the country of supplies, yet the Union soldiers, by the exercise of their characteristic inquisitiveness, succeeded in securing from the neighboring plantations plenty of fowls and rasters, which, in connection with hard-tack and coffee, furnished the officers and privates with respectable Christmas dinners."

The officers saw what side their bread was buttered on. After the rules changed and called for restraint, if ever the men were caught red-handed with stolen goods for "a sumptuous evening meal," Colonel Avery protected them. *Oh, that chicken?* Colonel Avery would say. *That one over there? Nah, they picked that chicken up in Brownsville. They've been carrying that chicken a hundred miles.* "For this cunning manner in which the colonel shielded his men from accusations of foraging which, if traced up, would, in many instances have been found true: they called him Colonel Pap."

It makes me very happy to think of Albert leaving the famine of his childhood behind and having so many new friends to kick through plantations with, so many of the enemy's hams and chickens and lush gardens and liberated bottles of wine. The reporter Charles Dana wrote of the Union experience of Vicksburg,

> We were in an incomparable position for a siege as regard the health and comfort of our men. The high wooded hills afforded pure air and shade, and the deep ravines abounded in springs of excellent water, and if they failed it was easy to bring it from the Mississippi. Our line of supplies was beyond the reach of the enemy, and there was an abundance of fruit all about us. I frequently met soldiers coming into camp with buckets full of mulberries, blackberries and red and yellow plums.

The confederates were down to eating rats and songbirds, but Albert could have all the berries he could eat.

Scrounging is a hard habit to break. On one long steamer journey to New Orleans, commanders couldn't keep men on the boats. Every time they stopped for fuel or fresh orders, "a few mischievous and unruly soldiers scoured the area for food and goods to take." When they arrived in New Orleans just after St. Patrick's Day, they saw rebel forts made entirely of oyster shells. This delighted them almost as much as the oyster beds they were camping by at Cedar Point, where, according to one account, "the surf was alive with wading soldiers, skirmishing not with rebels, but after oysters, of which they brought skiffs-full to the shore, and furnished the camps with large supplies of this luxurious article of food." Can't you smell the wood fire and the water, the roasted oysters and beer I hope they had? I love knowing about this night for Albert, loving this sweet dinner at a journey's end, all the careless laughter and sandy hair.

Right after Vicksburg they took Natchez, no problem, and quickly understood that there were a ton of Texas cattle nearby on their way to becoming delicious rebel soldier meals. So they found some horses, ran off the Confederate guards on cow-duty, and drove the cattle back to Natchez. While they had the horses, they decided to chase down a train. They were soldiers, gleaners, thieves, architects, builders, engineers, diggers, prison guards, re-inventors of siege warfare, inventors of trench warfare, even oyster-men. And now they were train robbers. America! Why not? What's next?

They took 150 wagons of rebel ammo, 5,000 Texas cattle, 312 new Austrian muskets, 3,000 rounds of cartridges, 11 boxes of ammo. And they blew up a bunch more, it being just too heavy to carry. (Plus, blowing shit up? Men love that.) They exploded and destroyed 207 rounds of infantry ammo they found hidden in a gully, 56 boxes of artillery ammunition, 17 hogsheads of sugar, 150 saddles, 1 artillery carriage, 1 government wagon, 50 stands of small arms, a cotton factory with 40 looms that made rebel army cloth, 2 locomotives, 14 freight cars, 2 passenger cars, 250 barrels of molasses, a French six-pounder gun. And bale upon bale upon bale of Confederate cotton. And that's just the stuff they wrote down.

They destroyed a fort with explosives, almost killing themselves in the process. The air was filled with timbers, great clumps of red clay, everything that had been the fort and the ground beneath it suddenly flying around. They tore up railroad communications and arsenals, found and raided Confederate stores.

All through the war they got better and better at playing it by ear, figuring out problems and solving them with whatever was at hand, without worrying much about things like who owned what. They traveled all over the known country by boat and train and on foot, saw Spanish moss and crocodiles and oyster forts and butterflies and strange new birds and freed slaves training as soldiers and season after season of horrors: piles of amputated hands and feet, rotting in the sun. You get shot in the hand, you cut the hand off. You get stuck under a corpse, you stay there till dark. You make a way through the swamp out of no way, you clear the steamers' decks of wild animals none of you has ever seen before. You get caught by the enemy, you tip your hat and run like hell the other way.

What could be more American, under these circumstances, than pretending to be a man? Pretending to be a man is exactly the kind of thing a man would do.

THESE MEN DIED, in great numbers. There are instances of women who signed up for the Civil War and saw death and rot and explosions and turned tail and fled. But Albert Cashier made a life out of survival.

Sometimes survival for women is about putting up with it when your boss hits on you. Being coerced to concede that actually, maybe that wasn't rape, after all. Quitting your waitress job in Lubbock so you can drive all night to the clinic in El Paso. Having ten miscarriages and only five babies. But sometimes, at least for

Al, it's about years of serving with men you quickly come to love. And then it's about watching those men die, in horrible ways—torn in half by cannon fire, wasting away in camp. Like the famine, so much was unspeakable.

After the fall of Vicksburg, one of the greatest Union victories, Al marched on with his fellow soldiers, and he survived one of the greatest Union defeats. Near Guntown, Mississippi, exhausted after a long, hot march and in no shape to fight, they met Lieutenant General Nathan Bedford Forrest. And Forrest had them right where he wanted them: close to the Confederate supply and far from the Union's. The Union called it Guntown. The Confederates, who won, called it Brice's Crossroads. There's a monument.

Forrest had 4,787 men against Union Brigadier General Sturgis's 8,100. In Ken Burns's beautiful documentary about the Civil War, historian Shelby Foote talks about Forrest being one of that war's two geniuses—Lincoln and Forrest, Foote thinks. He cites this battle as his favorite example of Forrest's abilities. Forrest knew the Union forces coming to attack him were double the number of his own men. But it had been raining for six days, and the roads were a muddy mess. He figured the Union cavalry would arrive way ahead of the infantrymen. So he took his time, beat the shit out of the cavalry, waited around for the rest of the exhausted northerners to show up on foot, and whipped them too. The Confederates lost 492 men. The Union lost 740, and 1,500 were taken prisoner.

Al made it out alive and free. When the 95th was told they needed to pick up the pace, cover five or six miles to help out their cavalry, they were lucky: their commander, Colonel Humphrey, was one of the few leaders that didn't tell his men to march double time; he just told them to be quick. So they were somewhat less exhausted than many of the soldiers from the other regiments when they showed up for the fight, though they still lost men to heatstroke before they'd even arrived.

Humphrey was shot dead on arrival and was replaced by Captain Stewart. Then Stewart was shot through both thighs and carried off the field. Captain Bush took over and was shot dead, and then Captain Schellenger was in charge, while the fighting "continued with indescribable desperation." Enlisted men and officers "were falling thick and fast from right to left of the regimental line; the ammunition was fast giving out, and none arrived from the rear to replete the empty cartridge-boxes." They ran away, those who weren't captured, and kept running from June 11 to June 13. "[W]hen the knapsack became too onerous, the men unslung and abandoned it, and around many a tree did they bend and break their faithful guns to prevent capture both of themselves and firearms by the enemy."

The 95th had never been beaten before. They'd had hard times and long marches and dirty work and death and disease, but they'd never marched right into getting their asses handed to them. When they loved their leaders they let them know it, but when leadership failed they weren't afraid to call it out, either: "The true cause of the great misfortune was plainly incompetency and lack of courage on the part of one who should have been the leading spirit of the occasion." During the war, the men of the 95th defined themselves, made themselves men of courage, men who weren't afraid to call out hypocrites and cowards, men happy to throw a bad leader under the bus.

After the war, waiting to muster out, they ran through their flawless dress parades again and again, showing off their freshly cleaned blue uniforms, sunlight glinting off the rows of buttons and crisp turns of bayonets. Their last camp, in Opelika, Alabama, had plenty of fresh air and clean water, so nobody got sick, or was even scared of getting sick.

On the Fourth of July, 1865, the soldiers slipped out before sunrise and fired a God-knows-how-many-gun salute without getting it cleared by anybody. It startled their commanders, scared the bejesus out of the locals, and made the men so happy they no doubt told and retold the story at their reunions for the next fifty years.

They deserved that salute. Albert had arrived on our shores with hundreds of thousands of other Irish immigrants, without food, clothes, money. And there he was five years later, a Union hero, a fighting man who helped keep our country together, helped define it.

When they finally got their orders to muster out, they were told they'd be marching from Opelika, Alabama, to Vicksburg, Mississippi, to end their service. Marching 350 miles in Alabama and Mississippi in the heat of July. Al and his buddies got together and said no way, forget that mess. They chartered a train, orders or no orders, and rode into Vicksburg, the site of their greatest victory, ending their war together.

THE MEN OF the 95th Volunteer Infantry went back to Illinois, and Albert returned to the life he was living before the war started. He was twenty-two. For a while he grew and sold plants with a war buddy, and he had a lot of other jobs—lamplighter for the little town of Saunemin, farmhand, handyman and laborer for the Chesbro family. There he had dinner with Mr. Chesbro, who was a farmer, his wife, and their two daughters most nights.

Eventually they bought him a house and gave him a spot in their family cemetery. He lived alone and still got teased for being so small; neighbors remembered that boys in town would call him little drummer boy, and Albert would lose it and yell, "*I was a fighting infantryman!*"

In 1890 a lawyer in town helped him get his veteran's pension, increasing it once he was fifty-five and couldn't work so hard anymore. In 1900, when he was fifty-seven, Albert's doctor told the Pension Bureau that he was totally disabled. Years came and years went and nobody found out Albert was a woman until 1911. At the time he was working for Illinois State Senator Ira Lish as a chauffeur. Lish needed a driver: one of the few times he was behind the wheel he managed to hit poor Albert, breaking his leg. Albert begged his boss to leave him alone, not to call a doctor. But the doctor came and soon discovered Al was born a woman. Lish's interest in keeping the story out of the papers probably helped keep Albert male for the next couple of years. The only people the senator and doctor told were the Chesbro sisters, who came out to help Albert get well again, and they promised not to tell.

Some while later, Senator Lish and the doctor worked to get Albert into the Illinois Soldiers and Sailors Home. The home either was told or discovered he was a woman, but they let him in anyway, on April 11, 1911. He kept wearing men's clothes and received visitors from his regiment, remembering together what they'd been through.

ROBERT HORAN, A corporal in the 95th, corresponded with his former sergeant, Charles Ives; we still have those letters. His spelling is terrible, but I love it too much to fix it for you. When word got out about Albert's being born a female, Horan told Ives, "I supose I have resived from defereon ones some 10 or 12 clipping of pappers & no to alike." No two articles alike: nobody could get this story straight, and Albert wasn't much help. He told so many different stories about his motivation. But what he decided to tell each person gives you a sense of the kind of calculating intelligence it took to live that life.

He told Charles Ives, his commanding officer, that he dressed like a boy from childhood, that he had a twin brother, and their mother always dressed the two of them the same. He was used to wearing pants "and later found it easier to get work that way." There is no evidence that Albert had a twin brother, but it's a terrific story to tell a commanding officer. You're an old lady, and he may be looking at you like you're crazy, freaked out you were a girl the whole time. But then you give him a sort of blurred double vision of a young male twin, the young boy that was, according to Ives's own memories. After all, Albert Cashier was a good man to have around in the tough spots they found themselves in during the war. In this twin version Al was never female-acting, always looked the part. And at a simpler time, when wearing pants and carrying a gun was enough to make you a man, this version might have been the kindest way to let Ives keep his vision of Al intact.

Albert gave a very different explanation to the Chesbro sisters, the two neighbor women he ate dinner with most of his life. In this story Jennie Hodgers had a gallant and handsome boyfriend, and put on a uniform so they could enlist together and never be apart. The unnamed boyfriend gets shot early in the war, someplace, and pulls Jennie to his deathbed. He loves her, he says, and his dying wish is that she be true to him forever, even after he's gone. He wants her to stay in the army, dress as a man forever, to forever be not just true to him but unavailable to all other men. So Jennie honors his dying wish and lives the rest of her life as a man. So romantic! Nobody else got this version, but it's not the only time Albert talked about romantic interests to help people see him in the way he needed to be seen.

Albert was illiterate, so any letters he exchanged during the war, someone helped him to write. It looks like he spent two years of the war talking about having a girlfriend whenever he wrote to the Morey family, neighbors back in Illinois. Three of their letters to him ask if he's going to bring his sweetheart back to Illinois when the war's over. If I were running with a bunch of Union soldiers who were teasing me about not shaving and never going to the brothels with them, inventing a sweetheart and letting word get around by talking about her in the letters I've asked someone else to write wouldn't be such a bad idea. But there's no other proof to support this idea of an early sweetheart, and there don't appear to have been any boyfriends or girlfriends later back home in Illinois over the next fifty years.

When a psychiatrist talked to him about it, Albert said he was born a bastard in Clogherhead, Ireland, and worked as a shepherd with his uncle. When his mom married Somebody Cashier, they all immigrated to New York together as a family. The stepfather— with no first name and a made-up-sounding last name, who never appears later in Albert's life—dressed Albert up like a boy and got them both jobs in a shoe factory. Albert's mom died, so he got the hell out of there and came west.

Okay. What a great story to tell a psychiatrist! By 1913, even podunk psychiatrists in Nowhere, Illinois, would have been influenced by Freud, right? Nobody else gets all these details about a single mom and shadowy older male relatives telling little Jennie what to do. Look at Albert helping each of these people find a little of themselves in his life: He tells his commanding officer a story of brotherly love and maternal devotion. He tells the sisters a love story, a story that will connect them to Jennie Hodgers, believing they too would have made the same romantic choices. Maybe when you are illiterate, you develop strengths to help make up for that deficit— reading people like a book, telling them what they want to hear. Maybe when you are a woman trying to make it as a man, you make fun of yourself for being short, compensate for being short by being brave. The bottom line, though, is that the sheer variety of the stories Albert told, each seemingly tailored to its audience, makes it hard to believe in any one over another.

ON MAY 20, 1913, the *Omaha World-Herald* published a story titled "Ives Identifies the Woman Veteran of War." "She is Albert D. J. Cashier all right," said Mr. Ives. "Of course time has made a big change in her appearance, just as it has in mine, but I recognized her, and she also knew me. She is considerably broken, and her mind is rather weak. She rambles in her talk, but at times her memory seems very keen." Albert didn't recognize Charles Ives at first—Ives and the folks around Albert seemed to take that as further evidence of how crazy Albert had become—but then Albert pointed out that Charles had gotten new teeth.

"Cashier is still wearing men's clothes and will remain at the home. Her old comrades regard her with even more honor than before they knew she was a woman," the paper reported. "She has never shaved, but has considerable hair on her upper lip and some on her face, about the same as is found occasionally on a woman."

In March 1914, Albert was among the small group of soldiers

who were transferred to an insane asylum in Watertown, Illinois. Our bad speller, Horan, wrote to Ives that

> a Cathlick Preast had been coming in to see him, and it was through him he was taken to Watertown in Rock Island County. He says he think the[y] can keep him cheaper. Cashier has some money in his old home and it In care of J. M. Lish, the man he worked for & who broke his Leg with his auto & took care of him & then took him to the Home. The Preast have heard of him having some Money they don't care of Cashier. It his money thare after.

I know that's hard to read: A priest had been visiting Al and learned that Al had some money saved up. Horan thought the sneaky priest was putting Al into an asylum to get his hands on Al's savings.

Albert's condition was the same as ever, but he was sent to the asylum anyway. The commitment papers give his name as Jennie Hodgers, say he'd lost his memory, was weak and loud, had trouble sleeping. All of the transferred soldiers were described as "distracted." This does indeed seem like some sneaky shit. DeAnne Blanton is one of the authors of *They Fought Like Demons: Women Soldiers in the American Civil War* and works at the National Archives. Check out this "neither confirm nor deny" statement she put in the endnotes of her book: "The State of Illinois refuses to release the Watertown State Hospital's case file on Cashier and will not even verify whether such a file still exists (Joseph R. Buckles, Rules/Records Administrator, Illinois Department of Mental Health and Developmental Disabilities, to DeAnne Blanton, 19 Nov. 1991)."

I figured it's been a long time since 1991, so I tried to contact the State of Illinois about the Watertown file, but they didn't give me any information either. So I couldn't find out what was up with the "Preast," but if Horan thought it was fishy, and they still don't want to talk about it, what kind of place could it have been? In the home, he was allowed to wear pants, but in the asylum, they made him bunk with the female patients and wear skirts. Albert couldn't stand it; he kept trying to fasten the skirts together somehow, fashion some pinned-up sort-of pants. He tripped over the skirts and broke his hip, a painfully typical end event for an old woman. The broken hip never properly healed and led to an infection—and Albert D. J. Cashier, living at the end as Jennie Hodgers and hating every second of it, died on October 10, 1915.

Albert's fellow soldiers got permission to give him full military honors at his funeral. He was buried in uniform in the Chesbro family plot, a flag draped over his coffin, a standard veterans' marble marker for a stone. In the 1970s, the local women's club and historical society started collecting money and working on doing more for Albert, to better acknowledge the range of his extraordinary life. Clearly, the debate about just who he was, at least in regard to something as frivolous as gender, still continued. They started with this gravestone, dedicated on Memorial Day, 1977, and placed next to the military marker he was buried under:

ALBERT D. J. CASHIER

CO. G 95 ILL. INF. CIVIL WAR

BORN

JENNIE HODGERS

IN CLOGHERHEAD, IRELAND

1843–1915

THE MUCKRAKER

Samuel S. McClure (1857–1949)

BY MICHAEL MOORE

STOP ME IF YOU'VE HEARD this one before: America, swept up in an era of innovative technology, exploding economic inequality, and deep political turmoil, falls prey to wretched corporate greed and men with maniacal, narcissistic egos. Labor unions are battered, and wages are far too low. Small businesses, factory workers, and farmers get screwed over and squeezed out by robber-baron schemes and massive industrial monopolies. Prejudiced cops roam the streets and enforce their bigotry with unchecked violence. Judges selectively dispense justice, and immigrants are vilified by angry white men as foreign radicals or parasites sucking on the national economy.

If this sounds depressingly familiar to you, it's because the

America of today looks a lot like the America of the early 1900s. To be sure, there are plenty of differences between the two eras, but there's one important thing that the United States right at this moment does not have—a crusading journalist by the name of Samuel S. McClure.

S. S. McClure may be just a footnote in history textbooks at this point, but he's someone we need now more than ever. As the founder, editor, and publisher of *McClure's Magazine*, McClure invented a new form of investigative journalism in the United States. He is the godfather of the muckrakers, a type of journalist you will be hard-pressed to find these days. Seymour Hersh is one of them. So is James Risen. Woodward and Bernstein used to be. And in the far-flung reaches of the Internet there are those few unknowns who try to do that work with the minimal resources available to them. But the muckrakers of McClure's era have become a near-extinct breed. And we, as citizens on the verge of a fading democracy, are all the worse off for it.

Throughout his lifetime, McClure took the pulse of the nation and felt there a real hunger for the truth, for the full story—a wish to examine the corrupt institutions that were dominating people's lives. And for a little while at least, he got the press to stop stumbling and fawning over powerful people. He discovered writers, gave them the time and space to work, and pushed them to produce articles using real facts and deep reporting. For several years, McClure published stories that forced Americans to pay attention— to look at themselves and say, Holy shit, our government is corrupt and our politicians are for sale! Our food is lethal to eat! Working conditions for men, women, and children are horrible! Also, why the hell are children working in the first place? McClure's efforts

jump-started an entire generation of progressive politics that turned
out quaint things like antitrust laws, the eight-hour workday, and
protections for children and the elderly.

In a lot of ways, the story of S. S. McClure is an unusual and
unlikely one. He was born in 1857 into deep poverty in County An-
trim, Ireland, in a tiny two-bedroom house with a dirt floor and a
straw roof. He and his three younger brothers shared a room, with
the kitchen doubling as the living room. His mother, Elizabeth,
worked on the family's small farm. His father, Thomas, worked as
a farmer too and also a master carpenter. It was what you'd call a
Spartan upbringing, governed by the stern rules imposed by his
strict Protestant parents. While McClure would later describe it
as a contented, if not mirthful, childhood, that was most likely because he found some measure of escape.

Young Sam relished education. The little Irish schoolhouse was
his oasis, and he would get there as early and leave as late as he
could. An intensely curious boy, he read constantly from a young
age, staying up to study until his parents forced him to go to bed.
This drive for knowledge was always there, and friends from his
early days could see a clear through line from Sam's dogged work
ethic, rapacious curiosity, and omnivorous tastes to his eventual
success as a bold and visionary magazine editor.

But that was much later. In 1886, life was still very harsh. Unable
to pay the bills, Sam's dad was forced to leave the family for work in
the Glasgow shipyards. One day a coworker left open a hatch door
on a ship Sam's dad was working on, and he tumbled all the way to
the bottom of the hold. That was that—he died in an instant. Sam
was only nine.

For the McClure family everything quickly went from bad to

worse. Now their poverty was acute. Elizabeth and her four boys were passed between relatives, staying at a house as long as they could before moving on. Naturally, she craved stability, and so, like many of the desperate families around her, she found herself ready to take a big roll of the dice. Elizabeth had relatives in America, specifically in rural Indiana. This, she decided, was where the McClure family would find a new start. And so in 1866, Sam, his three brothers, and his mother boarded a ship and took off for America.

If the United States was a place of promise, it was not without its challenges. The McClures were fresh-off-the-boat Irish, and little Sam had to be scrappy. It took hustle, and not just because the McClures were poor. It took hustle because they had arrived in a country that wasn't terribly hospitable to the Irish. The family settled on another small farm, now in rural Indiana. With his hunger for learning undiminished, Sam's grades were so impressive that he left home to attend nearby Knox College at age fourteen. The college was a serious, no-nonsense place. There he would meet the core group of fellow writers and curiosity hounds who would go on to help run his news syndicate and later his magazine. He was so young that he had to study at Knox for three years before even reaching freshman standing. But McClure made the most of his time. He edited the student newspaper and started a news service, worked every summer to pay the next year's tuition, and debated competitively.

During one debate, McClure delivered a powerful and telling speech that praised the efforts of American abolitionists. He said, "It was when they believed in what seemed impossible that the abolitionists did the most good, that they created the sentiment that finally did accomplish the impossible." He was celebrating the power of the public to topple institutional corruption and laying out his own vision for taking on long odds.

As a young student, McClure was brash and energetic—the kind of kid who is, and was, frequently compared to a whirlwind. He once told a college friend, "I feel like a chained tiger. I fret against my chains." On the romantic front, McClure didn't make life any easier for himself. He fell in love with the whip-smart and beautiful Harriet Hurd, whose father, Albert, was a leading professor at Knox and detested the cocky and impulsive McClure. Professor Hurd fought hard to keep Sam away from Harriet, for whom he envisioned a much more stable partner. (To his beloved daughter, the professor once wrote about McClure: "His personal appearance, his bearing & his address are not pleasing to me. I think him conceited, impertinent, meddlesome." Ouch.) But McClure, unsurprisingly, never backed off and, after a marathon seven-year courtship, eventually persuaded Harriet to be his bride. Professor Hurd, on the other hand, would remain unconvinced and didn't let his son-in-law into his house until years after they had married.

The young couple moved to Boston, and after a successful stint there editing a bicycling magazine called the *Wheelman*, McClure was lured down to New York to take a job at a printing house. He discovered that he was fascinated by the printing process but hated doing the work himself. He also realized he was a terrible employee and dreamed of building a career where he was his own boss.

In so many ways, S. S. McClure lived that special kind of mythical story that Americans know well and love obsessively—that of a self made man who creates his own luck through masochistic determination and hard work. McClure first attained real financial success by creating a system that syndicated the work of fiction writers to hundreds of newspapers across the country. Later, he would fancifully boast that he had invented the very concept of a syndicate, but that wasn't true. What he did was create a formula for tenaciously wooing writers who showed unheralded skill. He read magazines and newspapers voraciously and fought for writers whose work he coveted. Though many warned him that journalism and fiction were a poor fit, he would impulsively hop on trains or buses to chase far-off writers, and would even board ships to cross the Atlantic to hunt down his prey. A result of this, his syndicate is credited with introducing Americans readers to the likes of Robert Louis Stevenson, Sir Arthur Conan Doyle, and Rudyard Kipling.

But what separates McClure's Horatio Alger story from everyone else's Horatio Alger story is that McClure learned a better lesson from his climb up the social ladder: success had to be moral. And though he was an immigrant, he learned that to question power is inherently American. Accordingly, McClure didn't use his newfound influence to lobby Congress for tax breaks; instead, he embarked on an endeavor that would actually change the course of history by holding the powerful accountable and by asking readers to think for themselves.

By 1893, with the syndicate in sound financial shape, McClure's restlessness began to push him beyond the business. He was sending so many articles from his desk over to the desks of newspapers and magazines that he began to feel he was already effectively an editor—a magazine editor. And from there, the dream grew bigger. "I would rather edit a magazine than be President of the United States a hundred times over," he told his wife. In June of that year, he launched *McClure's Magazine*.

McClure's was created at the worst possible time—in the dead middle of the Panic of 1893—but it survived and flourished anyway because the work was good. And the work was good because, by basically all accounts, McClure was a genius—an obsessive, idealistic, imperfect one, but a genius nonetheless. Lincoln Steffens, who was empowered by McClure to write an entire book's worth of blockbuster stories on the unchecked corruption in city government, once described the job of the *McClure's* staff as putting "four-wheel brakes upon the madness of McClure's genius." In his autobiography, Steffens praised McClure as "the receiver of the ideas of his day," adding that "he was a flower that did not sit and wait for the bees to come and take his honey and leave their seeds. He flew forth to find and rob the bees."

At the time McClure was building his career, yellow journalism was all the rage. Yellow journalism exaggerated, trumped up, and sensationalized stories to raise circulations and to serve its masters instead of serving the public. It was clickbait in an era long before the Internet. Back then, newspapers were not only affiliated with political parties but also cozy with big business and corporate interests. And you did not bite the hand that fed you. If a story was bad news for your boss, you didn't dare report it.

The principles behind the muckraking movement, which seem so obvious now, were at the core of who McClure was. Just as sincerity, modesty, and perhaps the occasional affair with whiskey are practically Irish birthrights, so too is the love of language and storytelling. Long before *McClure's Magazine* had a truly investigative bent, the magazine scored a reputation as a respectable and popular place to read good fiction and incisive biographies. Early issues of *McClure's* featured some bylines you might be familiar with: Willa Cather, Mark Twain, Stephen Crane, Émile Zola, and Jack London, to name just a few. By 1899, the circulation had surged to four hundred thousand, making it one of the most popular magazines in the country. One year later, *McClure's* had secured more advertising per issue than any other magazine in the world.

But McClure's coworkers and contemporaries didn't call him a genius just because he was creative or fearless or more than a little bit crazy. Part of what made McClure brilliant was that he understood what he could and couldn't do. Sure, he could write well enough and could edit brilliantly, but as he explained in his autobiography, he also knew his "real capital was my wide acquaintance with writers and with what they could produce." McClure has been described by some as "a Columbus among editors," the idea being that he discovered so many major talents. But in truth, it wasn't so much about discovery; rather it was that he had been paying attention all along. Throughout his life, McClure identified smart people, collected them, and then put them to their best use for as long as they could stand him. With his writers, he was known to be gruff, blunt, and erratic at times, but he was also attentive, persuasive, and a superlative listener. His whole career was marked by his adeptness in cajoling, but also nurturing, talent.

Certainly, part of the success of the magazine was due to the fact that McClure's writers not only wrote with obsessive accuracy but also displayed an uncanny radar for examining deep social problems their readers often had yet to perceive themselves. The Civil War had ended a few years before McClure and his family arrived in Indiana, and the aftermath of that bloody war had given way to the Second Industrial Revolution. In America, the national issue of the day was no longer slavery but the concentration of wealth and power in the hands of the few—and uncertainty for everybody else. Sound familiar? In the wake of what was then the country's worst-ever economic depression, millions of people were suddenly jobless, banks and railroads were closing or failing, and farmers burned their crops in the fields rather than sell them at a loss. As we all know too well, income inequality is a complicated problem and difficult to see clearly. Americans in the middle class were losing their sense of economic destiny and didn't know why. Meanwhile the wealthy elites (believe it or not) were mostly clueless and largely responsible for the problems of the country.

According to McClure himself, it had never been the plan for his publication "to attack existing institutions." Instead, he called what he and his writers accomplished "the result of merely taking up in the magazine some of the problems that were beginning to interest the people a little bit before the newspapers and other magazines took them up." But once McClure's got started, the powerful in America were finally put on notice.

Part of what made McClure's special for its time is that it was specifically designed for a working-class readership. Most of the highbrow literary publications of the day cost thirty-five cents an issue, a price that connoted luxury, and their coverage didn't reflect the urgency of the moment. Using new technology to keep costs down, McClure and his staff priced his magazine at fifteen cents so that it would be accessible to the masses. He also set the mission dials of the magazine "to deal with important social, economic and political questions, to present the new and great inventions and discoveries, to give the best in literature."

Most important, he wanted it to be a force for good in the universe. Gradually, more and more hard-hitting investigative stories began to appear in the magazine, pointing out corruption and exploring issues that the entire country was dealing with in one way or another. These stories illustrated the national anxiety and clarified how raw the deal was for most people. And wouldn't you know it, before long, the real shitshow began.

The coming-out party for the journalists later known as the muckrakers happened with the publication of the legendary, earth-shattering, orgy-of-corruption January 1903 issue of *McClure's*. It featured a number of classic exposés that are still part of the journalism canon today. One was "The Shame of Minneapolis," a study of municipal corruption. In it, Lincoln Steffens uncovered graft schemes that implicated a connected cast of shady characters including the city's mayor, some local politicians, and the police force, all of whom conspired to take bribes from illegal brothels, saloons, and gamblers. Steffens also throws some of the blame on the citizens, who either looked the other way or didn't bother paying attention to what was going on around them.

The story was a triumph of reporting, and Steffens went on to cover similar corruption scourges in Pittsburgh and Philadelphia in future installments of *McClure's*. But perhaps the most gob-smacking aspect of "The Shame of Minneapolis" is how chilling it sounds in the context of America today. Here's one part of Steffens's indictment of the greed and destruction wrought by the mixing of business and politics in America:

> The business man has failed in politics as he has in citizenship. Why? Because politics is business. That's what's the matter with it. That's what's the matter with everything—art, literature, religion, journalism, law, medicine—they're all businesses. Make politics a sport, as they do in England, or a profession, as they

do in Germany, and we'll have—well, something else than we have now—if we want it, which is another question. But don't try to reform politics with . . . business men.

The January 1903 issue also featured one the most famous investigative stories of all time: the third installment of Ida Tarbell's groundbreaking series dissecting in detail the extent of Standard Oil Company's vicious industrial monopoly. Here we were, nearly two decades before women could even cast a ballot in the United States, and Ida Tarbell was taking on John D. Rockefeller, the richest man in the country and head of a company that controlled 90 percent of America's oil supply.

"The History of Standard Oil" was a thorough, fact-based nineteen-part takedown of Gilded Age capitalism at its very worst. Tarbell's series was as much about greed and injustice as it was a reflection of McClure's personal ideology about success and power in America. "They had never played fair and that ruined their greatness for me," Tarbell wrote of Standard Oil: "Everybody did not do it. In the nature of the offense, everybody could not do it. The strong wrested from the railroads the privilege of preying upon the weak, and the railroads never dared to give the privilege save under the promise of secrecy."

The public's enraged response to the Standard Oil series forced the political levers. Lawsuits were filed, and the Supreme Court eventually ruled that Standard Oil had to be broken up. Meanwhile, Tarbell, who had grown up in Pennsylvania oil country, was widely celebrated for her feat and even dubbed "the most popular woman in America" by one magazine.

McClure sensed that a wake-up moment in America was

underway, and so, just before the January 1903 issue was released, he did an unusual thing and penned a call to arms. Homing in on the anticorruption themes of the stories, the editorial was titled "Concerning the Articles in This [Issue] of *McClure's*, and a Coincidence That May Set Us Thinking." It was, in essence, the muckrakers' manifesto:

> Capitalists, workers, politicians, citizens—all breaking the law, or letting it be broken. Who is left to uphold it? . . .
> There is no one left; none but all of us. . . . We are all doing our worst and making the public pay. The public is the people. We forget that we are all the people; that while each of us in his group can shove off on the rest of the bill of today, the debt is only postponed; the rest are passing it on back to us. We have to pay in the end, every one of us. And in the end the sum total of the debt will be our liberty.

I can see you shaking your head right now. Maybe you are thinking, What a perfect foil S. S. McClure would have made for Donald Trump. If so, you're absolutely right. Can you picture it? A self-made man who worked his way off of a farm in the Midwest without so much as a $14 million loan from his dad? A leader who, rather than aspiring to be a petty autocrat, sought to collaborate with talented men and women to produce the best ideas. How McClure would have loved to assign several detailed investigations into a narcissistic billionaire stiffing blue-collar contractors, denigrating female employees, lying about his charitable donations, and not paying his taxes. And he wouldn't have waited years, or even months, to do it. He would have taken the threat seriously, from day one. After all, a full five years before he was elected president by the Electoral College, Trump announced his racist beliefs by suggesting that the first African American president was not an American but was perhaps a Muslim from Kenya. The media either ignored it or laughed it off, but they never failed to keep him on primetime TV with his weekly show, *The Apprentice*. There were no editorial calls for his removal. The network loved him, as did tens of millions of Americans. At the height of his powers, McClure would have dispatched his staff to take down this fraud. They would have already sniffed out all the rotten things, the dirty deals we don't know about even still. Where are you now, Sam McClure? A nation turns its lonely eyes to you.

Maybe most symbolically, McClure would have served up the best rebuke to Trump's racist and nativist campaign, because he himself was an immigrant, an immigrant whose life became the ultimate success story. It's not much of a stretch to say that all the vicious rhetoric that Trump and his supporters churned out— toward Mexicans, Middle Easterners, and any brown or black people—during the 2016 campaign wasn't really very different from what a lot of people used to say about the Irish in America throughout McClure's entire life and beyond. Like most immigrants, the McClures came to the United States because they wanted a better life. Like most immigrants, they dreamed of finding opportunities that weren't available to them elsewhere. But what the glib, blustering politicians want you to forget is that America also benefited from this deal. It was true then, and it's still true today. The truly smart American cities that are moving our culture and our technology and our society forward—not just places like New York or Los Angeles but places all over the United States—are doing so because the more diverse the population, the more the ideas and the art and the science flow. Midsize cities are now fighting to lure more immigrants—because they know that, for instance, Nashville has thrived as a twenty-first-century town in part because so many Kurds are thriving there. Meanwhile, Mexican and Vietnamese communities are putting down successful roots in Houston. Turkish immigrants are wonderfully reshaping small cities like Dayton, and Somalis are revitalizing Main Streets all across Minnesota.

What made Samuel McClure a special figure is that he wasn't simply content to make a good life for himself as an immigrant; he wanted everyone around him to do well and suffer less. Muckraking was only the start of this process. Once people finally started paying attention to all the corruption in our institutions, McClure moved on to his next mission: finding solutions to improve the government and arguing for them. McClure not only wanted the nation to be more efficient, but he wanted to make it harder for politics to return to a dirty game of profit that only served the rich. With badly needed progressive reforms underway, McClure did another crazy thing: he publicly started pushing Americans to consider ideas that were working well in Europe. As his autobiography shows, McClure was a passionate champion of the idea of America, but he knew that it wasn't doing what it was supposed to do:

> As a foreign-born citizen of this country, I would like to do my part to help to bring about the realization of the very noble American Ideal which, when I was a boy, was universally believed in, here and in Europe. I believe that the dishonest administration of public affairs in our cities has come about largely through carelessness, and that the remedy is as simple, as easily understood, and as possible of attainment, as the

remedy for typhoid fever. The remedy is no dangerous experiment. It was adopted in Germany in the latter part of the last century. As a matter of self-protection it was adopted by Great Britain in the first third of the last century, and it lifted the nation out of as corrupt conditions of government as had ever existed. It was adopted by Galveston, after the great flood of 1900, to enable that city to continue its existence as a city. This very simple remedy is the establishment, in every municipality, of what, in a railroad, is called a board of directors, in a German city is called the Council, and in an American city is called the city commission form of government.

The commission form of government was a simple idea. No more party elders, no more smoke-filled rooms, less political horse racing or horse trading. A set number of people elected by all the citizens run a city with "efficiency as the watchword." Simply put, it was governance—get this—without ego. There would be multiple winners and broader minds, instead of fewer hands and narrower ideas. *McClure's Magazine* would feature numerous stories about the possibilities of change; McClure himself would travel around the country delivering talks on the topic. In that classic way, his concepts had vision, they gave context, and they were accessible enough for a listener or a reader to understand. Most important, everything was presented in a way that diagnosed the problem and expressed the urgency of it all.

[D]uring the century more new inventions and discoveries were made than in all human history. These inventions, especially that of the railroad, brought new problems of government. . . . The railroads had formed the habit of buying franchises from

legislatures and city governments, and a great system of political corruption had grown up. This is the first cause of our
political corruption today, the corruption that we have been
fighting for the last twenty or thirty years.

This was in a speech McClure gave at Stanford University in
1912, and he spoke in a way that would probably stun anybody who
has been subjected to the last several years of American politics.
Instead of deploying easy sound bites and quick attacks, he offered
actual information and a true accounting of how America stood to
gain by thinking about things a little bit differently.

Our government is inefficient because it isn't properly organized to meet the problems of government. Why are the
fire losses in our great cities seven times as great as those of
Europe—in structures of absolutely the same material? Why?
Because our building inspectors are bribe seekers and takers.
In America, 100,000 people suffer violent deaths every year.
This exceeds the yearly losses in the Civil War. Eight thousand
people are murdered every year here, ten times as many as in
other countries of the same population in Europe.

All this is the product of inefficient government. The effect
of government, like that of Tammany Hall, is as bad as that
of the despot. In the countries of despots, young girls may be
burned at the stake in the market place, but in America they
are burned to death in the factories through insufficient fire
protection.

Can you imagine a modern American politician delivering a
speech like this? Connecting special interests and the greed of big

business with death and destruction? Just a simple argument for good, humane government. "The true function of the masses," Mc-Clure would write, "is criticism and restraint of officials. But first you have to have efficient officials."

In addition to his ambitions to contribute to the American project, McClure also maintained a sincere devotion to his birthplace. In 1876, ten years after leaving Ireland for America, he made the long trip back, accompanied by his mother, first taking an eleven-dollar train from Chicago to Philadelphia, then once again boarding a boat. Of the visit he would write:

> I spent a good deal of time with my grandfather McClure. He was then an old man, and he had never got over the loss of his son. The affection he had felt for my father he seemed to transfer to me, and I think he got great pleasure out of my visit. Before I returned to America he begged me to stay in Ireland. I told him that I would come back some day, but he said he would not live to see that day—and, indeed, he did not.

An affection for Ireland and his Irish identity was something McClure carried with him throughout his lifetime. As Irish Americans continued to be harassed and targeted and discriminated against in the United States, McClure continuously commissioned stories about his native country. He wanted an American audience to care about and understand Ireland's complicated aspirations in the same way they would hopefully care about and understand the aspirations of a Pennsylvania coal miner or an Ohio farmer.

One of these stories was "What Ireland Wants," by John Redmond, the famous Irish statesman whose life's work was dedicated to the ultimately impossible job of keeping the peace between

Irish unionists and nationalists, as well as the English. In his story, Redmond would lay out the argument for a form of self-rule, explaining, "What Ireland wants is the restoration of responsible government, neither more nor less. The Irish demand is, in plain and popular language, that the government of every purely Irish affair shall be controlled by the public opinion of Ireland, and by that alone."

Reading a story like this in 1910 in the United States would be something like finding a copy of the *Nation* after being forced to consume *Breitbart* all your life. At that point, negative stereotypes of the Irish were alive and widespread. The Irish were a "treasonous lot," "disloyal," "backwards," and worse. The Irish in Ireland were seen as troublesome elements bucking against dear old England, just as the Irish in America were considered "primitive" or "subversive," even by those at the very top levels of the U.S. government. In his personal diary, Colonel Edward M. House, who was a close adviser to President Woodrow Wilson, wrote of the president's own bias against Irish Americans, "In speaking of the Irish, he surprised me by saying that he did not intend to appoint another Irishman to anything; that they were untrustworthy and uncertain."

As the political situation turned tense and violent in Ireland around the time of World War I, McClure was careful to understand that if the image of Ireland suffered as it fought with the English, the lives of the Irish in America would suffer from the stigma—much like those of modern-day Syrians or Somalis. In a later issue of *McClure's*, he would write a story called "The Real Ireland," which promised "a few words in praise of Ireland." It appeared among a series of poems and a short story by W. Somerset Maugham. "We find in history many records of human delusions," the piece began. "Today, probably the largest single delusion is the average man's opinion of Ireland. I propose in this place to give a few facts about Ireland."

As when McClure compared America to Europe to make his points stronger for American readers, he now put Ireland and its politics in American terms (perhaps a bit too optimistically at times) to make the defamed country more relatable.

> There are few peoples in the world who, for a generation at least, have been as prosperous as the Irish. A larger percentage of the Irish people than of the American people own their own homes. In studying a mass of statistics in many fields dealing with Irish economics, the only statistics in which the figures grew smaller were the statistics of the poorhouses and of those in receipt of outdoor relief and in this matter the Irish made a considerably better showing than the State of New York.

And sure, while he might have promised just a few words, the story goes on like this for several pages, with tables and statistics to back up his arguments. It was more or less the opposite of a dumbed-down news story written in today's alternative-fact America. And because of the syndication system he had mastered all those decades earlier, the story went far and wide, appearing in far-flung newspapers like South Carolina's the *Watchman and Southron* and the *Nebraska State Journal*.

But the sad truth is that while *McClure's Magazine* spawned an entire movement of imitators and laid the groundwork for the rise of progressive politics in the United States, the carcass that once was the American press is a huge part of why we elected an arrogant, ignorant clown to the White House. As we all know, much of the media failed to call Trump on his lies. They didn't challenge him; they let him insult their reporters and phone into their Sunday news shows. The media allowed Trump to show that he took the press about as seriously as the press took him. They let tweets stand as unchallenged news and heightened meaningless scandals for clicks and ratings. In other words, America has entered a new era of Non-Journalism. It is perhaps, sadly, the final chapter, even though journalism as an institution is barely a couple hundred years old. Maybe anthropologists centuries from now will dig it up and study it as a curiosity. If there is a "centuries from now." Because without muckrakers, do you honestly think we're going to stop the polar ice caps from sinking into the oceans, or nuclear weapons from destroying us? The journalist was to be our last buffer against the profiteers who have homes in the Hamptons built on the money that carbon and missiles gave them. We need a hundred thousand S. S. McClures if we are to make it. I'm sorry if this story doesn't have a happier ending, but I am not hopeful.

And so, given that the institution of journalism has been gutted, let me point out one last thing I think S. S. McClure would want me to say. One of the biggest failures of modern-day journalism has been the journalists themselves. They, like most humans, are sadly too seduced by, too enamored of, celebrity, power, and money. They like the perks. They like to be liked just as much as the rest of us. They crave and need access so they are willing to get close—too close—and then they end up not knowing where or when they blurred the line.

McClure's journalists, by comparison, were like celibate priests. They were given the time and resources they needed instead of quotas and word counts. They were encouraged to master their subjects and to know a thing or two about the world. They were expected to read books—lots and lots of books. The rise of *McClure's Magazine* inspired a civic curiosity that actually became a profitable business model. In the decade or two of true muckraking journalism in the early twentieth century, nearly two thousand examples of muckraking were produced by American magazines—magazines that were following McClure's lead. During that time, when the U.S. population was just a third of the size that it is now, each of those muckraking magazines on average sold about three million copies a month.

Even before Trump came down the escalator of his gilded fortress in June of 2015, America needed a stronger press. One that would never report that Saddam Hussein helped finance the 9/11 attacks or tried to buy uranium from Niger or sought out some aluminum enrichment tubes. Journalist Judith Miller said, "My job isn't to assess the government's information and be an independent intelligence analyst myself, my job is to tell readers of *The New York Times* what the government thought about Iraq's arsenal"—that's how we got into Iraq. Remember how we didn't see the biggest downturn since the Great Depression coming? Or how the water crisis in Flint in 2014 made national news and then nothing happened to fix it? These were disasters for the country, but also disasters for the press—failures to investigate, failures to pay attention, failures to follow up.

But it is in this very dangerous moment that journalists have to try and save us from our self-inflicted doom. To start, the press has to earn back the trust that it has fumbled away. It also has to generate and publish reporting that isn't a reflection of public opinion but rather something that shapes it. And to do this, the media already has a blueprint: follow the lead of S. S. McClure and his band of muckrakers. These were men and women who were not only fearless but also creative and moral. Journalists who wrote timely stories that got the attention of disenchanted Americans in forgotten industrial centers. Journalists who reached out to those who had watched the slow-motion decimation of the American working class from the very front row and inspired them to stand up and do something about it.

THE FATHER

Father Edward J. Flanagan (1886–1948)

BY MARK K. SHRIVER

"He ain't heavy, Father . . . he's m' brother."

I don't remember the first time I heard that line. And I don't remember the first time I saw that image of an older boy carrying a younger boy. But the words were always there in my consciousness, and so too was the image.

I was raised in a large, tight-knit Irish Catholic family in the late 1960s and 1970s, and I know that line was mentioned in our house as much as, if not more so than, Notre Dame football, which was a lot. There were four boys and a girl under our roof. We were proud to be of Irish descent, and somehow those words and that image seemed a part of our story. Family mattered—your brothers and sisters, not to mention aunts, uncles, nieces, nephews, cousins, and so on. But the word family was interpreted in a much broader way, broader than just shared DNA or common ancestry.

To my father and my mother, we were all bound together by a shared humanity. Not just as a family, or even as Irish Americans, but as part of a collective whole that included Italians, Greeks, Germans, Swedes, Jews, Christians, Muslims, blacks, whites, Latinos—you get the idea. This meant people with developmental differences too—the men, women, and children that my mother worked with through the Special Olympics movement. And it meant the poor and disempowered living across America and in countries strung across the globe, with whom my father worked through the Peace Corps and the War on Poverty. We were all responsible for each other—and that was perhaps the principal lesson of my childhood. "He ain't heavy, Father . . . he's m' brother": those words were a call to all of us.

So it is ironic, though not surprising, that however much I heard that refrain throughout my childhood, it wasn't until I was an adult that I became even vaguely aware of the man who had written the words—Father Edward Flanagan of Boys Town. After all, by then Father Flanagan had been dead for over a quarter century, and though his legacy was still running strong, a great many other ideas and organizations had emerged to address the needs of children. In the shuffle of time and progress, it can be easy to forget the men and women who came first. It shouldn't be that way, but it often is. And so Father Flanagan, the tall, rangy priest from Ireland who did so much to carve the path, was lost from the telling.

But then life is something of a circle. And in moving forward, it seems you often end up returning to the place where you started.

This was true for Father Flanagan. And as for me, I guess I had heeded my parents' call. I ended up going to work for Save the Children, a nonprofit that, much like Father Flanagan's Boys Town, is committed to improving the lives of children here in the United States (we are now in 120 other countries too). I joined the organization in 2003, creating early childhood development and school-age literacy programs that serve children and families in some of the poorest and most remote communities in the United States, as well as domestic disaster preparedness and response and recovery programs. Ten years later, to strengthen our ability to effect systemic change, I started Save the Children Action Network, which seeks to build bipartisan will and voter support to ensure that every child has an equal opportunity to succeed. In many ways, it is the same fight that Father Flanagan was waging in what now might seem like ancient history.

But it isn't history at all. The struggle is very present. I see it every day. "He ain't heavy, Father . . . he's m' brother"—these are words worth remembering, just as when I first heard them over fifty years ago. And the man behind the words, the life he led and the great many things he accomplished—he's worth remembering too.

EDWARD JOSEPH FLANAGAN's birthplace was a whitewashed limestone farmhouse with a thatched roof, wooden floors, and flagstone fireplaces. Despite its simplicity and modest size, the homestead, located in County Roscommon, bore the impressive name of Leabeg House. It proved to be a comfortable, nurturing home for all fourteen of its inhabitants: John Flanagan, a farmer, his equally hard-working wife, Nora, their eleven children, and John Flanagan's father, Patrick.

Edward was born on July 13, 1886, the eighth child. He suffered a convulsion when he was only a few weeks old, turning blue in the face. His grandfather Patrick, a large, brawny man respected countywide for his skill as an amateur healer for both livestock and people, wrapped his tiny grandson in a blanket, cuddled him next to his chest, and sat by the large kitchen fireplace for hours, praying. The family—tightly knit and devoutly Catholic—firmly believed that prayer was what saved the infant Edward's life.

When Edward Flanagan came into the world, he had five older sisters—Mary Jane, Nellie, Kate, Susan, and Delia—as well as two older brothers, Patrick A. and James. He later would have two younger sisters, Nora and Theresa, and a younger brother, Michael. All of his siblings except Mary Jane and Kate eventually would immigrate to the United States.

The Flanagans of Leabeg House were well-off by community standards. John Flanagan oversaw a three-hundred-acre stock farm owned by an absentee landlord. Everyone in the family worked the farm, including Edward, who in a 1942 letter to a friend remembered himself as "the little shepherd boy who took care of the cattle and sheep . . . as I was the delicate member of the family and good for nothing else."

The largest room in Leabeg House was the kitchen, where a huge teakettle hung above the constantly lit fireplace, ever ready to provide hot tea. It was there that the Flanagans gathered for their daily prayers and sometimes performed small family concerts on the instruments—a piano, an accordion, a violin, and a flute—that were kept in the house. It certainly paints a lovely picture. Edward had a fine baritone voice and enjoyed singing.

He always considered his boyhood home a model for what he later would build at Boys Town—a self-contained community in which everyone worked to address its needs and advance its cause. He wrote, "The old-fashioned home with its fireside companionship, its religious devotion and its closely-knit family ties is my idea of what a home should be."

In the same 1942 letter in which he described himself as "good for nothing else" but being the family's shepherd boy, Edward also claimed that he probably had "a poorer brain than most of the other members of the family." The fact was his family realized early on that he was extremely smart, even scholarly. His older brother Patrick, who soon would begin studying for the priesthood (and thereafter always be known as Father P.A.), recognized his younger brother's sharp mind and began tutoring him, enabling young Edward to skip three grades in the two-room, forty-student Drimatemple National School.

As early as the age of eight, Flanagan said that he wanted to become a priest. Maybe he was inspired by his older brother's example, or perhaps, as family lore would have it, by the prediction of an elderly traveling priest who, upon meeting Edward at their church, noticed the boy's thoughtful appearance, put his hands on Edward's head, and said, "Someday Eddie will be a priest." Certainly, Edward was nothing if not determined. He sought additional tutoring in Latin, Greek, and French from his pastor and, at the age of fifteen, entered a private high school called Summerhill College, located in the Atlantic seacoast town of Sligo, about fifty

miles from his home. It was the same school Patrick A. had gone
to before entering the seminary.

Edward had never been so far from home, never experienced
the strict, harsh, and seemingly uncaring regimentation of an institution such as Summerhill, and never seen sights such as hungry, homeless boys rummaging for food in the garbage behind the
houses of Sligo's wealthy residents. It seems to have had a profound
effect on him, as he never forgot the deep loneliness he felt at Summerhill. He buried himself in his studies, graduating in three years
with honors in Greek, history, and geography. He also took time to
play handball, a sport he loved, and ran track, until an ankle injury
ended that. He put his fine baritone voice to use in the Summerhill
choir.

In January 1904, the same year Edward received his high school
diploma, his older brother Patrick graduated from the Dublin
Seminary and became a priest. Because at the time Catholicism
was so central to Irish identity and a religious career so highly regarded, there were too many young Catholic priests for the country's parishes. Many newly minted priests agreed to serve overseas,
including Patrick, who was sent to far-off Omaha, Nebraska, to
become the founding pastor of the Holy Angels Parish. Although
Omaha had a wide variety of immigrant communities, some said
the immense Irish population made it simply just another Irish
town—"O'Maha" without the apostrophe.

Edward had expected to attend the same Dublin seminary as
Patrick, but his journey to becoming a priest would have many
more twists and turns. Shortly after he graduated from Summerhill,
his sister Nellie—already happily living in New York—returned to

Leabeg House for a visit and recommended that the family send
Edward to the United States to complete his studies.

Edward's parents agreed, and late that summer, when Nellie was
ready to return to New York, her younger brother accompanied her
and Father P.A. aboard the SS *Celtic*, a ship owned by the famous
White Star Line—later owners of the doomed *Titanic* and equally
doomed *Lusitania*. Thankfully, their crossing proved less event-
ful. On August 27, 1904, Edward Flanagan—a lanky, six-foot-tall
eighteen-year-old with light-colored hair and intense blue eyes under bushy brows—went through the gates at Ellis Island, as had
tens of thousands of Irish immigrants before him.

NEWLY ARRIVED IN the United States, Edward stayed
with his mother's relatives in Yonkers, New York, just north of
Manhattan. He applied for admission to St. Joseph's Seminary, also
known as Dunwoodie, which was located in Yonkers. He was told
that he had to get an undergraduate college degree first, so he enrolled at Mount St. Mary's College in Emmitsburg, Maryland (now
known as Mount St. Mary's University). After Edward graduated
with a BA, he again applied for admission to St. Joseph's. This time
he was accepted and officially became a seminarian in the Archdiocese of New York.

Unfortunately, Edward's long struggle with poor health resumed. He developed double pneumonia and was bedridden for
much of his time at St. Joseph's. One of Flanagan's teachers, Father Francis Patrick Duffy—who would earn national fame during World War I as the chaplain of the Fighting 69th, the New
York–based Irish-immigrant infantry regiment founded in 1849

and noted for its battlefield bravery in every conflict since the Civil War—often visited the sick young man to help him with his courses. Edward's physicians, though, urged him to drop out of St. Joseph's. The future Monsignor Aloysius Dineen, who would succeed Duffy as the Fighting 69th's chaplain, was a classmate of Flanagan's at St. Joseph's and recalled that no one at Dunwoodie "would ever have voted Flanagan the one most likely to succeed. I think the majority view would have been that he would wind up as a pastor of some little country parish, where the world would never hear of him."

Edward left school and made his way to Omaha to join his brother. While he recuperated there, the New York Archdiocese sent him a letter releasing him to the Omaha Diocese. By the late summer, the supervising bishop in Omaha thought Edward's health had improved enough to send him to the prestigious Gregorian University in Rome. Flanagan arrived in Rome in October 1907, but within a few months, the damp and cold winter had affected his frail lungs. He returned to Omaha just a few months later, determined to rebuild his strength.

In all of this, one can't help but feel how desperate Edward was to become a priest. But this time, he decided not to rush his recovery and instead became a bookkeeper for the Cudahy Packing Company. Cudahy was then among the largest meat-processing plants in the country. As it turned out, this would prove a critical period in Edward's life. During his nearly two years at Cudahy, he received excellent business training—a whole different skill set that would come in handy down the road.

In the fall of 1909, his health restored, Edward enrolled at the University of Innsbruck in Austria, where the brisk, clean mountain air proved good for him. His family also believed that Innsbruck's water changed the color of his hair from blond to dark brown and caused it to begin thinning. Almost three years later, on July 26, 1912, Flanagan was finally ordained a priest at St. Ignatius Church in Innsbruck. The next day, after saying his first mass for his fellow seminarians, Father Edward J. Flanagan began his journey back to the United States. He was twenty-six years old.

INITIALLY, THE BISHOP of Omaha assigned Father Flanagan to a small, rural parish in O'Neill, Nebraska, largely populated by Irish immigrants (who had named it), but within a year he was transferred to St. Patrick's parish back in Omaha. There he began what many considered a foolhardy effort to help the huge number of homeless migrant farm workers who were flooding into the city. It is funny, but ideas that we've come to think of as visionary often start off as foolhardy. Maybe audaciousness requires you to discount reality. Regardless, this would not be Flanagan's last such effort.

With the approval of his bishop—but with no financial support from the diocese—Flanagan founded what he called the Workingman's Hotel in an abandoned two-story, forty-bed hostelry in an unsavory part of town. Decades later, he told biographers, "I was a very rash and enthusiastic young man. I'd never thought much about money before, you know. Now I was to find out it could be mighty important."

He may have been "rash and enthusiastic," but he was also clearly an intelligent, driven entrepreneur. He raised funds from a variety of sources, including the St. Vincent de Paul Society, his own family, friends, and local merchants. He also enlisted the farm workers to fix up the old hotel and managed to round up additional cots. All told, his total initial expenses came to $150, and before long, more than one hundred men had moved in. Those who had money paid ten cents for a bed and five cents for a meal, but Flanagan never turned away anyone who needed shelter or food. He manned the front desk, and before long, the Workingman's Hotel became a refuge for not only migrant farm workers but destitute men of every kind—from alcoholics to drug addicts to the chronically homeless, all were welcome. It was not uncommon for him to cram one thousand men a night into the hotel, including the attic and basement.

When Flanagan made a detailed study of some two thousand of the men who had stayed at his hotel, he found that many had come from broken homes or large families unable to care for them. They had been unloved and abandoned, beginning in their childhoods. As he would later write, after three years of operating the Workingman's Hotel, he realized he had "put the cart before the horse." He now wanted to shift his focus to helping youngsters "still in their formative years."

And so it was that in the fall of 1917, Flanagan began searching for a place he could convert into a home for boys. He was soon introduced to a real estate agent named Catherine Dannehy (who would go on to spend more than twenty-five years working for Boys Town). Dannehy knew of an old, dilapidated two-story redbrick house that she thought would serve the purpose. The monthly rent was ninety dollars, in advance—a large sum for a poor priest. But Flanagan was nothing if not scrappy, and he quickly found an anonymous friend who was willing to loan him the money.

Though he never revealed the name of that friend, it is almost certain that the founding benefactor of Boys Town was a prominent Jewish attorney in Omaha named Henry Monsky. Monsky, who was one of Flanagan's closest confidants, shared the priest's interest in caring for poor children—religion was beside the point. Flanagan's sister Nellie would later say that the money had come from a Jewish friend of her brother's. In fact, Flanagan himself once let slip that a Jew had been the one to help him found what became Boys Town. In 1937, when Flanagan was talking to the movie studio MGM about a scriptwriter for a potential movie about Boys Town, he told the studio, "Don't send me any Catholics. Why don't you get hold of a young Jewish kid? He'll know what I'm talking about." When Flanagan got his wish and screenwriter Dore Schary, an Orthodox Jew, was assigned to write the script for *Boys Town*, he told Schary why he had asked for a Jewish screenwriter. "How do you think I got into this business? How do you think this place was built? Because a Jewish man understood what I was doing and gave me the money."

As for Monsky, he would later become the international president of B'nai B'rith, as well as the head of the American Jewish Conference and a member of the Boys Town board. He and Flanagan would remain close until Monsky's death in 1947.

On December 12, 1917, with the borrowed ninety dollars, Flanagan opened Father Flanagan's Boys' Home at Twenty-fifth and Dodge Streets in Omaha. The first residents were five boys aged eight to ten; three of them were orphans, and two were homeless youngsters paroled to his care by the city's juvenile court. Flanagan's staff consisted of two nuns and a novice from the School Sisters of Notre Dame. All the furnishings—aged chairs, tables, cots, and beds—were obtained by Flanagan, who had gone asking door-to-door.

By Christmas Eve, about twenty-five boys were living in the house. Flanagan didn't have food for a proper Christmas dinner, or even a simple meal, when a large barrel filled with sauerkraut arrived from a local grocer. "I wish it were something else, boys—dear," said Flanagan, who habitually addressed each child as "dear." It didn't matter—the kids gobbled it right up.

Segregated Omaha had a wide variety of immigrant communities, and the cast-off kids from all were welcome. So too were the "tagged boys," who arrived on foot from far away with a card pinned to their clothes that simply said "Father Flanagan Boys Home, Omaha, Nebraska." One Omaha politician, outraged that black children lived alongside white ones, complained, "If God had intended people to be all the same, why did he make them of different colors?"

Flanagan had a potent reply: "And could you tell me—what is the color of a soul?"

"I see no disaster threatening us because of any particular race, creed or color," Flanagan later wrote. "But I do see danger for all in an ideology which discriminates against anyone politically or economically because he or she was born into the 'wrong' race, has skin of the 'wrong' color, or worships at the 'wrong' altar."

A year later, the number of children in the Boys Home had grown to at least 150, far too many for the residence. And so Flanagan moved to a much larger building, the abandoned German American clubhouse on South Thirteenth Street. No one wanted the two-story, half-block-long building because of the fierce anti-German sentiment during World War I. Over the next three years some 1,200 boys would live there, only 386 of whom were Catholic.

By 1919, the year Flanagan became a United States citizen, most of his family had settled in New York—and a few had joined him in Omaha. His nephew Patrick was now working alongside him, and his sister Nora would become his lifelong secretary. He would soon be on the move again, this time to Overlook Farm, some ten miles west of the city. The 160-acre site would come to be known as Boys Town and would ultimately expand to encompass 1,300 acres. And when Flanagan's father died at the age of ninety-four, his mother, who was ten years younger, also moved there to live with him.

AT ABOUT SIX feet one inch in height, with ramrod-straight posture, Father Flanagan seemed tall even when seated. He had a large brow and long jaw, but despite this, his soft eyes, warm smile, and smooth baritone voice conveyed a remarkable tenderness. "When you first met him, you could feel this warmth," recalled Margaret Takahashi, a Japanese American who encountered Flanagan during World War II. "I've never felt that from another human being. He was so full of love that it radiated out of him." That said, Flanagan could also be tough, and brusque, especially when dealing with juvenile authorities or state officials whose actions frustrated him. "When he spoke to you, his piercing eyes under thick eyebrows, studied you eagle-like," recalled Father Clifford Stevens, a 1944 graduate of Boys Town who went on to become a priest. "When he laughed, the whole room rocked with his laughter, and when he was angry, he was like a bull."

Flanagan knew that to raise money for what was to be an entirely self-funded endeavor, he needed to increase the home's profile. As fate would have it, he turned out to have an uncanny talent for promotion, what one biographer referred to as "the Flanagan Flair." He launched the *Father Flanagan's Boys' Home Journal*, which was sold on street corners by the boys in the home, many of whom had once earned what little money they had as newsboys. There was often an article by Flanagan, explaining in simple, plain English the youngsters' needs, their achievements, and how he hoped to help them.

Flanagan's efforts captured the imagination of Louis Bostwick, one of Omaha's most prominent society photographers. Bostwick donated his time and talent to record every aspect of Boys Town's activities. Whenever Flanagan needed a photo of his boys attending the home's school, which was launched in 1920; or playing baseball or football or wrestling; or tending to the animals on its substantial dairy farm; or learning another vocation by working in the printing house or carpentry shop; or playing in their band or singing in their choir; or meeting celebrities who came to visit, Bostwick was there. His photos went not just to local newspapers but all over the country.

According to Boys Town lore, early in their association, Flanagan told Bostwick how he had once encountered an older boy carrying a younger one piggyback, and the boy explained, "He ain't heavy, Father . . . he's m' brother." Bostwick was as moved as Flanagan had been by that simple statement and later had two youngsters reenact the scene and took a picture of it. Although that image—and that declaration—did become the iconic Boys Town's trademark, the official telling of events is slightly different. In the official version, Father Flanagan saw a picture of two boys in *Ideal* magazine (one piggybacking the other) with the statement in the photo's caption. Flanagan was reminded of the earlier Bostwick photograph and only then moved to make it the Boys Town trademark.

In 1922, Flanagan created a children's circus—grandly promoted as the "World's Greatest Juvenile Entertainers"—that traveled the countryside in colorfully painted wagons pulled by horses. It lost money, but it certainly made Flanagan's boys well known. On its inaugural tour, when a restaurateur in South Dakota insisted that the lone black performer in the circus eat in the kitchen and not with the entire group, Flanagan marched the children out, saying, "If we don't eat with him, we don't eat." That night, the owner of the restaurant went to the show and gave the group a check for $500.

Flanagan also quickly recognized the potential power of radio, and by 1926, he had an hour-long program called *The Boys' Period*. The program featured the Boys Town Band and later its choir, advice to families and children, and inspirational talks by an upbeat young boy billed as Johnny the Gloom Killer. (Over the years, several different kids filled that role.) Johnny had a nationwide following, and Flanagan somehow arranged for Will Rogers, the former cowboy turned political commentator and the era's most popular stage, screen, radio, and newspaper celebrity, to accept "election" as president of the Gloom Killer Club. Naturally, Flanagan had Rogers photographed shaking the hand of the young boy then portraying Johnny. Flanagan would also use radio to promote his philosophy and urge clemency for youngsters who he had learned were going to be jailed or executed.

Omaha was a major railroad hub through which many top performers and national figures touring America's heartland passed. Flanagan "became shrewd, clever and calculating as a fox," according to one of his protégés. He kept an eye on the local newspapers for any report of a visiting celebrity and then made it his business to corral these figures into visiting Boys Town or at least meeting its residents, if only at the train station. The first such prominent visitor was Éamon de Valera, a leader of the movement for Irish independence and later prime minister of Ireland, who visited Omaha in June 1920 while on a fund-raising tour. He was photographed with Flanagan, several senior Catholic clerics, and a group of barefoot Boys Home residents. It is unclear why the children hadn't worn shoes—perhaps a not so subtle way of indicating the home's needs?

Drawing on memories of his childhood home—that whitewashed farmhouse in County Roscommon where Flanagan and his ten siblings put on their family concerts—Flanagan had a strong belief in the power of music. "I like to think of music as being the language of the soul," he once wrote, and in time the Boys Town Band was joined by a Boys Town Orchestra and, most prominently, the Boys Town Choir. The Boys Town Band greeted John Philip Sousa, the March King (composer of "The Stars and Stripes Forever"), at Omaha's train station in 1926; three years later, they welcomed band leader Paul Whiteman, dubbed the King of Jazz (and the man who commissioned George Gershwin to write "Rhapsody in Blue").

New York Yankees Lou Gehrig and Babe Ruth, fresh from their 1927 World Series triumph, also visited. As a child, Ruth, the son of a Baltimore tavern owner, was considered by his parents to be ungovernable. When he was only seven, they sent him to be raised by the clergy at St. Mary's Industrial School for Boys, a Catholic orphanage and reform school in the city. There, Xaverian brother Matthias Boutilier taught him how to play baseball and became his surrogate father.

Ruth told the youngsters that they should never be ashamed of their time at Boys Town. He would visit them several more times over the years, with his last visit near the very end of his life, when he was dying of cancer. Ruth said he simply wished to see Flanagan and his community one more time.

Flanagan believed sports were essential to a boy's development. Baseball had been the first team created, but the Boys Town football program was particularly successful. In the 1930s, they had one of the country's leading high school teams, going undefeated in forty games between 1935 and 1940. Huge crowds filled the stadiums at out-of-town games. Flanagan himself was part of the draw, often appearing before the games began to demonstrate his skill at placekicking.

As with every other activity at Boys Town, the football team was integrated. This led to a showdown in 1946 with the Blackstone Hotel in Miami. The Boys Town team, with a 10-and-0 record, was supposed to play the Florida state champions, Sts. Peter and Paul Catholic High School of Miami. The hotel offered to let the Boys Town team stay there for free—provided no black players were on the roster. Flanagan and his coach said they would never leave any of their players behind, including their African American quarterback, Tom Carodine. The hotel backed down, and Boys Town went on to win 46 to 6.

Flanagan also was not shy about finding prominent people where they vacationed and showing up with his boys. In August 1927, the Boys Town Band serenaded President Calvin Coolidge at his vacation retreat in Rapid City, South Dakota. Coolidge apparently liked the concert enough to ask the band to come back the next year. (Flanagan also made sure that two African American members of the band were in the photo with Coolidge, just to emphasize that they were as much members of Boys Town as the white children.)

Not long after the second concert for Coolidge, Flanagan began to impress upon his boys the remarkable rise to the presidency of Coolidge's successor, Herbert Hoover, a poor farm boy orphaned in childhood. In August 1929, a year after Hoover's election, Flanagan took forty boys to West Branch, Iowa, the president's humble birthplace, and gave a speech noting that Hoover's ascent "beckons to America that it must not be inattentive to its unfortunate young. . . . It is a forceful reminder that tucked away in an orphan mind may be the genius to guide the destinies of a great nation."

Of all the presidents during his time, Flanagan would develop his closest association with Franklin D. Roosevelt. In November 1932, while campaigning for the White House, FDR and his wife, Eleanor, stopped at Boys Town for a tour. Mrs. Roosevelt said it was "one of the most beautiful places" she'd seen while crossing the country, and FDR was equally impressed. After becoming president, Roosevelt would meet with Flanagan a number of times and seek his advice on juvenile issues.

But no matter how crammed his schedule, Flanagan never lost focus on the children in his care. Oscar Flakes, an African American youth who arrived at Boys Town in 1922, recalled that Flanagan "was mother, father, everything to a young boy. He would wrestle with us, run with us, horse-ride with us . . . do anything a youth would care to do . . . shoot marbles with us."

Flanagan would even spar with some of the boys. Once, when a boy knocked off his eyeglasses, Flanagan's mother, who was living at Boys Town at the time, shouted, "Come on you big kid, get in the house. Get in the house!" Flanagan dutifully obeyed.

In 1936, Boys Town was incorporated as a village and placed on all of
Nebraska's maps. "Boys Town is not by any stretch of the imagination
an orphanage," Flanagan would write a decade later. "It is a complete
community in itself—the smallest incorporated city in the country—
with its own first-class post office, its own grade and high school,
trade school, print shop, gymnasium, church, movie theatre,
swimming pool, farm, infirmary, athletic field, dining hall, and
apartments."

The town also had its own government and held elections for a
boy mayor, who then appointed other boys to various town positions. True to form, Flanagan once arranged for one of Boys Town's
newly elected mayors to meet with New York City's colorful Mayor
Fiorello La Guardia in Manhattan and be photographed together
at La Guardia's desk.

Regardless of his far-flung activities, Flanagan's priestly duties
remained central to his being. At Boys Town, he maintained a regular schedule of religious services. Recitation of scriptures, spiritual reading and prayer began at 6:00 a.m., with Flanagan always
the first to arrive in the chapel. Similar services were held daily at
noon and after the evening meal. Following the morning service,
Flanagan met with his staff to discuss the day's upcoming events,
then headed off to other meetings. As Rev. Peter Dunne, a Boys
Town school dean, recalled, "He was a whirlwind of activity."

THROUGHOUT MY OWN career focusing on the needs
of children, I have tried to attract sports stars, movie stars, music
stars, business leaders, and politicians much like Father Flanagan
did, though with much less success. I've written articles under my
own byline, coauthored opinion pieces with famous people, and

regularly posted about Save the Children's work on Facebook and Twitter—all in an attempt to call attention to children's needs. I have even produced videos with Hollywood stars for Save the Children's website and YouTube. Despite all this work—and believe me, while it may seem a little glamorous, it is still work—there are large swaths of Americans I have found very difficult to reach.

For Flanagan, on the other hand, Hollywood came calling. It seems the seed for a movie was planted by a story titled "The Boy Who Shot His Father" published in the then-popular magazine *Liberty*. The article, by a prolific journalist named Edward Doherty, recounted not only the tale of a fifteen-year-old boy who murdered his father because the man had abandoned his family but other stories of abused and neglected children who found sanctuary in Flanagan's Boys Town.

A screenwriter for Metro-Goldwyn-Mayer named Eleanore Griffin thought the story on Father Flanagan would make a terrific movie. She went out to Omaha to interview the Irish priest, now over fifty years old. Initially, Flanagan was cool to the idea because he feared MGM would turn the story into another *Oliver Twist*. But when Dore Schary came onto the project, he convinced Flanagan that a great film could be made. It would next take some persuading to get the internationally renowned movie star and Academy Award–winning actor Spencer Tracy to accept the role of Father Flanagan. Two years earlier, Tracy had won much acclaim portraying a priest in MGM's 1936 blockbuster *San Francisco*. Now, despite the rave reviews, Tracy said he didn't want to play another man "with a collar turned backwards." He finally relented when his good friend Eddie Mannix, MGM's powerful general manager and vice president, convinced him to do it.

Flanagan worked closely on the *Boys Town* script with Griffin and Schary, who won an Academy Award for best original screenplay in 1939 for their work. The story has some basis in fact but is mostly filled with fictional characters. Among them is a tough, streetwise kid named Whitey Marsh, played by then-seventeen-year-old Mickey Rooney, who comes to realize the value of Boys Town, and a small child nicknamed Pee Wee, portrayed by seven-year-old Bobs Watson, who idolizes Rooney's character and forms an unlikely bond with him that is the sentimental center of the story. (Watson's signature talent as a child star was his ability to cry buckets of real tears on cue. He had ample opportunity to display it in *Boys Town*.)

Although well experienced in the ways of publicity, Flanagan agreed to sell the movie rights for a scant $5,000, believing that a successful film would prompt a flood of contributions. Instead, the public who flocked to the theaters assumed Boys Town already had plenty of money. The movie earned MGM more than $2 million. But Boys Town had to spend the full $5,000 it received to fix up the campus after the fifty-eight-member movie crew had left. Flanagan ruefully told a reporter for the *New York Times*, "Next time I come to Hollywood, I'm going to get myself an agent."

But Flanagan didn't have to go to Hollywood, as, once again, Hollywood came to him. Having hit box office gold with *Boys Town*, MGM naturally wanted to make a sequel. It was to be called *The Men of Boys Town*, with Tracy again portraying Flanagan. This time, instead of an agent, Flanagan got something better—his old friend, attorney Henry Monsky, who negotiated a $100,000 fee for the movie rights.

Over the course of these productions, Flanagan and Tracy

formed a genuine friendship that endured for the rest of Flanagan's life. When Tracy won the 1939 Academy Award for his portrayal of the priest, he sent the gold statuette to Flanagan with an inscription on it: "To Father Flanagan, Whose Great Human Qualities, Kindly Simplicity and Inspiring Courage Were Strong Enough to Shine Through My Humble Efforts. Spencer Tracy." It is still on display at Boys Town.

The success of *Boys Town* did much to inform a vast audience of the guiding principles behind Father Flanagan's efforts. He had been writing and lecturing about them for decades—and battling against bureaucrats and politicians who ignored or opposed him—but now his name truly was box office gold, and his words, and his philosophy of focusing on the individual boy, carried extra weight.

In a 1940 speech titled "To Cure, Not to Punish" given to the National Conference of Catholic Charities in Chicago, Flanagan summarized his philosophy:

> The juvenile court, which a generation ago was greeted with much enthusiasm as a cure-all for juvenile delinquency, has utterly failed. . . .The reformatories the nation over, instead of rehabilitating youth, actually have become schools of crime. . . . It is the duty of each family to provide security, protection, and direction for their children but when the home fails it is necessary for the community to devise ways and means to prevent delinquency. . . .
>
> Further, I would say that each police department should assign a certain number of picked men in plain clothes to work with juveniles exclusively, under the direction of this social

service bureau. These men are to visit the homes of these boys from time to time and seek out the causes of their misdeeds and work to an end of helping the boy, instead of carrying a club of punishment over his head. . . .

Of course, it will cost money, but even now thousands of dollars are being squandered in the manner in which we are handling juvenile delinquency through our juvenile courts and reformatory system. There is an old saying, "Crime does not pay," but the public is finally learning that it pays the crime bill in taxes. I am certain that under such a set-up as I have outlined here, the cost of rehabilitating youth will be greatly decreased.

I have reread these words countless times, and each time they give me goose bumps. They are so prescient and powerful, reflecting the very experience I had working with juvenile delinquents in Baltimore in the late 1980s and early 1990s. The juvenile court system was under-resourced and overwhelmed. The facilities where the kids were sent were called "training schools," but they were little more than jails. And instead of plainclothes policemen who visited and worked with troubled juveniles "from time to time" with the goal of "helping the boy," Baltimore hired social workers who too often were able to do little more than push paper because of an overwhelming caseload.

Flanagan was clearly not in favor of the state supplanting the role of the family, but he was a hard-nosed realist who understood that sometimes the family needed help. And his realism recognized the reluctance of the electorate to invest in rehabilitating troubled youth, so he made an economic argument: pay now or pay a lot more later.

When he spoke these words, he was still running Boys Town. To speak up against the power structure and prod people to do something they don't want to do takes guts, especially when the victims of the situation are overwhelmingly poor and powerless. And it takes special courage to do that while trying to raise funds for your own work from the very people you are prodding. It is much easier to complain privately, while still seeking both the private and public resources to do one's work. I often hear colleagues say words to that effect: "Do the best you can, but don't rock the boat." "The system will eat you up, and then you won't be able to help any kids." Or countless times, "You can't push rich people too hard to change their lifestyle, or they're not going to help you at all." Clearly, Father Flanagan thought otherwise.

WHEN THE JAPANESE attacked Pearl Harbor on December 7, 1941, the news had a personal impact on Father Flanagan: four Boys Town alumni were serving in the military there, two of whom were killed—George Thompson, on the USS *Oklahoma*, and Donald Monroe, on the USS *Arizona*. Just six months earlier, Monroe had written to Flanagan that the movie *Boys Town* had been shown on the ship. "Everyone enjoyed it," Monroe wrote. "All the boys on the ship ask me was Boys Town just like in the picture? I told them that was you up and down." Monroe was an African American cook on the *Arizona*; his body remains entombed on the sunken battleship, now a national monument in Pearl Harbor.

Ultimately, at least eight hundred former Boys Town residents served in the military during the war, fighting in practically every major theater of combat, and some forty of them gave their lives. Flanagan mourned them all. To the mother of a Boys Town alumnus who died on Bataan, he wrote, "[W]hile perhaps you may think that, after all, these boys are not as close to me as they would be to a natural father, still, let me assure you, my dear Mrs. Clark, they are very close and I feel the loss of each and every one very deeply."

Though Flanagan was named national chaplain of the American War Dads Association and instituted a military training program for the youngsters at Boys Town, he did not hesitate to again stand up to injustice, this time on behalf of the Japanese. He was greatly upset by President Roosevelt's Executive Order 9066 forcing some 120,000 Japanese Americans, many of them United States citizens, to evacuate their homes and be relocated to one of ten internment camps located in remote areas of Wyoming, Colorado, and Arkansas.

As his own countermeasure, Flanagan offered jobs and housing to any Japanese families who wished to come to Boys Town. It is estimated that about three hundred Japanese Americans managed to get there between 1943 and the end of the war, with Flanagan often paying for their transportation. When one of the Japanese Americans was hired as a psychologist in the Boys Town welfare department but found his efforts to buy a house nearby blocked by racial prejudice, Flanagan enlisted Monsky's law firm to take on the case. They won.

Shortly after the end of the war, Flanagan expressed his belief in racial equality in a letter to a Jesuit priest in Detroit: "Who am I that I should think that Christ, when he died on Calvary, died only for the Catholics living on millionaire row and white Catholics at that. My understanding of Catholic doctrine is that Christ died for the Negroes, for the Mexicans, for the Germans and for the Japanese, and for all of these other nationalities."

Despite their differences, Flanagan and Franklin Roosevelt remained friends. In August 1944, just two months after D-day, Flanagan wrote to FDR about the necessity of planning to help homeless European children once the fighting ended.

> If these children are neglected, they will constitute a very serious problem in the immediate future and in the years to come. During adolescence, and before they reach maturity, they will be easy prey to temptation and crime, and to infection from the various noxious isms. . . . If, however, they are properly cared for, trained and educated in the true traditions of their respective countries, and if they are given Christian care and love, they will become the most able leaders in the peaceful rehabilitation of their countries.

Roosevelt responded promptly, saying the issues Flanagan had raised were a major concern and that "I am sure that in developing any such plans . . . [we] will wish the benefit of your experience."

Before turning his attention to postwar continental Europe and Asia, however, Father Flanagan decided to fulfill a long-standing wish to return to Ireland. He wanted to see the members of his family who remained there, but he also had unspoken reasons for making the trip. He had heard about the horrific conditions in Ireland's industrial schools for youths and reform schools, known as Borstals, and intended to see them for himself.

What he found appalled him. During a monthlong trip in the summer of 1946, he visited a number of such schools and was sickened to find that severe physical punishment and what amounted to slave labor were inflicted routinely on the children. In one Belfast school, he found youngsters under the age of eleven making shoes in a windowless basement room lit by a single lightbulb. He also received a detailed report on a boy who had been brutally whipped at a school in County Limerick. Flanagan spoke out forcefully while in Ireland, calling the industrial schools "a disgrace to the nation" and the Borstal system "a scandal, un-Christlike and wrong."

Irish authorities were infuriated. The minister of justice, Gerry Boland, said on the floor of the Irish Parliament that Flanagan had used "offensive and intemperate language" to challenge "conditions about which he has no first-hand knowledge." James Dillon, another political leader, said, "Monsignor Flanagan turned up in this country and went galumphing around . . . got his photograph taken a great many times and made a variety of speeches to tell us what a wonderful man he was and of the marvels he had achieved in the United States. He then went back to America and published a series of falsehoods and slanders."

In public, Flanagan would only say that he realized his remarks had made Irish officials "rather uncomfortable," adding that "avoiding facts and appealing to clichés and individual prejudices is as futile as trying to settle a dispute by seeing who can shout the loudest. Little is gained unless argument leads to inquiry."

In a private letter to a friend, however, he wrote, "We have punished the Nazis for their sins against society. . . . I wonder what God's judgment will be with reference to those who hold the deposit of faith and who fail in their God-given stewardship of little children?" A year later, he wrote sadly, "I don't seem to be able to understand the psychology of the Irish mind."

For an Irish-born priest who spent the first eighteen years of his life there, those are damning words. It is hard to know exactly why

Flanagan felt so different in his thinking. Perhaps our memory of home is always partly fictionalized. Maybe Flanagan had chosen to remember only the positive aspects of his birthplace—the big, loving family in the whitewashed farmhouse—and had cast aside the memories of homeless boys rummaging for food in Sligo.

For its part, the Irish government ignored Flanagan's charges. It was not until a major public investigation in 1970 finally revealed the terrible conditions in these schools, including malnutrition, child labor, and physical and sexual abuse, that corrective actions began. It took another exposé, a three-part 1999 television documentary and the book that followed, *Suffer the Little Children: The Inside Story of Ireland's Industrial Schools*, by Mary Raftery and Eoin O'Sullivan—which recounted the details of Flanagan's trip and accusations—to finally move the Irish Parliament to offer an official apology for the decades of mistreatment to which it had turned a blind eye.

Flanagan had intended to return yet again to Ireland, but that trip was postponed by a request from General Douglas MacArthur. The general, then essentially ruling Japan as head of the U.S.'s occupying forces, wanted Flanagan to go there and also to Korea to examine the conditions of war orphans and other destitute children and offer recommendations on how to help.

Beginning on April 24, 1947, Flanagan spent an exhausting sixty days touring sixteen Japanese and South Korean cities, visiting devastated areas and orphanages and even wandering through the cold and dark underground railways of Japan, where homeless children found shelter. He discovered sweatshops masquerading as "homes" for children as young as eight who worked long hours, six days a week, to make products, for which they received little pay.

Returning to the United States in late June, he quickly completed a detailed report, "Children of Defeat," and on July 7 delivered it personally to President Harry Truman in the White House. In it, he "heartily recommended" creation of a foster home system in Japan, with the help of U.S. occupation forces, since the Japanese had little experience dealing with the problem of homeless children. He also suggested tough regulations to eliminate the "orphanages" that in reality were child labor rackets.

Truman was so impressed with Flanagan's report that a few months later he asked him to undertake a similar fact-finding tour of Austria and Germany. Although exhausted, Flanagan felt he could not turn down a personal request from the president of the United States. He made arrangements to leave for Europe on March 5, 1948.

On the day before he left, Flanagan sat down with two of his friends, the writers Will and Fulton Oursler, for another long interview about his work. "We asked him . . . an indiscreet question, but one that had to have an answer, although how urgently we could not suspect," the Ourslers wrote in their biography of Flanagan. "What would happen when he passed on? Was there someone so passionately devoted to children that the work would be carried on?"

"'God will send,' was his answer. 'We have already started an endowment fund. Someday in the far, far future that may make us self-supporting. Anyway, the work will continue, you see, whether I am there or not, because it's God's work, not mine.'"

Arriving in Vienna on March 11, Flanagan spent the next two months traveling thousands of miles through Central Europe. He estimated that in Vienna alone, some forty thousand children were homeless and in terrible shape physically and emotionally. He made a prescient proposal for the creation of day care centers in which the children of single mothers could stay while their lone parent worked.

He returned to Berlin on May 14, held a number of meetings, learned that an estimated ten thousand homeless children were in the city, and finally went to bed. In the early morning hours of May 15, he knocked on the door of his nephew, Patrick Norton, who was there working with him. "Pat," he said, "I have a pain in my chest. Please get a doctor right away." He died of a massive heart attack only a few hours later.

MUCH AS FATHER Flanagan predicted, the work of Boys Town continued. In 1972, the Boys Town National Research Hospital for the study and treatment of hearing and speech disorders was started. The endowment fund he began is still going strong today, and his successors have expanded Boys Town's reach to communities in more than half a dozen states, serving an estimated eighty thousand children and families a year. And Boys Town also now operates a 24/7 national suicide hotline to provide counseling to hundreds of thousands of callers a year in more than one hundred languages.

At the time of Flanagan's death, one of the most eloquent eulogies came from Rabbi Edgar Magin of Los Angeles, who wrote of Flanagan's love of children in the *Boys Town Times*: "He reached out his arms, took them to his bosom. He counseled with them. Some were black. Some were white. There were Jews, Catholics, and an infinite variety of Protestants, and those who called themselves by no name and knew no God because they had never been taught there was a God until they met Father Flanagan."

On May 21, 1948, Flanagan was buried in a crypt at Boys Town. He had been brought home. Not to the whitewashed farmhouse in Ireland, but to the home he had created—the shelter he had given to thousands and thousands of boys. It didn't matter who the boys were or where they came from—they were his brothers. And he was laid to rest among them.

Two weeks later, President Truman traveled there to place a wreath on his grave. Upon the news of Father Flanagan's death, the president had issued a public statement: "American youth and youth everywhere have lost an ever faithful friend in the untimely death of Father Flanagan. His unshaken confidence in the love of God and in even the least of God's children found eloquent expression in the declaration that there is no such thing as a bad boy."

Amen.

THE DIRECTOR

Rex Ingram (1893–1950)

BY PIERCE BROSNAN

I WRITE THIS FROM MY home in Los Angeles—Malibu, more specifically. I've spent the morning painting. I like to paint every morning when I'm home, as I am now—enjoying a bit of down time before I leave in a few weeks for a film in Italy. I can hear my wife, Keely, downstairs. She's probably reading the *New York Times*, the print version, which we just can't seem to shake.

I close my eyes and try to imagine this city of Los Angeles roughly eighty years ago—this would be in 1936—and a scene found over the hill from here, on the southern edge of the San Fernando Valley in what was then the sleepy little suburb of Studio City.

On a tree-lined street, in an ordinary house, a forty-three-year-old man is walking around his property. He's handsome—Irish American, with a strong nose and high forehead, his short black hair combed back. The man steps into his studio, just as I'm in mine, and dips his hands into a bucket of clay. He begins to sculpt a mythical creature—a satyr of sorts. His wife keeps her own company inside.

Watching him, it would be hard to guess that just a few years earlier this man—Rex Ingram—was Hollywood's hottest director. He was responsible for some of the silent film era's biggest commercial and critical hits, with his wife and creative partner, Alice Terry, as their star. Bringing an artist's sensibility to what was a new directing style, he lit up movie marquees and popular magazines across the country, launching silver-screen stars like Rudolph Valentino and Ramon Novarro, and making himself and his movie executives wildly wealthy along the way. But here he is, alone in his studio.

I suppose—you go up, you come down.

From my window, I stare out at a wide expanse of blue ocean. Ireland feels a long way away. It's not easy getting here; this I know. Certainly, ending up as he did in Los Angeles, it had been a long journey for Rex. There were incredible highs and some lows too, and at least four remarkable films to show for it, but overall, it was a long journey indeed.

REGINALD INGRAM MONTGOMERY HITCHCOCK—later to be known as Rex Ingram—was born in Dublin in 1893. I myself was born only an hour's drive north in Navan, County Meath, more than half a century later. Navan was then a little rural town on the banks of the River Boyne and worlds apart from the city. Not that any of this matters much: I realize Rex is the star of this story, and even though we are both Irish, both in the business of film, and both artists independent of that work (for Rex, in sculpting, and me, painting)—I'm only supporting.

The Hitchcock family was middle-class Protestant. Living there in the Dublin neighborhood of Rathmines, they represented what's known as the Ascendancy, a privileged class of Protestants carrying the British flag, as it were, among us Catholics. His mum, Kathleen, was culturally refined, demure, and warm. His father, Francis, stern and demanding, was a divinity scholar at Trinity College preparing for a career in the Church.

When Rex was three, his brother, Francis, was born. Two years later, his father got a job as a curate and the family moved to the countryside in Tipperary. Now this was rural for sure—and young Rex and Frank, as his brother was called, took to the outdoors, riding horses and trampling over hill and stream. You could do this then in Ireland. In fact, this was one's childhood when I was a boy.

Myself, I was an only child. My father left us when I was an infant. (In fact, I only met him once in my life, when I was thirty-one years old and shooting *Remington Steele*.) My mother then went to England to make a better life for us both. If she had not had the courage to do that, I wouldn't be the man I am today. But it came with the price of loneliness and separation. My grandparents took care of me.

I too was raised in that pastoral Ireland. I lived across the river from town, and I remember great access to the forest and woods. Grandfather had built our house on the banks of the Boyne. He was a gentle man by the name of Philip. Together we would walk hand in hand up the dirt road on a summer's evening, the sunlight dappling through the over-canopied trees. He would every now and then stop and look for the "little people." He loved to show me where they lived. Yes, they were real to me as a boy—part of what I call Irish dreamtime. We had a plot of land my grandparents would let out to a family of tinkers, as we called Irish travelers then—old Ma Crutchie was their matriarch. The family had a painted wagon and a couple of horses, and old Ma would fix our pots and pans and sharpen knives. Her two boys taught me how to make bows and arrows, and off I went into the woods each day. This was the late 1950s, so one can only imagine the country life for Rex some fifty years earlier. A young boy with a great deal of dreamtime—and you wonder what filled his head.

In 1903, when Rex was ten, his father was again promoted, now to rector, and the family moved to Kinnitty, a postcard-perfect town in the central part of the country with more green hills to explore, and an abundance of castles and mansions to spin romance around. Living with a rector, naturally there was a lot of religion in the home. But Francis also encouraged the arts—readings and performances of Shakespeare and the classics—while Kathleen played piano. It was a good deal more than I got. Young Rex would sit sketching and doodling for hours, developing skills that would figure in the notoriously detailed storyboards he created for his films years later. These delicious details, by the way, and many others, come courtesy of the wonderful biographer Ruth Barton, whose masterful *Rex Ingram: Visionary Director of the Silent Screen*, is considered the last word in all things Rex.

As a boy I too loved sketching, from very early on. Acting came much later. My first performances, when I think on it, were really at St. Mary's church. It was there I made my first communion and, in some ways, my first public appearance—as an altar boy serving mass. Certainly, there were the Christian brothers in their black soutanes of holiness and despair. They could be cruel. But to serve communion was a joy for me. My grandmother would plaster my hair down with Brylcreem, the radio playing Chuck Berry in the background, and down the road I would go, over the bridge and up into town. Mass on a Sunday morning dressed in my red cassock, white shirt, and white plimsolls, the smell of the incense in the church, along with the sound of the choir, would fill me with the greatest of comfort. Those days as a boy have stayed with me.

Rex's experiences with the Protestant church were no doubt also profound. Despite what seems a pleasant enough home life, Francis was intense and demanding—and apparently he and his eldest never much got along. In 1905, when he was twelve, Rex's parents sent him to St. Columba's College, a boarding school just outside Dublin. This is often how it goes in Ireland. Life in the countryside was isolated, sheltered—adults kept everything from you. If somebody was having a baby, they'd spell it out. Rosie's having a B-A-B-Y. But you were king of the mountain with fields to roam. And then it was off to a traditional private school and hardly enough room to breathe.

St. Columba proved a bad fit for Rex. Socially, Rex was considered a bit of an outcast. He preferred drawing to studying and produced a trove of illustrations of lavishly dressed women. It's hard to imagine that going down very well in a turn-of-the-century all-male boarding school. Like Rex, I didn't take much to formal education. It can be difficult for an artistic soul—the life of an outsider. But in those early drawings of Rex's, you can see a flair for extravagance that, so much later, his film fans would come to appreciate.

Rex's school woes were greatly compounded by the sudden death of his beloved mother, in the fall of 1908. The two had been extremely close, and she was a lifelong shield of warmth and affection against his father. Rex was devastated. It was a terrible loss. My own grandparents had passed away by the time I was seven, so I know something of a child's heartache. That coming Easter, in very much a mutual decision, Rex left St. Columba's. He would return home to figure out his next steps, a state of affairs he commemorated with this grim poem:

> I am going back to father.
> Back to dear old Dad.
> Although I made him sorry
> I now will make him glad.

As for me, my last few years in Ireland were spent with my Aunt Eileen in a house in town, number 2 St. Finian's Terrace. I remember these as happy times. Eileen had a son and a daughter who were teenagers—Donal and Ann. I was seven. I always received great presents from my mother at Christmastime should she not be with us. I loved to skate and had the best pair of roller skates on the street. They were called GoJos with black rubber wheels. I was the fastest kid in the neighborhood with my GoJo skates. On a weekday, Eileen would bake the most magnificent soda bread. When I came home from school it would be sitting on the windowsill cooling. Then she would slice off a chunk and put lashings of butter on it, which I would then dunk in the sugar bowl and wash down with a glass of milk from the local cows.

But the little house on St. Finian's was bursting with all of us:

Eileen and her own children, and then two lodgers to whom she rented a room upstairs. My bed was at the end of that room, with a shiny green curtain around it. Eileen would pin newspapers to the curtain as to block out the light when the lodgers would come in at night. This tiny space was all mine, and I would gaze at those papers, imagining a life beyond. For me it would be London. But Rex, he fantasized most about South America, and even tried to teach himself Spanish. He was also entranced by the Arab world, which would figure prominently in his later films.

Don't we take our leaving in stages? Whether it be from a place or a person—it begins in the imagination. The morning I left Ireland it was gray and wet. I was by then eleven. The date was August 4, 1964—the same day that Ian Fleming died, ironically. My dear Aunt Eileen packed my tiny cardboard suitcase, and I wore a gray V-neck hand-knitted sweater with a tartan bowtie. In one hand a set of rosary beads and in the other an aspirin bottled filled with holy water. Eileen cried when we parted; she knew I was never coming back. But I was to be with my mother at last. And I could not have been happier.

My Uncle Phil drove me to Dublin airport in the rain, where we met a priest at the bar having a pint. We struck up a conversation with the man of God, who said he would take care of me on the flight. The plane was a twin-engine prop. When we landed in London, the priest disappeared, and I just followed the crowds to the gates. Customs asked me if I had anything to declare. I said no. I could see my mother through the glass, waiting.

FOR REX, AS it turned out, his father had a friend in New Haven, Connecticut, who could set him up with a job. Both Francis and Frank hated for Rex to leave, but they knew there was no holding him back. "My mind was made up. I was going to try my luck in the United States," he would write in his memoirs. (He titled them "A Long Way From Tipperary." Curiously, they were never published.) Just nineteen, Rex boarded the SS *Celtic* in late June 1911. It was his own sad farewell, a scene that Rex would recall emotionally: "My brother . . . just clung to my arm and bit his lips to keep from crying."

Rex couldn't have realized he would never see Ireland again.

He landed in New York about a month later and found his way up to New Haven, where his dad had arranged work for him at the dockyards as a night messenger. He started his shift at 6:00 p.m., bringing a sandwich in his pocket for dinner. It must have felt romantic to a romantic young man, but it was likely tough too. The characters at the docks were a colorful bunch, visitors from the world over—a rollicking cast of misfits.

One such regular was a girl named Daisy who apparently reminded Rex of his mother and with whom he instantly fell in love. This would become a pattern for our man. Although not yet twenty, he pestered Daisy to marry him. She refused over and over and ended up leaving the docks altogether. But Rex's ruminations over his mother loomed large, and throughout his life he often compared girlfriends and prospective lovers—unfavorably—with her.

Back home in Ireland, Francis was unamused by his son's debauched dockside adventures. If Rex pressed for marriage, his father pressed for college and eventually won out. Rex had heard about a university right nearby with a good reputation. It was called Yale, and in 1912 he enrolled in the fine arts school there.

One of his teachers at Yale, the famed sculptor Lee Lawrie (perhaps best known for the sculpture of Atlas that stands at the front of Rockefeller Center), would become a lifelong mentor. The two men would correspond throughout the next thirty years and collaborate in the promotion of Rex's most famous film. Rex made lots of friends at Yale and wrote and drew illustrations for the humor magazine. Foreshadowing his imminent rise as a master storyteller, one fellow student recalls him "spending the whole afternoon regaling me with the wildest and most varied tales, all stories created on the spur of the moment." But in barely a year, Rex had dropped out. The culprit? The strange and blossoming world of motion pictures.

There are chance meetings that can change the direction of your life. As Rex had initially wanted to be a sculptor, I once wanted to be a painter. I left school in London at age sixteen with nothing but a cardboard folder full of drawings and paintings. After pounding some pavement, I found work as a graphic artist in an advertising shop called Ravenna Studios, just off Putney High Street. There I was in a room working alongside three other artists. It was a low-slung room, sort of retro 1950s, not unattractive, with windows all down one side. I spent my days drawing straight lines, making cups of tea, and watering the spider plants. I was quite happy. Like Rex, I was pursuing an artistic life. And then one day, I was hanging up my coat, and there was this coworker, Alan Porter, from the photography department. We were talking about movies, because I loved the movies, and Alan said I should come to these actor workshops at the Oval House. And that was it—my chance meeting.

For Rex, his chance meeting was over Christmas break from Yale in 1913. A classmate took him back to his Long Island home and introduced him to Charles Edison, son of the inventor and movie pioneer Thomas. Conversations with the younger Edison stoked Rex's passion for movies, and that was it—he was off. He and his Yale friends began to frequent the nickelodeons. His first movie love was *Man's Genesis*, made by D. W. Griffith.

Soon, Rex wanted not just to watch films but to make them. He got a job with Edison Studios in the Bronx, in what was then a young, freewheeling industry. The kid was handsome, so it should come as no surprise that with his sharp eyes and soft features, he was quickly thrown in front of the camera as an actor. Rex had done some writing too, and he was further tasked with helping shepherd through some scripts. A strong young man, he was also put to building sets. The movie industry was like this—fast, frenzied, and—for a restless Irish lad looking to make his mark— wide open.

During a busy year or so with Edison, Rex appeared in a string of long forgotten films, with titles like *The Necklace of Ramses*, *Witness to the Will*, and *Borrowed Finery*. He wrote scripts too.

A whirlwind, those first years in film. I remember mine. After the fractured childhood, fighting your way through whatever calamity was thrown upon you—by nature, by your parents, by your lack of parents—and trying to work your way through the pain, until suddenly you arrive at a place where you belong. And where you are going to do something big.

Rex was soon to give up his dream of becoming a professional sculptor. It was not easy, and part of the decision was certainly driven by economics. As he wrote to his Aunt Lizzie in 1913, "I can make enough to live in a kind of way in this [movie] business—I could not at sculpture." A few months later, he left Yale.

It is worth noting that by the time Rex took leave of Yale, he had already managed to piss off most of the people he was working for.

Rex just couldn't help but rile his directors and executives. It might have dashed all his hopes, but then another chance meeting intervened, this time with the famous director D. W. Griffith, who wrote a letter of reference for Rex that he could take around to studios outside the Edison orbit.

These are the steps and half steps and steps backward that would mark what was, for a good while, a fairly steady climb. Rex landed at Vitagraph, a top-notch studio, and there he kept acting. This seems to have been unfortunate. Because while Rex had the looks, he was clearly self-conscious on screen. Whether by his own design or not, he was frequently cast as an artist and often a sculptor, as in films like *The Spirit and the Clay* and *Eve's Daughter*. But despite his real-world experience, Rex struggled to give a convincing performance. And then, in 1914, World War I came along. Thousands of his fellow twentysomethings were sent off to the front lines, and Vitagraph, hit by the wartime economy, as many studios were, had to let Rex go.

A year later, his younger brother, Frank, was sent into battle. This while Rex was looking for a new movie studio to put him in front of the camera. And thus played out the divergent journeys of the Hitchcock brothers, a pattern that would last their whole lives. Frank—rooted, disciplined, and a realist; Rex—restless, rebellious, and a fantasist. As if to thumb his nose at his disapproving father, Rex now legally changed his last name to Ingram, in honor of his late mother.

Rex ended up getting a job at Fox, where he was assigned to work with directors on sharpening up unwieldy scripts. It might be hard to imagine that a studio would hire a director, cast, and crew, build sets, scout locations, and design costumes without a final shooting script in place, but it happened then and it happens now. Still, despite his first steady paycheck, Rex wasn't interested in coasting along as a master script doctor. He was ready to direct. And when Fox told him to stay in scripts, he walked away, a decision that he would recall ruefully. "And so ended one of the happiest associations of my life," he wrote. "One from which I learned more than any other in my motion picture career."

Still just twenty-three, Rex next set his sights on Universal, then led by the formidable Carl Laemmle. He persuaded Laemmle to give him a shot as a director and quickly set out to make his own script that he'd been kicking around, a *Pygmalion*-like tale called *The Great Problem*. Rex soon made clear to his crew the obsessive attention to detail that was to prove paramount for him. He recreated New York's famed Bowery slum on a Universal lot, making sure that everything from the fire escapes to the natural stench were authentic. Rex fans will notice too that one of the waiters in a restaurant scene is a dwarf, or little person. This was a character type that for some reason endlessly fascinated him and would turn up in his films throughout his career.

The Great Problem was released in April 1916, and the reviews were not kind. "A consistently commonplace scenario," wrote *Variety*. But in those days, turnaround times were fast, and sour reviews could be quickly steamrolled by better ones. So Rex just threw himself into his next project, a story called *Yellow and White*, a wild tale of "white slavery" that jumped between China and America. Here, to achieve the authenticity he craved, Rex and his crew visited real opium dens and rented some of the pipes they saw being used, and Rex even bought and smoked some opium himself. Reviews for the film, retitled *Broken Fetters*, were better, with particular praise for the quality that would propel Rex forward from here on out—his detailed and florid visual style, and beautiful camerawork.

AT THIS TIME, the fast-changing movie business was making its biggest move yet—uprooting itself from the east to the west coast, to what would soon become Hollywood. Carl Laemmle put his vast empire, which included the young director Rex Ingram, onto train cars and headed three thousand miles across the country. In California, the wild and open landscapes, the craggy rocks and wide sandy beaches, offered up visual and aesthetic possibilities Rex had never imagined—a different kind of dreamtime.

My mind was blown too when I first got off the plane in Los Angeles in 1982. Because anything did seem possible. Any stigma of being Irish, or not-British, simply evaporated into the blueness of the California skyline. My late wife, Cassie, and I stayed on North Havenhurst, in the shadow of the Chateau Marmont and just around the corner from Schwab's deli, where I ate my first LA breakfast. I rented a lime green Pacer from Rent-A-Wreck—the right bumper hanging off and a pillow cushion on the seat so the springs didn't go up my ass. It didn't matter. I felt lucky.

The first two films Rex made in his new Southern California home—*The Chalice of Sorrow* and *Black Orchids*—starred Cleo Madison, an actress whose career Rex would help launch. Critics were enraptured. A true contrarian, in both films Rex resisted the uplifting endings that were in vogue at the time. If a character needed to lose a lover or a fortune or to simply die off—so be it. Rex didn't have patience for the all-tied-up-in-a-bow happy ending. Critics noted this tendency, but they seemed to forgive him because of the films' rich production values and imaginative narratives. A twisted love story, *Black Orchids* featured violent du-els and ruthless killings, dungeons, a strong erotic undercurrent, and even an ape. Despite its strange and saucy content (or perhaps because of it), it opened on New Year's Day, 1917, to immediate success.

Rex Ingram was now a full-fledged A-list director, and Univer-sal rewarded him with a whopping $300-per-week salary. At the same time, he'd further developed his prickly reputation. He went on to knock out a few lighter films for Universal and demonstrated a flair for creating drama and emotion with his use of lighting. Still, his stubbornness and his temper were continuing to cause trouble. That same year, Carl Laemmle fired his hot-tempered star.

At that time, Rex also suffered another bitter breakup. Cleo Madison had introduced him to a visiting Nebraska girl, an aspir-ing actress named Doris Pawn. Rex invited Pawn to his house for dinner. In his typically rash and impulsive romantic style, he ended the meal by asking her to get married. Strange? Perhaps even more so because not long after the dinner, they actually tied the knot. Almost as quickly, Rex became bored by her. "We had little in com-mon," he wrote. "She was beautiful to look at but I could not just sit and admire her all evening." Then, bang—divorced.

Something of a roller coaster—as I said, you're up and then you're down. As these shenanigans were taking place, Rex's brother, Frank, was off fighting Germans on the front in Europe and earn-ing distinctions for bravery. Inspired, or maybe ashamed of his own luxurious life, Rex finally decided to enlist. He tried to join the U.S. Signal Corps, but his citizenship papers were a mess. And so he enlisted instead with the Royal Flying Corps Canada, which was then part of the British Empire. Here things get murky. By some accounts Rex learned to fly, possibly becoming a flight instructor, and maybe even being badly wounded in a training accident. But the records are not clear.

What is known is that he was discharged in late 1919 after the war ended, and he returned to Hollywood that year with a host of injuries and, apparently, his money just about gone. Friends nursed him back to better health and helped him find physically untaxing, low-level work on sets. He made a half-hearted attempt to win back his estranged wife, Doris, but she would have none of it.

While Rex's adeptness at pissing people off never left him, neither did his uncanny knack to pull himself out of professional misery.

It's worth noting here that Hollywood and the movie business was an empire being built almost entirely by immigrants, men and women who had recently arrived in our country and who were in fact looking to reinvent themselves. For Rex, not yet thirty, it was not far from the rollicking cast of characters he had first found in the New Haven dockyards—perhaps not misfits, but outsiders nonetheless. One of those figures was fellow Irishman and co-founder of Universal P. A. Powers, from County Waterford. Powers helped Rex to direct two films back at Universal, *The Day She Paid* and *Under Crimson Skies*, which together showed the town he had not lost his touch. Around the same time, Rex met an actor who would play a starring role in the next few years of his life, a handsome young Italian immigrant named Rudolph Valentino.

On the heels of his latest two films, the studio Metro Pictures offered Rex a stage adaptation called *Shore Acres*. He chose to film it in Laguna Beach, because it reminded him of Ireland. He was also determined to cast a beautiful girl he had worked with once before, Alice Taaffe. In his work as a sculptor, Rex often created busts and even full figures inspired by people he met. As part of his courtship of Alice, Rex would ask her to model for a head he was sculpting, but she declined. Camera shy, only after much persuading did she even agree to appear as an extra in the film. But the two seemed to get along. So much so that on his next outing, *Hearts Are Trumps*, Rex pushed to make her the star. He also assembled a creative team that would prove vital in the coming years—ace cameraman John Seitz and editor Grant Whytock. The pair would remain Rex's go-to team for his finest films, both for their skills and for the fact that they were among the few crew in town who could actually get along with him.

Directing Alice on set one day, Rex had a thought and tossed her a blonde wig. She didn't see the need for it but agreed under pressure to put it on. They both ended up admiring how pretty the brunette looked as a blonde. It was a look she would keep throughout her career. But there was something else about Alice that the perfectionist Rex didn't entirely appreciate: her last name, Taaffe. From now on, he told her, you're Alice Terry. Terry was his mother's mother's name.

Hearts Are Trumps won warm reviews and strong box office. And, crucially, it turned a Metro studio powerhouse named June Mathis into a believer in all things Rex. Mathis had worked on the script for the film and would champion Rex for the next picture under her wing—the one that would become Rex Ingram's masterwork.

THERE WAS A bestselling book in 1921: the multigenerational antiwar epic *The Four Horsemen of the Apocalypse* by Vicente Blasco Ibáñez. June Mathis urged Metro to buy the rights and was

then asked to write the script and oversee production. She chose
Rex to direct.

Mathis and Rex also pushed the studio to allow the very green
actor and dancer Rudolph Valentino to take a leading role. Mathis
offered him an impressive $100 a week, a windfall for the young
man. Rex successfully fought for Alice Terry, now his lover, to play
a leading role. Another Rex Ingram discovery—a Mexican actor
named Ramón Samaniegos, later Ramon Novarro—plays an extra.

Nearly everything about *Horsemen* grew wildly out of control:
massive and lavish sets, ferocious battle scenes, and a notoriously
demanding twenty-eight-year-old director led to a production
that lasted an ungainly six months—unheard of in that era. About
twelve thousand people worked on the film, and there were single
sets that cost as much as many of the studio's entire films. Officially,
the final budget was $650,000, a staggering amount at the time and
a Metro record.

Rex put his artistic talent to work creating detailed storyboards
for key scenes. Coming on the heels of the Great War, *Horsemen* featured full-pitch battle scenes with hundreds of extras that
shocked many viewers for their raw power. To achieve these effects,
Rex let loose the camera department, sometimes deploying more
than a dozen cameras for a single scene.

And for many viewers, there was one scene that stole the movie
and made a superstar of Rudolph Valentino. A smoldering Valentino, whip in hand, seizes his partner on the dance floor of a
raucous saloon and dances a tango with her that melts the screen.
If you haven't seen the actual scene, you have seen imitations and
parodies, so it is surely lodged in your consciousness. Audiences
devoured the film. President Warren Harding requested a private
viewing. *Horsemen* made a tidy fortune for Metro, Rex, and its top

stars, grossing about $4 million. This was the pinnacle, the high-water mark for this Irish lad who had arrived on our shores barely a decade earlier.

It was at this time that the press started to focus on Rex's art world background and his time at Yale. He was becoming known as a "sculptor of the screen," an image that Metro worked hard to promote. The studio commissioned Rex's former mentor, Lee Law-rie, to make a sculpture of the four horsemen of the apocalypse—exhibiting the piece at the premiere and using the image in the press. Yale was more than willing to embrace its celebrity alum (never mind that he'd dropped out), bestowing on the director an actual fine arts degree. Rex himself saw a very clear connec-tion between the influence of sculpture and his work in film: "As time went on I began to realize how valuable my training in the art school was going to prove." Indeed, even then, during his directo-rial prime, Rex still found time to keep up on his sculpting.

How he managed, I can't say. For me, I'm drawing all the time and, when on set, will cover my scripts with sketches. But I am rarely painting. That is for home, for the recovery. My painting comes from a need to make something beautiful, and it gives meaning to my time between acting, between making movies. But Rex was different.

At this point, professionally speaking, Rex could write his own ticket. But he and Valentino had predictably quarreled on the *Horsemen* set, as Rex's rough and controlling style rankled the young heartthrob. Filmmaking is in fact a far cry from sculpting. Given how many people actually share in the production, it de-mands almost unceasing collaboration. There are directors like Rex (and I have worked for them) who are just so incredibly specific in their vision—unwavering. I have the greatest admiration for that, although I am not of that cloth. I feel it's essential to always try to keep your ego in check, to be generous of heart. Though of course that is easier said than done. Rex was an artist, in his studio or on a film set, a true artist of chisel and hammer and clay. He seems to have wanted that control always. But in Hollywood, I have to say, it helps to get along.

In the end, Metro was able to keep their lucrative team together, Rex and Valentino, along with Alice Terry, for at least another film. Rex was also able to keep together the key crew that had crafted so much of *Horsemen*'s visual power.

Next up was a picture called *The Conquering Power*, and Rex's fighting with Valentino continued. To complicate matters, there were rumors of a possible love triangle involving the Metro exec June Mathis, Valentino, and Rex—this though Rex was still very much involved with Alice Terry. In the end, both Mathis and Valentino decamped for rival Paramount, leaving the star director on his own. Metro's publicity machine put a clever spin on the departure: "Ingram was a very independent Irishman." But surely it must have hurt.

To close out the frenetic year, Rex took on the duel-filled, swash-buckling adventure story *The Prisoner of Zenda*. Perhaps missing Valentino, he was eager to groom another Latin heartthrob, and so he coached Ramón Samaniegos, that extra from *Horsemen*. Formerly a singing waiter, Samaniegos restyled himself Ramon Novarro, played a sexy villain in *Zenda*, and another star was born. *Zenda* was a clear winner, both at the box office and in the press. But the most memorable event surrounding the film was personal. One Saturday after shooting, Rex and his star, Alice Terry, quietly walked off set and decided to get married. They spent the next day watching movies and then jumped right back into production on Monday. They wouldn't announce the event until after the film was finished and they were on their honeymoon.

Rex's marriage would last the rest of his life. But though he and Alice seemed to keep a fairly stable series of homes, it'd be hard to call theirs a storybook romance. Long separations were frequent. Rex's memoirs tell stories about romps with prostitutes, and he wrote of Alice that "my feeling for her was platonic." As for Alice, she told a biographer that "we were very good friends." Friends said they seemed to enjoy each other's company, got along well, and that each provided a sounding board for the stresses of Hollywood. Alice was sweet, capable, and levelheaded—a calming force for the anxiety and rages that often overcame Rex.

Soon after their marriage, in 1921, the two also began to talk openly and with studio heads about their desire to move to Europe and set up a studio in the South of France. Was Rex done with America? Or was he just a restless soul? He claimed to crave greater autonomy from the studios, and he hungered to shoot in southern European and northern African locations. Surely this was part of it. But there is to Rex the aura of the perpetual outsider. His tribe was nomadic. I am not exempt from this. I love to work as an actor, and part of that is you pack your bags and hit the road. Because after two or three months here at home—yes, even with the blue Pacific and my painting—I need to get onto a movie set or I lose the thread of who I am. For Rex, well, he had been in Hollywood an awfully long time. And given that his earning power was now huge, it was the right time to push.

In the breakneck pace of the silent era, Rex and Alice decided to make just a few quick films before the move. *Where the Pavement Ends* was another hit. But while making the film, he was dealt a bruising blow. Rex had been expecting to direct the big-budget *Ben-Hur*, but his former partner, studio exec June Mathis, held the keys to that one, and she chose a lesser-known director. Rex was crushed. Adding salt to the wound, Novarro, the star he had created, would be cast in the lead. Rex was so enraged that crew noticed he began drinking heavily, unusual for him. Too broken up inside, he was unable to finish *Pavement*, and Alice was brought in to close it. Rex made a vow: one more film, and he was done with Hollywood.

It was 1923, and for his final American-based film ever, Rex set his sights on the French Revolution epic *Scaramouche*. For his last hurrah, Rex worked in perfect sync with his cinematographer and editor, and showed himself to be at the height of his powers. Not only did *Scaramouche* score with viewers, but many critics praised it for a new level of visual artistry. But despite this success, Rex was weary of Hollywood, and, to a degree, of directing as well. Still a young man, he found himself at a crossroads. He bought a house, an old Moorish villa in faraway Tunis, and in March of that year declared that he was quitting filmmaking altogether to focus solely on sculpture. Was this ever really Rex's intention, or just a fantasy? Lord knows, a long, hard production will plant dreams of escape. But in the end, Rex and Alice would set sail for the South of France—a place of true enchantment.

REX MOVED TO Europe in part to be closer to home. Political violence was shaking Ireland and Britain at the time. Rex's father, a Protestant minister, had found himself in the crossfire. Rex had wanted to visit him and Frank in Ireland for several years, but work commitments never allowed. By 1924 Reverend Hitchcock had finally had enough, and he fled Ireland for a parish in southern England. Rex's brother, Frank, soon followed. Rex and Alice stopped in England to visit them—the first encounter between father and son in thirteen years.

At this point, Rex needed a physical film studio to use as a base. He found the perfect location in southern France. Victorine Studios, on a hill overlooking Nice, had been built a few years earlier but was run-down and in receivership. Rex rented it and set out to craft the studio of his dreams.

He brought over to Nice his core production team and as many additional players as the studio would send. For the first production at Victorine, Rex wanted to make maximum use of the Mediterranean setting. Novelist Vicente Ibáñez, author of *Four Horsemen of the Apocalypse*, had written the romantic Great War espionage tale *Mare Nostrum* (Latin for "our sea"). But Victorine's crude and deteriorating facilities proved a tough fit for Rex, leading to near-constant production hurdles, delays, and budget overruns. The oceanic melodrama required two submarines and a huge water tank to shoot battle scenes.

It was a high-stress production, but Rex also found himself the object of attention from a number of Europe's movie luminaries and his studio something of a global salon. Many would make the pilgrimage to Victorine and his sets, eager to see the working methods of the famously prickly but charming Irishman—Henri Matisse, F. Scott Fitzgerald, Charlie Chaplin, European royals, Douglas Fairbanks, Mary Pickford, and a parade of others.

What they saw was a stubborn, obsessive go-it-aloner who

would do anything to craft a perfect shot. French filmmaker Jean de Limur observed that "Rex was quite stubborn . . . Nobody could cross him. He was his own producer." On the other hand, Rex's overbearing style was a relief to some on the team. "Rex knew what he wanted and visualized it. Most of the film directors of those days made their films without a real script, but Rex Ingram knew what he was going to shoot," noted actor Andrews Engelmann. Rex held such clout with the studio by now that he was even able to retain a tragic ending to the film, continuing to buck the wider trend of tidy, pat endings served up to the moviegoing masses.

Mare Nostrum took more of Rex's time than any other film he made. Over the course of the fifteen-month production he shot more than a million feet of film. When it came out at last in 1926, it won strong reviews, and French audiences were so smitten that they made Rex a Chevalier of the Legion of Honor. Victorine also suddenly became available for sale, and Rex, by now extremely wealthy, bought it up. He paid $5 million and said he would lease it back to what was now Metro-Goldwyn-Mayer for productions. But buying such a complex foreign property would end up backfiring, as the investment over time would become a knotty mess.

By the late 1920s, Rex, sometimes accompanied by Alice or friends, sometimes alone, would travel throughout North Africa whenever he had a chance. Rex found Algeria and Tunisia as magical as he had imagined when he was a boy, and he grew extremely fond of Arab cultures and the Islamic faith, coming to feel that life in the West was decadent and suffering under the self-inflicted blows of the Depression. Finally, he officially converted to Islam, rejecting the faith of his father and family to embrace what he saw as a beatific spiritual outlook. He even adopted an Arabic name,

Ben Aalem Nacir ed' Deen. In his memoirs, he spells out his attractions to Arabs and Islam: "The desert nomad can pack all his earthly goods in a couple of camel bags. He is richer, more free and happier than the richest man in the world."

But material matters also consumed Rex. Although his next film, *The Garden of Allah*, was a modest success, it was a struggle for Rex in many ways. He was plagued with health problems, including chest pains and stomach ulcers that had dogged him for years and were getting worse. Just before making it, his longtime cameraman and editor both told Rex they were through with him and Victorine, and returned to Hollywood. Strife on the set led to widespread sour feelings.

He also had a visit from his father while shooting, which can't have helped. Reverend Hitchcock was alarmed at his son's drift into Islam and wanted to advise him on some of the religious aspects of the film. Perhaps tellingly, Rex would produce during this time one of his most enigmatic sculptures—a sleeping Christ in the arms of Buddha. His father was said to detest it.

After this film, MGM told Rex it wouldn't be renewing his contract unless he returned to America, but Rex refused. At the same time, Rex's ownership of Victorine was also proving enormously costly—in 1930, he was forced to sell it at a loss.

It is a capricious game, filmmaking. Now isolated, without the studio he had built, shunned by many of the industry's top players, and financially troubled, Rex nonetheless tried to carry on. Alice, though, had lost her appetite for acting. She could not reconcile herself to the era of talking films and called it quits.

Unmoored, Rex plunged ahead with one last film. He cobbled together funds to make his first and only talkie, *Baroud*. Unable to

find a leading man (and maybe to save money as well), Rex decided
to take the lead himself. The rest of the cast was a mishmash of
unknowns speaking in multiple tongues (which mattered in talk-
ies) and seemingly disconnected from one another. Rex found it
hard to radically alter his directing style to accommodate synced
sound, and the bumpy results show up on screen. By the end, for
various reasons, Rex was unable even to finish *Baroud*, and Alice
had to step in again to direct. The film, retitled *Love in Morocco* for
American audiences, was a flop, both critically and in theaters, and
Rex's performance was panned as well.

Rex had finally reached the end of his career. While Alice returned to the United States to visit her ailing mother, Rex spent the
next few years exploring North Africa. He returned to California
in 1936, and the couple settled in their house on Kelsey Street, in
the Valley. Was he home? To some degree, I think, more so than in
Ireland or England. But then Rex really seemed to live in his art.

Rex's time in the San Fernando Valley in the late 1930s and 1940s
was marked by some socializing and a good bit of travel around
America, as well as sculpting and writing. That is in fact where we
found him at our open, puttering about the studio, his hands deep
in clay, while inside Alice kept her own company. In 1939, he had
a novel published, *Mars in the House of Death*. No one seemed to
give it much notice. But in that same year a far more successful
book came out, James Joyce's *Finnegans Wake*. Rex must have been
delighted to see a reference in it to "Rex Ingram, pageant-master."

When the United States entered the Second World War in 1941,
Rex became a naturalized U.S. citizen and offered up to the au-
thorities his knowledge of the Arab world should it be desired.
The timing strikes a chord in me. I myself decided to become an

American citizen the night of the "hanging chad," Election Day, 2000. My wife, Keely, and I rode our bikes down to the local polling station that evening. Al Gore was ahead. Keely voted as I stood outside the box, the silent partner with no vote. By the time we rode home twenty minutes later, George W. Bush was on his way to becoming president. I remember Keely saying, "We're going to war." That night was a turning point for me. After twenty years of paying taxes and living an American life, I needed to have a voice. So for Rex, what with the Second World War, and himself growing older, maybe that is some of what he was feeling.

Although he was not quite fifty, his health was getting worse. Along with his stomach issues, Rex suffered from high blood pressure. He kept a low profile, though Hollywood nobility like John Ford counted themselves among his friends, and sculpted more or less full time. He kept in touch with Lee Lawrie, who would later write that Rex's "discerning judgment on the Fine Arts used to astonish me." And he stayed in close contact by letter with his father and brother, still in England. Neither was physically well—his brother, Frank, wracked by war injuries, and his dad by old age. He frequently sent them money and well wishes. He also still nurtured dreams of returning some day to visit Ireland. "I must go," he wrote them, "having been away since 1911. Maybe the three of us could meet in Dublin." But it was not meant to be. He sailed to see them both in a joyous reunion in London, in 1947. From London, he returned to Egypt and Morocco, but his health was getting worse, and he was beginning to suffer heart attacks. In 1948, he struggled to make his way back home to Los Angeles.

In early July 1950, Alice took him into the hospital for some heart tests. On her birthday, July 24, Rex told her to go shop for something pretty for herself. When she got home, the hospital called. Rex was unconscious. Alice rushed there, and he died soon after she arrived. He was fifty-seven.

THE GREAT FILMMAKER Erich von Stroheim called Rex "the world's greatest director." Directing legend Michael Powell (whose career, incidentally, Rex had helped launch) once admitted, "Rex was all-powerful and acknowledged no master." By the time of his mid-1930s suburban exile, it would have taken Rex's giant Auburn 851 Supercharged Speedster barely twenty minutes to get to most of the big movie studios. But by then his film career had crashed to a halt. Despite his massive talent, his obsessive perfectionism and contrarian creative style had finally pushed him out of Hollywood's innermost sanctum.

Fair enough, I suppose. Remington Steele also drove an Auburn Speedster what seems to me like a long time ago. We are all allowed to stay at the table only so long. But still, and most important, by then Rex Ingram—a wanderer, a restless soul, a true artist—had left his mark on Hollywood and at a time when Hollywood was just discovering who it was and what it could become. So it is a shame that his life and work are not better remembered.

Of course, I realize that this may be something of a sad ending. And having lived in Hollywood now for over thirty-five years, I know well enough that sad endings are not welcome. Better to say, wasn't it grand—for an Irish boy, the son of a minister, raised in the little town of Kinnitty—wasn't it one hell of a life? And it was. But still—it was sad too. And Rex, likely, would not have wanted it told otherwise.

THE AUTHOR

Maeve Brennan (1917–1993)

BY KATHLEEN HILL

Yesterday afternoon, as I walked along Forty-second Street directly across from Bryant Park, I saw a three-cornered shadow on the pavement in the angle where two walls meet. I didn't step on the shadow, but I stood a minute in the thin winter sunlight and looked at it. I recognized it at once. It was exactly the same shadow that used to fall on the cement part of our garden in Dublin, more than fifty-five years ago.

Here is Maeve Brennan hanging on, recording a solitary encounter in her last published piece in *The New Yorker*. On the sidewalk of the city where she had come to live in her twenties and spent the rest of her life, she recognizes, that sunny winter's day in

1981, the stamp of the house in Dublin where she had passed her childhood. Maeve Brennan and her work had already been lost to public view when she died in 1993. Never eager to establish a home, moving from one rented room to another, staying in friends' places while they were away, she disappeared by degrees, at last joining the ranks of the homeless. But four years after her death, with the publication of *The Springs of Affection: Stories of Dublin,* her work appeared in a new edition. For the first time the Irish stories could be read in a sequence that made strikingly clear the remarkable depth and originality of her art.

An exile whose imagination never abandoned its native ground, Maeve Brennan was in perpetual transit. Her emigration was not chosen, although in time it became so. She would not have left Ireland at the age of seventeen if she'd been given the choice, and yet in her adult years she didn't choose to return. A displaced person, always on provisional ground. When writing about New York City she described herself as a "traveller in residence." She was staying for a while, poised to depart. And in that displacement she may be a figure for the Irish American a little disoriented as to notions of home, or for any immigrant who finds herself elsewhere without having chosen to leave where she came from. In time, Maeve Brennan's status as traveler had become a habit, a preference, an identity. But at one time there had been a home, a fixed address at 48 Cherryfield Avenue. Lost, it could only be remembered.

The particulars of Maeve's wandering life were often elusive, even to her friends. But in her art, for which she sacrificed so much, she is everywhere felt in her dedication to the poetry of place, whether in Dublin or New York. It is in her work we find her.

In almost every one of the Dublin stories, the house on Cherry-field Avenue in Ranelagh, on the south side of Dublin, provides the setting. Sometimes the characters who live in the house are called Rose and Hubert Derdon. In another sequence, they are Delia and Martin Bagot, a couple who in many ways resemble Rose and Hubert. Or, in the earliest brief autobiographical stories published between 1953 and 1955, the children living there are called Emer and Maeve and Derry. But the house they variously occupy never changes. The front door opens onto a narrow front hallway that passes a staircase to lead down a few steps into a kitchen with a coal-burning stove. In the front sitting room, where there is a fire-place, a large bay window looks out on the houses across the street, as does the bay window in the bedroom just above it. The stairs are covered by a red runner held in place at each step by a brass rod. The back sitting room, or dining room, as it is sometimes called, is warmed by a gas fire and overlooks the small garden in back. Rose, or it might be Delia—both passionate gardeners—step outside through a heavy wooden kitchen door painted green. In spring the laburnum tree in back explodes in a profusion of tiny yellow blossoms.

Every corner of the house is meticulously cared for by the un-ceasing labors of the women who live in it. In one of Brennan's earliest published stories, "The Day We Got Our Own Back," writ-ten before Rose Derdon or Delia Bagot appeared on the scene, the terror inflicted one day during the Irish Civil War when the Free Staters raid the house looking for evidence of the father's Repub-lican activities is measured by the chaos they leave behind: the beds torn apart and the mattresses bundled together, the books taken from their shelves and shaken out for suspicious notes and letters, the drawers emptied, the tins of tea and flour and sugar dumped onto the red tiles of the kitchen floor, the scarred oilcloth on the dining room floor the mother had been polishing when they burst in with their revolvers. "*Still* they had found nothing, but the house looked as if it had suffered an explosion without bursting its walls."

Maeve Brennan was almost five in 1921 when her parents, Bob and Una Brennan, bought the house in Ranelagh at the outbreak of the Irish Civil War. The year 1921 had marked the end of the Irish War of Independence; a truce had been struck in July, ending what had been largely a guerrilla war of attrition. A few months later, however, when the terms of the treaty Michael Collins had negotiated in London became public, a civil conflict erupted perhaps even more terrible than the one waged against the Crown: fellow patriots who'd shared prison cells and fought alongside each other for years became bitter enemies. It was de Valera who led the opposition to the new treaty that required of elected representatives an oath of allegiance to King George V and allowed Britain to retain the six counties in the north. These terms, for members of the Anti-Treaty Irish Republican Army, like Maeve's father, Bob Brennan, betrayed the Irish Republic as declared in the proclamation of 1916.

For safekeeping during this desperate time, Maeve's parents sent her, along with her older and younger sisters, for long spells to Coolnaboy in the Wexford countryside, where her mother had grown up and where they were fondly cared for by their grandmother and young aunt and uncles. Emer, Maeve, Deirdre: these were the names—all taken from ancient Irish sagas—that Bob and Una gave to their daughters. Between her older sister Emer and

Maeve there'd been another child, a boy, Manus, who'd lived less than a year. Later on, in 1928, Robert was born and, like his father, was called Bob.

Maeve Brennan's years at 48 Cherryfield Avenue were her school-going years: first at St. Mary's National School, a short walk away, then later on with her sister Derry (Deirdre) for a couple of years at a boarding school in County Kildare called Cross and Passion. After she returned to Dublin at thirteen, she attended Scoil Bhrighde, a Catholic Irish-speaking day school run by Louise Gavan Duffy, the daughter of the Irish rebel Charles Gavan Duffy. It was housed in Duffy's townhouse on St. Stephen's Green and distinguished by the fact that it employed only lay teachers and that all of its classes were taught in Irish. The school encouraged the use of that language outside the classroom, and years later Brennan's school friends wrote to her in Irish. Here she distinguished herself in English and laid the foundations of a lifetime interest in French language and literature.

During the summer holidays, after she and her sisters had spent a couple of weeks at Coolnaboy, where their Bolger cousins, who included Ita—the future mother of Roddy Doyle—were also visiting, they would be driven to Wexford, where Bob had grown up, to stay with their father's mother and two of his grown sisters. Later on, both places and the people who lived in them would come to figure in her stories, in fact, counterpointing each other in her last published story, "The Springs of Affection."

When in 1934 the Brennans moved out of the house in Ranelagh after more than a decade, Maeve was turning eighteen, and de Valera had become head of the Irish government and had appointed Bob Brennan as the first Irish envoy to the United States. Long afterward, when Brennan's life had come apart, she told a friend who visited her in the hospital that she had felt "desperate about being uprooted" when the family left Ireland to relocate to Washington, DC. You could say the house at 48 Cherryfield Avenue was her only home, irreplaceable. When she lost—or found—her way and after her many years at *The New Yorker* began to wander the streets, it seems she could locate its shadow on the pavement beneath her feet, anywhere.

MAEVE BRENNAN WAS born in Dublin on January 6, 1917, eight months after the Easter Rising. Her parents, both early members of the Gaelic League, were Republicans, sworn members of the secret Irish Republican Brotherhood. They took part in the rising not in Dublin but in County Wexford, in Enniscorthy, one of the few towns outside Dublin that engaged in armed struggle. By the end of Easter week, following Patrick Pearse's surrender to the British, Bob and Una, along with other Wexford patriots, were taken to Mountjoy Prison and charged with "armed rebellion." Although Una was released after a few days, Bob, like his Dublin counterparts, was quickly court-martialed and sentenced to death. On May 3, Pearse as well as Thomas MacDonagh and Tom Clarke were shot. But as the executions rolled on day after day and as the tide of sympathy in Ireland and the United States turned toward the insurgents, Bob's sentence along with others' were commuted to five years of penal service in Britain.

On the January day Maeve was born, the Feast of the Epiphany, Bob Brennan was serving his sentence in Lewes Prison in Sussex.

Under a general amnesty in June 1917, the Irish prisoners were released, and Maeve's father returned home and met his five-month-
old daughter. During the following years he'd be arrested again and
again, serving prison time both in Ireland and Britain, using false
names, spending nights in one safe house or another, rapidly skip-
ping between places to avoid arrest, seldom at home with his wife
and little daughters. In 1918 he produced the *Irish Bulletin*, a daily
paper whose purpose was to counteract British propaganda and
make the underground-elected government's political positions
known. As a Republican during the Irish Civil War, he continued
his life on the run and had a breakdown during that time, perhaps
more than one. It wasn't until later, after the hostilities had ended
and the state was established, that Éamon de Valera asked him to
be managing editor of the Irish Press.

As an adult, Brennan would distance herself from the ardent nationalism of her parents' generation. But she made distinctions.
William Maxwell, her editor and close friend at *The New Yorker* for
more than twenty years—editor also of J. D. Salinger, Eudora Welty,
John Cheever, Isaac Bashevis Singer, and Frank O'Connor—writes
in his introduction to *The Springs of Affection* that he and she
became friends over shared literary affinities: Tolstoy, Turgenev,
Colette. "The only bone of contention between us I was aware of
was that she refused to read the novels of Elizabeth Bowen because
Bowen was Anglo-Irish. On the other hand, she venerated Yeats,
who was also Anglo-Irish, and she knew a good deal of his poetry
by heart."

But Yeats had thrown in his lot with the cause for Irish independence. Indeed, he later worried that the early play he'd written
with Lady Gregory, *Cathleen ni Houlihan*, had sent men to their

deaths. On the other hand, Bowen's feelings about the rebellion were more ambivalent, a fact Maeve would have carried in her bones but that may have been lost, sometimes, on even her closest American friends.

MAEVE AT SEVENTEEN had no choice but to move with her family to Washington, DC, in 1934. Though later on she visited Ireland a number of times, she couldn't have known when she left that she would never live there again, nor even return for many years. At twenty-four she moved by herself to New York City, where she lived for the rest of her life. During the years in Washington, she'd graduated from Immaculata Seminary, a junior college run by the Sisters of Providence, and then from American University, where she'd completed the final two years of her bachelor's degree. Afterward she studied library science at the Catholic University of America.

Years later, she told a friend that in Washington she'd been in love with Walter Kerr, who would later become a noted drama critic, that he'd broken their engagement and married someone else. Whether it was for this reason or another she moved to New York, it seems she left home against the wishes of her parents. Her break from them wouldn't be permanent, but when they returned to Ireland, she didn't go with them.

Long afterward, in about 1970, she described in a letter to William Maxwell a terrifying dream she'd had of that initial rupture with her family.

I woke with the most painful feeling of irrevocable separation from something I could put my hand out and touch—I was

in New York City and had come from Washington and they
were in Washington & the sense of time drawing tight from
nowhere to nowhere was . . . agonizing, as if the feeling I woke
up with was incurable and would last for every minute as long
as I lived. It was as though I could see them & they were wondering about me & didn't know I was dead. And I didn't want
them to know.

Could these words describe some deep and terrified aspect of the
emerging writer Brennan remembered herself to have been at the
time, the horrified anticipation of chasms that would widen as she
wrote from the place of family pain and loneliness? Of antipathies
that refuse to soften? Inconsolable longings that neither disappear
nor give way to something else?

On the other hand, perhaps this letter written in her early fif-
ties, so soon before her own unraveling, is in itself a cry of warning, an anguished premonition of what lay ahead. It may have
been the expression of some dreaming part of herself that both
feared and longed for the destruction of memory—in itself a kind
of death—that had risen up at last to signal the approach of what
people call madness. Brennan herself might have named it the "delirium of loss," the affliction suffered by Rose in one of the Derdon
stories, "An Attack of Hunger": "The only ease that could come to
her would come if she could just get down on the floor and put her
face in the corner and let her mind wander away into sleep, very
deep and distant, where there was no worry and where her mind
would not be confined in dreams but could float and become vague
and might even break free and sail off like a child's balloon, taking
her burden of memory with it."

By 1970 Brennan had carried the burden of memory for years, had labored to give those memories shape, trace in them the pattern it was hers alone to decipher. She gave everything of herself to her stories. She worked very hard, producing little. Sometimes she labored on a story for years, refusing to release it to publication if it seemed unfinished to her or if William Maxwell's editorial hand had seemed to disturb its integrity, as was the case with "The Rose Garden." The meticulous beauty of her sentences is spun out of the chaos of the past. Their disturbing grace must have been personally costly to herself, but while she was at work on them, it can be hoped she was in a state of vibrant tranquility.

BY THE TIME Bob and Una were at last recalled to Dublin, the war was over and with it Bob's uneasy diplomacy in the face of Ireland's declared neutrality. In June 1948, Maeve's father wrote to her referring to the recent visit she'd made to see them not long after their return. By then, she'd lived for five years in New York City, working briefly at the public library on Forty-second Street before being hired at *Harper's Bazaar* in 1943 by the editor Carmel Snow, also Irish. There she'd been drawn into a world that included writers and editors, some at *Harper's* and others, like Brendan Gill, at *The New Yorker*. She frequented Tim and Joe Costello's, at Fortyfourth and Third Avenue, a favorite drinking and eating place for Irish writers, and increasingly writers of any stripe. As a young man Tim Costello had known her father as a fellow Republican in Dublin, and he now kept an eye out for her. While she'd adopted many aspects of American fashion and culture, her speaking voice remained the one she'd grown up with. She was "effortlessly witty," as William Maxwell wrote of her later, had a lively sense of the ridiculous. She was generous, sometimes extravagantly so, bestowing lavish gifts, pressing on friends things of her own they admired. Costello's was only a few blocks away from *The New Yorker*, and on the basis of a few short pieces she'd written for that magazine she was hired there by William Shawn, in 1949, at Brendan Gill's urging.

But during those years at *Harper's* she began and completed a novella, *The Visitor*, that was only discovered years later, in 1997, in the library of the University of Notre Dame among the papers of Maisie Ward—of Sheed and Ward—who with her husband had founded a Catholic publishing house in London that had moved to New York. The manuscript can be dated by the address—5 East Tenth Street—written on its cover sheet. Brennan was living there in 1944, when she was twenty-seven and working at *Harper's*. By the late 1940s she'd moved. Maisie Ward must have read the manuscript or at least received it. But who else? And why was it never published? Did Brennan, who sometimes worked on a story for decades, never revisit it? Did she keep a copy herself? This novella announces her great themes and obsessions, and who can say but that she herself was shy of it.

With *The Visitor*, the harrowing novella that seems to have been Maeve Brennan's first completed work, the reader, with a jolt of recognition, enters a world that is at once new and strangely familiar. How simple the writing, evoking the crowded but lonely mood of a train arriving in Dublin on a rainy November evening. And then, seamlessly, the story opens, and we're in a place known better in dreams, in the murkier places of the unconscious. "Home is a place in the mind. When it is empty, it frets. It is fretful with memory, faces and places and times gone by. Beloved images rise up in disobedience and make a mirror for emptiness. Then what resentful wonder, and what half-aimless self-seeking. . . . Comical and hopeless, the long gaze back is always turned inward."

Anastasia, an orphan, twenty-two years old, arrives on the train from Paris following the recent death of her mother, desperate to find a home in her grandmother's house in Dublin. It is the house in which her parents' unhappy marriage had been played out under the cold eye of the grandmother, whose ferocious grip on her only son remained unshaken, the house in which Anastasia had grown up. Now her grandmother, resolute in her intention to expel Anastasia from under her roof, is all politeness, all chained fury, exquisitely in control of herself, implacable, immune to any appeal to mercy or love. "There is no comfort in her," Anastasia quickly understands. For Anastasia has committed an unforgivable sin. At sixteen, she'd followed her mother, who, "like some kind of madwoman," her grandmother says, had fled the house for Paris, abandoning Anastasia's father, the beloved son. Now six years later Anastasia, aching for love, for a place to call home, is repelled. The chill of her grandmother's dislike, indeed of her hatred, surrounds her as the two sit silently, one on either side of the fire in the enormous, shadowy room. "There was no movement in the room except the wild movement of the fire-flames and the light they let go. The light washed up and down the room like thin water over stones."

There is an inside and there is an outside. Anastasia, condemned to be a visitor, is somewhere between. She is inside, but her lease is up. She is on her way out onto the streets, where the poor are to be observed from the windows, sometimes playing a violin or a tin whistle, but welcomed in by Katherine, Anastasia's grandmother's servant, who gives them a meal at her own table beside the roaring oven in the basement kitchen. "Don't ever say beggar," said Katherine in a fierce whisper. "He's a poor man, God help him." And in the final pages Anastasia becomes one of those on the outside. Evicted from her home, she is on the way to the mail train, by which she'll return to Paris, when she turns back for a final glimpse. Just outside the house, taking off her stockings and shoes, leaning against a lamp post, she steps barefoot into the street, her eyes fixed on the window—where her grandmother and Katherine will soon appear—and begins to sing, "loud and sudden as one in a dream, who without warning finds a voice in some public place":

> There is a happy land
> far far away. . . .

And those passing by stop to listen.

Anastasia cannot choose both parents: they are at odds, and therein lies her misery. She is excluded because she has chosen one. It is not the other, her father, who would have denied her; it is his mother, who cannot forgive her son for marrying at all. That is the primal sin, to choose outside the family. Yet what is the alternative if not incest, symbolic if not actual? Sexual choice comes with the charge of family disloyalty, with the fierce disapproval of those held longest and closest.

Again, the unyielding grudge, the unflagging sense of betrayal. Indeed, very like the spite to which, in one of the Derdon stories, Rose is subjected by her mother, who mocks her openly, maliciously, in front of her suitor, Hubert, names her a "poor soft thing with no respect for herself or her family." Or like Min Bagot in "The Springs of Affection," whose life is embittered by what she sees as her twin brother's betrayal of his mother and sisters by marrying, who slips her dead brother's wedding ring from his hand and puts it on the fourth finger of her own left hand. To save it from grave robbers, she tells herself.

The ones set adrift, the outsiders, are doomed by coldness of heart, the pinched refusal to take in another's ravenous need. They are the dispossessed, in silent sympathy with the poor, the wanderers. But the punishment for holding out against the needy is claustrophobia, confinement to the prison within: slow suffocation between ever narrowing walls.

And what is to be found in the spaces outside, where Anastasia is exposed to wind and weather? For one, the laburnum tree in the back garden that is seen in so many of the Dublin stories. And the parade of seasons as Anastasia broods on the passage of time: "Next winter and next winter and next winter. In the mind they passed all slowly, like clouds across a summer sky, but a sudden call or turn of the head and they disappeared in a rush, shuttling quickly one after the last till nothing was left but a strangeness in the mind, a drop of thought that trembled and was gone, perhaps."

It is on the street that Anastasia finds her voice "loud and sudden as one in a dream," not within the confines of the house. In taking off her stockings and shoes, she joins the poor and the dispossessed. The ones who stop to listen to her are not her longtime familiars but those she meets in passing, strangers all.

WHEN DID MAEVE Brennan become an exile? And for what or where is she homesick? It seems she returned to Ireland for the first time after fourteen years away, exactly the same number of years the missionary bishop in one of Brennan's last published stories, "Stories from Africa," was first absent from Ireland. "You could say that an exile was a person who knew of a country that made all other countries seem strange," the bishop thinks. But then he stops himself:

> Anyone listening to him would imagine he thought Ireland to be a pretty little oasis of one kind or another, a kind of family paradise. He thought of his country, where terrible pride and terrible humility stand together, two noble creatures enslaved, enthralled, by what defines them, the bitter Irish appetite for humiliation. No, there was no complacency there, no complacency and no chance of any. He thought of his country and sighed in admiration, and grinned, although he knew he was being guilty of self-satisfaction.

Is exile, then, a question of geography? Is it distance—chosen or compelled—from a state of mind particular to the place that has shaped you? A national temper that can lucidly be seen for what it is but neither renounced nor embraced? And is Anastasia's wrenching departure a condition for her song? Surely she would have remained if she could. "There was no comfort there."

And in time it may have been that distance became a necessity for Brennan, a writer whose preoccupation with the close interior spaces of her childhood drew her always more deeply into the inexhaustible lives of those she imagined moving in the same rooms, dreaming in them, looking out at the ever-shifting clouds through their windows.

In 1949, the following year, Maeve was hired by *The New Yorker*, and her life changed again. While *Harper's* had been a woman's world—run by a woman who hired other women—*The New Yorker*, arguably the most powerful literary magazine in America at the time, was a magazine dominated by men. As elsewhere during the 1950s, a woman's value—however that might be assessed—would have been assumed to be different from a man's. In her early thirties Maeve wore her thick auburn hair in a ponytail that made her look younger than she was. Later she piled it on her head. Just a little over five feet, she wore high heels, usually dressed in black, a fresh flower, often a white rose, pinned to her lapel, a bright dash of red lipstick across her mouth. Several of her colleagues would become good and constant friends—Joseph Mitchell, Charles Addams, Philip Hamburger, and, of course, William Maxwell—and some lovers as well. But she was an outsider, a stylish and beautiful Irish woman in a world of American men. As Roger Angell put it, "She wasn't one of us—she was one of her." Although she would live in an assortment of furnished rented rooms and hotels in Manhattan—and as the years went by, increasingly obscure ones—her place at *The New Yorker*, however alien at first, provided a kind of sanctuary where her work would be fostered and edited and published.

Early in 1954 Brennan began writing the unsigned pieces for the "Talk of the Town" in the voice of "the long-winded lady." They would appear in the magazine for more than fifteen years, but only in 1968 would the writer be identified as Maeve Brennan when she chose some of her favorites to be published as a selection. In a foreword Brennan describes her persona:

> If she has a title, it is one held by many others, that of a traveler in residence. . . . She is drawn to what she recognized, or half-recognized, and these forty-seven pieces are the record of forty-seven moments of recognition. Somebody said, "We are real only in moments of kindness." Moments of kindness, moments of recognition—if there is a difference it is a faint one. I think the long-winded lady is real when she writes, here, about some of the sights she saw in the city she loves.

Indeed, she declares her love for the city in an ode to the ailanthus, New York City's backyard tree,

> that appears like a ghost, like a shade, beyond the vacancy left by the old brownstone houses . . . speaking of survival and of ordinary things . . . : New York does nothing for those of us who are inclined to love her except implant in our hearts a homesickness that baffles us until we go away from her, and then we realize why we are restless. At home or away, we are homesick for New York not because New York used to be better and not because she used to be worse but because the city holds us and we don't know why.

When Brennan was thirty-seven she married St. Clair McKelway and joined him where he lived in Sneden's Landing, a community just north of the city on the west bank of the Hudson. He worked at *The New Yorker* as a nonfiction staff writer, was three times divorced and twelve years older than herself, and known to be a compulsive womanizer. Like Brennan, he was volatile, hard-drinking. And like her too, incapable of handling money. "I think I feel as Goldsmith must have done," Maeve wrote to Maxwell, "that any money I get is spending money, and the grown-ups ought to pay the big ugly bills." During the three years she was married, her mother died, a death she grieved for a long time, and she and St. Clair fell into calamitous debt. Her stories from that period are often set in Herbert's Retreat, as she calls Sneden's Landing: unlike the Dublin stories, they tend to be ironic, even brittle, in tone; they have to do with affluent households looked after by knowing Irish maids who observe and appraise their employers' lives from the kitchen.

And on St. Patrick's Day, 1959, Brennan wrote a reply to a letter from a reader asking when more Herbert's Retreat stories would appear in *The New Yorker*, a letter that was making the rounds in the office. When it reached her, she wrote a reply on the back before passing it on.

I am terribly sorry to have to be the first to tell you that our poor Miss Brennan died. We have her head here in the office, at the top of the stairs, where she was always to be found, smiling right and left and drinking water out of her own little paper cup. She shot herself in the back with the aid of a small hand-mirror at the foot of the main altar in St. Patrick's cathedral one Shrove Tuesday. Frank O'Connor was where he usually is in the afternoons, sitting in a confession box pretending to be a priest and giving a penance to some old woman and he heard the shot and he ran out and saw our poor late author stretched out flat and he picked her up and slipped her in the poor box. She was very small. He said she went in easy. Imagine the feelings of the young curate who unlocked the box that same evening and found the deceased curled up in what appeared to be and later turned out truly to be her final slumber. It took six strong parish priests to get her out of the box and then they called us and we all went and got her and carried her back here on the door of her office . . . We will never know why she did what she did (shooting herself) but we think it was because she was drunk and heartsick. She was a very fine person, a very real person, two feet, hands, everything. But it is too late to do much about that.

IT WAS ONLY after she had amicably separated from St. Clair during the winter of 1959 and was alone once more that Brennan returned to the Dublin stories she'd been working on during the years leading up to her marriage. The solitary life had fostered her writing earlier, and now she would again live by herself, accompanied by her beloved black Labrador retriever, Bluebell. During the early 1960s when Brennan was writing steadily, she spent the summers in the city and the winters alone in East Hampton, renting houses off-season close to her devoted and nurturing friends Sara and Gerald Murphy, on whom F. Scott Fitzgerald in *Tender Is the Night* had modeled Dick and Nicole Divers. She wrote about the sea and shore and seagulls, and about children too. She wrote about the progress of the day as seen through the eyes of her animals—her cats and Bluebell—with the radiant simplicity of Colette.

And she continued to work on the Derdon stories, to publish them, and began to write about the Bagots. What she required, it seemed, was a room where she could be alone with her typewriter.

She would go on writing of lonely marriages as lived out in the house at 48 Cherryfield she'd grown up in. And though by this time she'd had her own intimate experience of marriage, and there are many echoes of her parents' lives in the stories, her portraits are originals. Both couples—Hubert and Rose Derdon and later on Martin and Delia Bagot—are shadowed by fear and regret and shame. They experience self-misgivings, a ravished sense of having made some first mistake, of having missed out on some crucial knowledge that everyone but themselves has grasped and so are condemned to solitude.

Because the sequence of Derdon stories is mostly set within about the same period in the Derdons' marriage—after their grown son, John, has gone off to be a priest—and because the backdrop is the same rooms looking out on the same garden, it can be hard, on first reading, to distinguish one story from another, to recall in which one a particular incident breaks the surface of their quiet, tormented life together, a memory takes hold. Or a shining image rises unbidden from the mysterious undercurrent of life itself. The dramatic confrontations between Rose and Hubert are often wordless, or rather the words break through only after long silent periods of brooding, of baffled efforts to make sense of themselves or each other. Their lives circle in a timeless space, heavy with misunderstanding and foiled attempts to catch each other out in trivial matters. There is Hubert, setting out to his job in a men's clothing store, subtly shaming Rose by failing to leave the household money as usual on a Friday morning because she isn't there at the doorway to ask for it. Her helpless fear of Hubert and his own anger at that fear; her cringing smile of defeat; her rough, dry hands, his daintier ones. Hubert's irritation with the way Rose eats, her greater appetite, her preference for poor people, her curiosity about them matched by his own dislike. Her grief at the loss of John, her fascination with the changing sky as the clouds "melted slowly into each other and slowly drew apart." His devastating assessments: "It is too late for Rose." Her clogged need for love balked in childhood by the death of a beloved father; her sly, tortured attempts to make of their child, John, an ally. Hubert's attempts too to make peace, to comfort her after the loss of John with the gift of a blue hydrangea, a tea tray after an illness. Or his sustained determination to hold out against her: a long moment of regret, a sky growing dark, and the understanding that there is nothing to be said.

Or a story too may be backlit by memories of their life as a couple, by glimpses of an inscrutable moment, as in "Family Walls," when Hubert, in the wake of a prolonged spell of silent recrimination, looks out the window and sees Rose working in the garden. She lifts her arm to smooth a loose strand of hair, "and as the sleeve fell back, her upraised arm gleamed. Hubert saw her wrist and her elbow and in that fragment of her he saw all of Rose, as the crescent moon recalls the full moon to anyone who has watched her at the height of her power."

"The bitter Irish appetite for humiliation": would that be an appetite for feeling humiliated, or rather an appetite for humiliating someone else? Rose is married to Hubert who has a "great gift for cutting people down when they got above themselves." Or so Hubert puts it to himself by way of naming his "great gift." As for Rose's life at home as a child, "her mother had always said she had too good an idea of herself." Called her "Miss Importance." In the face of Hubert's disdain, Rose's moments of passionate revolt exhaust themselves at last in a craven, trembling smile, her expressions of outrage more often than not giving way to a pitiful appeal for mercy.

A domestic version, perhaps, of the humiliated Irish subject's long history of rebellion, of furious uprisings against the colonial master followed by collapse into submission, into making-do. Of the calm and pitiless attempt of those in power to subdue another spirit when it rebels, as it is sure to do. Because sometimes the humiliated will look to humiliate another in turn: gross distortions in the exercise of power in the public sphere will find subtle echoes in the most intimate spaces, as in a marriage. For isn't this one of the ways of soothing injured pride? The blind attempt to shame someone else, someone close at hand? The Derdon stories, in particular, dissect the cruelties that spring from one person's settled assumptions of superiority over another, the damage done in the name of maintaining order, of keeping someone "in their place." But the personal costs to those who allow themselves relief of this brutal kind—as do Hubert or the grandmother in *The Visitor* or Min in "The Springs of Affection"—are dramatized as well: an anguished state of paralysis, a furtive retreat from the unpredictable and vulnerably human life of feeling.

Rose Derdon, like Anastasia, in the face of humiliation and banishment, makes common cause with those on the outside, "the poor." The man with the wounded hand, for instance, who comes to the door every Thursday afternoon: "His eyes, blue, seemed weary enough to die, but still the poor natural mouth, obedient to its end, a mouth so lonely it appeared to have no tongue, opened itself to her in a thin bashful smile of recognition and supplication. Never mind, never mind, never mind, no blame to you nor to me nor to anybody, the mouth said, only fill me."

Then one day she encounters him on a bridge over the River Liffey, and he looks at her with welcome, with the kindness of rec‑ognition. Much to her dismay, he fails to come to her door the following Thursday, then reappears the next week: "He held up his sore hand and gazed at her without a sign of the radiance that she had seen in his face on the bridge. If he felt ashamed that he had given himself away there was no sign of that either. He was too far gone in want. He was gone out of reach. It gave her great comfort to see him at the door again."

The Bagot stories were begun later—even while Brennan was still at work on the Derdon stories—and if Delia and Martin Bagot are less fiercely locked in opposition than the Derdons, it may be because the husband is less frequently on the scene. They have lost an infant son early in their marriage and now have two little girls. When Martin returns from work late, he sleeps alone in the box room over the kitchen. The lonely and neglected Delia may be found at home longing for her children's return from a holiday in the country or caring for the beloved dog and cats Martin would be rid of altogether. But these stories are less desolating than the stories about the Derdons, and Delia finds some comfort in her children, in a kindly shadow on the wall, in the little terrier "who brushes against her every chance he got . . . who lived in the blazing humility of perfect love."

Then one day she is introduced by a visitor—the exiled old missionary bishop, her dead father's long-ago boyhood friend in the Wexford countryside, where Delia too had grown up—to a life, her own.

The captive monkey, reduced by grief and age to the lowest and farthest corner of her cage at the zoo, watches the crowd that stares at her with an acceptance so profound it shines like sympathy. All struggle had vanished from the old Bishop's eyes, and Mrs. Bagot gave him a smile of tremulous indignation, showing how, one morning, she would face her own death.

"We have tea all ready for you, Your Grace," she said.

"God bless you," he said, "but never mind 'Your Grace.' I'm a very plain priest. 'Father,' or 'Father Tom,' whichever you like. Delia, is it? Am I right? You're the image of your grandmother, Delia."

He asked her about her life, and as they spoke she had the feeling she was talking about someone who was very well known to her although they had never met. She was talking about herself, and she was amazed to find how much there was to be said about this person, herself, who had come into the conversation from nowhere and who was now becoming more real, although invisible, with every word that was spoken. In response to the Bishop's trust in her she spoke as though in Braille, feeling her way eagerly and with confidence along a path that she found she knew by heart, every inch of it, in the dark. And as she spoke, that path, her life, became visible.

The bishop, who has thoughts about Ireland's appetite for humiliation, is the exile who has returned to Ireland to die. Like the monkey "reduced by grief and age to the lowest and farthest corner of her cage," like the man dying of want, he is now on the outside. It is he who recognizes Delia, as the poor man recognizes Rose. Is it, then, that the kingdom of heaven belongs to the poor in spirit? That grief and want are conditions for vision?

Maeve Brennan achieves a supreme mastery in these late stories: "Family Walls," "A Girl Can Spoil Her Chances," "The Drowned Man," and "The Springs of Affection." A single story may encompass an entire life, and the sequence of Derdon stories and the sequence of Bagot stories each has the artistic integrity of a novel. Alice Munro wrote that she counted "The Springs of Affection" among her favorite stories of all time, and it isn't hard to imagine that she may have learned something from Maeve Brennan about the possibility of folding the span of a character's life into a few pages. No wonder, either, that Edward Albee compares Brennan's stories to Chekhov's: In each the same luminous precision of detail, the same sense of suffering humanity. The tenderness toward the forgotten.

BRENNAN'S FIRST COLLECTION, *In and Out of Never-Never Land*, was published by Scribner's in 1969 and included the Bagot and the Derdon stories that had been published up to that point. It included neither "The Springs of Affection" nor "Family Walls," two of her greatest stories, which would appear in *The New Yorker* only three years later. In 1974, another collection, *Christmas Eve*, was also published by Scribner's that included these newer stories as well as several from the 1950s. There was no paperback edition of either one. And as she had no Irish publisher, her Dublin stories went largely unnoticed in Ireland where so many of them were set. At about this time William Maxwell said he thought her the best living Irish writer of fiction, but in her own country she was almost entirely unknown.

By the early 1970s Brennan's friends had become aware of painful changes in her behavior. She was no longer a young woman in a working world still dominated by men: she was middle-aged now and alone. Her father and Gerald Murphy had died within a few weeks of each other in the fall of 1964, and her nearest companion, Bluebell, was also dead. She was having trouble writing. Pursued by an accumulation of debts and creditors, she stayed in increasingly rundown hotels. She had always moved from place to place, but now she began moving rapidly, as her father had done long ago when he was on the run and staying in safe houses. Sometimes she camped out—like a similarly bereft Bartleby—in the offices where she worked: in the *New Yorker* offices in a little space next to the ladies' room, at one point tending a wounded pigeon. Then she had a severe breakdown and was in the hospital for a time. When things were better she returned to Ireland, thinking perhaps to remain there. But it must have been too late. For a few weeks she stayed with her cousin Ita Bolger Doyle. She wrote to William Maxwell from the garden studio on September 11, 1973:

> The typewriter is here in the room with me—I hold on to it as the sensible sailor holds on to his compass. . . . What I am conscious of, is of having the sense of true perspective . . . that is in fact only the consciousness of impending, imminent revelation. "I can see." But "I can see" is not to say 'I see.' I don't believe at all in revelations—but to have, even for a minute, the sense of impending revelation, that is being alive.

Sometime after her return to New York from Ireland, things again fell apart; her movements became increasingly hard to track. She'd always been known for her generosity; now she began rapidly to divest, handing out money in the street. She was occasionally seen by her old colleagues sitting around Rockefeller Center with the destitute. Then she fell out of the public eye altogether. She had unequivocally become an outsider now, one of the poor and afflicted among whom she'd always counted the visionaries. It wasn't until she seemed quite forgotten—until after her death in 1993 in a nursing home in Queens where she wasn't known to be a writer—that she again swam into view.

Christopher Carduff, a senior editor at Houghton Mifflin at the time, encountering Brennan's work by chance in the late 1980s, "fell in love," as he put it, and undertook to get it all in print, including the recently discovered novella *The Visitor*. In 1997, for the first time, the Derdon stories as well as the Bagot stories could be read in sequence when they appeared in *The Springs of Affection: Stories of Dublin*. William Maxwell wrote a foreword to the volume. One of the many writers who greeted the publication was Mavis Gallant: "How and why the voice of these Dublin stories was ever allowed to drift out of earshot is one of the literary puzzles. Now *The Springs of Affection* brings it back, as a favor to us all, and it is as true and as haunting as before."

One of the literary puzzles indeed: Perhaps her colleagues and friends at *The New Yorker* tried and failed to intervene on her stories' behalf when Brennan was unable to do so herself? To help see her existing volumes into paperback? Or press for the Dublin stories to be compiled and arranged, as did Christopher Carduff? Would things have been different if she had been "one of us"? A

man rather than a woman, a compatriot? Unknowable and com-
plex factors, surely, must have played their part, but it's painful to
remember that Brennan's furious dedication to her art had been
witnessed by so many.

At about the same time that Carduff's editions started to come
out in 1997, Mary Hawthorne, who'd been hired to work at *The New
Yorker* in 1981, wrote a piece about an encounter with Brennan that
sparked interest when it appeared in the *London Review of Books*.
Not long afterward Angela Bourke undertook the formidable task
of exploring Brennan's life while many people who had known her
were still alive. Bourke's biography, *Maeve Brennan: Homesick at
The New Yorker*, to which I am much indebted, appeared in 2004.
In 2012 Emma Donoghue wrote a play based on Brennan's life, *The
Talk of the Town*, for the Dublin Theatre Festival. And in the spring
of 2016, a new edition of *The Springs of Affection* was published by
Dublin's Stinging Fly Press, with an introduction by Anne Enright.

The paroxysms of the Irish rebellion that shaped Maeve's early life
have been given shape and voice by numbers of writers. Whether
in novels or poems or plays or memoir, many have written about
the era of the struggle for Irish independence with the authority
of witnesses. Maeve Brennan writes too as one who was there, as
child-witness, as girl-witness: the armed men breaking into the
house protected by the helpless mother, the heart-stopping search
for the father. But it may be that Brennan's own early terrors of
whatever kind were translated in her fiction into the anguish of
love withdrawn or love denied: these flash in and out of *The Visitor*
and the Derdon stories, in particular, like searchlights illuminating
a wasteland where disappointment and confusion rise up the more

terribly because it had been just here, on this island of home and security, that comfort had been most hoped for. It's the specter of want, "the delirium of loss," that stalks Maeve Brennan's Irish stories, the sense of something that is not there. They take their place in a long tradition of tales of exile and displacement, of spellbinding metaphor carried by song.

The lost and irreplaceable home can be restored only from within, painstakingly. And like the exiled bishop who describes for his African students over and over again the particulars of the beloved road leading to the house in the Wexford countryside where he was welcomed for so short a time, so that his students and he make a game of "Going to Poulbwee," so Brennan, spinning her sentences—scrupulous, lyrical, devastating—allows us to enter that first place. Only as irretrievably lost is it open to reclamation. It is hers to cultivate the ground of memory, to entertain the wealth of details that swarms restlessly until set down, one by one, in its destined place; to make something uncompromising and beautiful where love has been misplaced or betrayed and so to redeem that loss; to find solace in rendering whole what has come undone. Hubert Derdon, wearied at last by a long bout of simmering resentment against his wife, happens to look out, toward the end of "Family Walls," at the absorbed Rose working in her garden:

> She was intent on placing the plant in its exact place, and she was as anxious at her work as though she had taken the future of the world between her hands and must set it right once and for all because there would be no second chance—no second chance for her, at least—to prove that if it was left to her, all would be well. For this moment the weight of the world was off her shoulders and in her hands.

THE PEACEMAKER

Niall O'Dowd (1953–)

BY MARY JORDAN AND KEVIN SULLIVAN

A DARK HOTEL BAR IN Dublin. Just after Christmas, 1992.

Niall O'Dowd was new to the secret agent game, and more than a little awkward at it. He was an Irish-born journalist who had been living and working in America for thirteen years, and now he found himself in an odd and audacious position.

President Bill Clinton's White House wanted to make contact with the Irish Republican Army. Clinton was intrigued by the notion he could help bring peace to Northern Ireland, which had been wracked for years by violence between Protestants and Catholics known as the Troubles. Peace would only work if the IRA was interested in a cease-fire—but the American president couldn't exactly send his secretary of state to Belfast for a cheery sit-down with a group considered terrorists in Washington and London.

There needed to be a no-fingerprints, totally deniable approach to the overture.

And into that opportunity walked O'Dowd, a soft-spoken writer, illegal immigrant, Gaelic football player, and house-painter who had risen to become publisher of two influential publications based in New York, *Irish America* magazine and the *Irish Voice* newspaper.

O'Dowd offered to serve as a clandestine, off-the-books bridge between the two powerful and skittish players, who just might be interested in ending three decades of bloody misery.

After making his pitch to a man in New York with "friends" in Belfast, O'Dowd received a cryptic handwritten note. A man from Sinn Féin, the political party closely associated with the IRA, would meet him at 11:30 a.m. in the bar at Wynn's Hotel, just off Dublin's famous O'Connell Street. His contact would be reading the *Irish Times*, with a pint of Guinness in front of him.

O'Dowd arrived drenched with rain and twenty minutes late, frantic that he had messed up his first attempt at amateur spy craft. He stumbled into the half-empty bar, where a couple of regulars were drinking pints. There at a table was a tall, bearded man with thick, graying hair who was dressed in jeans and a casual jacket. He looked up over his *Irish Times*, a Guinness on the table.

"Ted," he said, holding a hand out and introducing himself.

"Niall," O'Dowd replied.

Ted started ordering more pints, but O'Dowd had long since sworn off alcohol. So he settled for a very un-007 mineral water.

O'Dowd felt out of his depth with his water and his proposal for peace, which began to sound wackier and wackier the more he explained it.

Ted just looked back at him, difficult to read. O'Dowd wasn't sure if he was interested or annoyed that O'Dowd was wasting his time.

O'Dowd made the pitch: He'd personally spoken to Clinton a few months earlier, and Clinton had made it clear that he wanted to get involved in Northern Ireland. But not publicly, at least not yet. O'Dowd was in contact with people in Senator Edward Kennedy's office who could relay messages to and from the White House. O'Dowd told Ted that he could put together a group of sympathetic Irish American businessmen and politicians who would come to Belfast and publicly meet with representatives from all sides of the conflict—including an unprecedented meeting with Sinn Féin.

The idea was to "internationalize" the issue—to give this domestic British problem the kind of international attention that had helped undermine apartheid in South Africa.

Sinn Féin's bloody campaign against British rule in Northern Ireland had left it out in the cold, isolated. In return for any thaw in relations, the IRA would have to first agree to a weeklong cease-fire during the American group's visit to the north, O'Dowd said. It would be a goodwill gesture to prove that it was serious about wanting to work toward peace.

Peace in Northern Ireland had always topped O'Dowd's list of priorities, and he wrote about it constantly. He believed in the IRA's cause of kicking the British out of Northern Ireland and reuniting it with the Irish Republic but disagreed with its violent tactics. At the same time, he knew how much blood had been spilled in the violent clashes between Protestant unionists loyal to Britain and the Catholic Irish nationalists opposed to British rule. Some thirty-six hundred people had died in the guerrilla war. And in order to have what he called "an honorable peace," an agreement had to be seen as respectful to those on both sides. An IRA official had once told O'Dowd that the IRA could only accept a deal "the dead can live with."

O'Dowd stressed to Ted that his group could have no official status from the White House, but that it would be "very well connected." If the IRA took that first step, O'Dowd said it was very possible that Clinton would buck pressure from London to not get involved and appoint a U.S. peace envoy to Northern Ireland. Britain, the United States' closest ally, was fervently opposed to U.S. involvement in what it considered its internal affairs. And, O'Dowd said, it was possible that Sinn Féin leader Gerry Adams might finally be able to break a long-standing logjam and receive a visa to visit the United States—a long-term goal in Sinn Féin's campaign to have the world hear its voice.

Don't miss the opportunity, O'Dowd told Ted. The conditions had never been this favorable.

Ted looked at his eager, idealistic partner—soggy from the rain, clearly nervous, a thirty-nine-year-old man of average build who did not stand out in any way except for the dimple on his chin. The rumpled journalist playing secret statesman listened as Ted said that Sinn Féin wanted to engage with America, wanted peace negotiations. "Part of our objective is that our movement is not isolated," he said, without committing to anything, but without rejecting anything, either.

Ted hadn't laughed at him, and he hadn't walked out. Trying to read the hard man sitting opposite him, O'Dowd sensed that Ted thought the idea wasn't totally crazy.

If it did go forward, Ted said, here's how communication would be handled: All documents would be destroyed after being read. There would be a code: the Irish American effort would be called "the project," Gerry Adams would be "chairman," letters would be hand-delivered by trusted couriers. The IRA would be "the local football team"; U.S. ambassador to Ireland Jean Kennedy Smith would be "dream woman," a reference to a mythical figure in Gaelic poetry; and Senator Kennedy would be "the brother."

Without another word, Ted got up and left.

O'Dowd felt overwhelming relief. "I had not been laughed out of the court," he would say later. "The American connection was up and running."

NIALL (PRONOUNCED "KNEEL") Oliver O'Dowd, born in County Tipperary in May 1953, was one of seven children and thought he would be a schoolteacher like his father. His family moved to Drogheda, an industrial port north of Dublin, when he was nine, and as he grew older, he felt the small island was too constricting. "The sons of lawyers became lawyers, sons of doctors became doctors, sons of teachers, as I was, became teachers," he says now. "A few hours' drive in any direction," he said, "and you fall into the ocean."

Like many young Irish around him, O'Dowd felt the gravitational pull of America that had moved so many generations of Irish before him. His imagination was fired by Superman comic books, and then by the works of Whitman, Faulkner, and Hemingway, which were brought to his attention by an inspiring teacher named Brother Nolan.

America seemed so endless, so full of possibility, a place where anybody could be anything. To O'Dowd, nothing represented the vast greatness of America more than Muhammad Ali. "I read a *Playboy* interview with him," O'Dowd said. "He was unbelievable. Giving up everything for his beliefs, basically. I thought he was an extraordinary person. He was magnificent in terms of what he achieved and what he was challenging. He was a hero. You couldn't do anything like it in Ireland."

One of his most vivid memories was waking up before dawn on May 26, 1975, and watching with his father Ali's much-anticipated second world championship fight against Sonny Liston. They turned on the TV just in time to watch Ali knock out Liston only two minutes into the first round. "We went back to bed 10 minutes later," O'Dowd said.

In the spring of 1976, when he was twenty-two, he flew to Chicago on a six-month student visa. He was a respectable Gaelic football player, fast on his feet and sturdy enough to absorb the game's brutal hits. And he found a local team in Chicago that was willing to sponsor his visa and pay one-way airfare for their new Irish recruit.

A couple from Kerry who helped run the team took him in. Later, a teammate invited him to live in his fraternity house at Loyola University during the summer. He found a job in construction with an all-Irish crew, spending his days shoveling mortar into a wheelbarrow in the hot sun. But the thick-necked foreman who had arrived in the United States before him didn't get on well with the college-educated newcomer. One day their argument—and O'Dowd's job—ended in a fistfight.

He returned to Ireland that fall and went back to University College Dublin, where he graduated in 1977 with a degree in

English and Gaelic. Despite his big dreams of faraway lands, he took a job teaching in an inner-city school in Dublin. He found himself frustrated and dispirited, teaching unruly poor kids who were too hungry to study. His father's noble profession now seemed like an exercise in keeping order in forty-five-minute chunks. In the summer of 1978 he set off for America again on a new student visa, this time for San Francisco.

A friend had a brother on a Gaelic football team there and they were looking for new blood. California. O'Dowd saw it as the most American of all American places. Besides, he was feeling a little like a hippie anyway with his long hair and beard. San Francisco sounded perfect.

After a stint painting California houses and even starting his own little painting business, O'Dowd decided he wanted to try something more cerebral. As a teenager back in Ireland, he had started a school newspaper. In the United States, O'Dowd was struck by the large Irish immigrant communities in Chicago and San Francisco and how hungry they were for information, not just concerning news back home but also about specific issues they, as Irish Americans, cared about. In the pre-Internet era, many would drive miles to get weeks-old Irish newspapers that had been mailed from overseas. O'Dowd saw an opportunity.

Eventually, his visa expired, and he was officially an illegal immigrant. But in the late 1970s, that seemed more like a detail than a serious offense, and he barely gave it a second thought. After nearly falling through scaffolding to his death while painting, O'Dowd decided it was time to start a new career.

He scraped together $952 with the help of a friend, Tom McDonagh, to start a newspaper. He called it the *Irishman* and launched the twelve-page first edition on September 14, 1979, with an editorial that he wrote: "This newspaper is born out of a hope that we can act as the link between the various strands in the community and strengthen the bond of birth and upbringing that we all can share."

O'Dowd already had a clear sense of living in two worlds, the land of his birth and the land of his choice. He rejected the notion that immigrants had to pick one or the other, and he argued that one of the great things about the United States was that it allowed him to be thoroughly American while maintaining his Irish identity.

His strategy for his business, and for the way he wanted to position himself as a bridge between two nations and cultures, rested on three pillars:

Be someone people can trust.

Be well informed.

Harness the untapped power of forty million Irish Americans, and urge them to think beyond St. Patrick's Day parades to work for the betterment of both nations.

He printed five thousand copies of the *Irishman* and sold them for fifty cents each, mainly at Irish bars. He was nearly broke most of the time, supplementing his income by freelancing for the *Irish Press* newspaper in Dublin under legendary editor Tim Pat Coogan, who was a mentor to him.

He had read that 90 percent of new publications fail, but a fear of failure, which holds back so many others, didn't weigh him down. If this venture didn't work out he would just move on to the next thing.

He interviewed Charles Manson and César Chávez and kept up with the U.S. news but mainly focused on Irish issues—including the immigration status of so many undocumented Irish. They were trapped without any legal protections and feared that if they went back home for funerals and other family milestones they might not be allowed back in the United States. The response from his immigrant readers was immediate and satisfying.

Along the way, he fell in love and moved in with another Tipperary native and immigrant to the United States, Patricia Harty, whom he had hired to work at the *Irishman*. He had also gotten himself legal. In 1980 the *Irish Press* sponsored him for a work visa; and in 1984 he was among several thousand Irish who obtained permanent residency—a green card—through the Donnelly visa program. (He became a U.S. citizen in 1989 and still holds both Irish and U.S. passports.)

In April 1985, after five and a half years of publishing the *Irishman*, O'Dowd, still broke, was ready for a change. He and Harty moved to New York City, married, and—with a $40,000 loan from a wealthy friend and journalistic pioneer, Brendan Mac Lua, founder of the *Irish Post* newspaper in England—launched *Irish America*, the first glossy magazine of its kind.

They sent out direct-mail solicitations to 250,000 people using contact lists borrowed from a wide variety of sources: the Irish Tourist Board magazine, companies that sold Waterford crystal and other Irish goods, and Irish groups including the Ancient Order of Hibernians. O'Dowd sensed that many were "tired of the shamrocks and green beer image" of the Irish in America and would subscribe to a smart magazine devoted to Irish events and issues. To their delight, about 10,000 people responded—a high hit rate for a direct-mail solicitation—all willing to pay $19.95 to subscribe to *Irish America*, which debuted in November 1985.

Harty recalled being amazed as the checks started showing up at their tiny New York office, including one from Los Angeles Dodgers owner Peter O'Malley.

"I thought, 'Wow, even the Los Angeles Dodgers believe in us,'" she said.

Two years later, O'Dowd and Harty started the *Irish Voice*, a newspaper aimed primarily at younger Irish immigrants. The paper began covering issues like AIDS in the Irish community and practical problems faced by the undocumented Irish, and it soon became a formidable rival to the more established *Irish Echo* newspaper that had been around since the 1920s.

O'Dowd was on his way to becoming what Bill Clinton later called "the voice of Irish America for this generation."

BY 1985, AFTER seven years in the States, O'Dowd felt he understood the complications and contradictions of being an Irish immigrant, and with his publications he made it his mission to help his fellow countrymen and women more fully celebrate their roots and their culture while at the same time embracing America.

"I was a man of two countries, one the land of my birth which I still hankered after, and yet somehow rejected," he wrote in a 2010 autobiography.

The other was my adopted home of the United States where I was happy but never fully a part, forever camped outside the mainstream. An immigrant is a stranger in both cultures.

When I returned to Ireland on vacations it had all changed, still recognizable enough for me to be at home, yet an outsider there. When I returned to the U.S., I was from somewhere else, no matter how much I tried to fit in. Emigration forces you to think about who you are but also to regret who you might have been if you stayed behind.

Because of his own experience, O'Dowd had the ability to understand the new arrivals, but he also proved adept at connecting with the more established community, who had ties to Ireland though their parents and grandparents.

He sought out meetings with influential Irish Americans, including Don Keough, then the president of Coca-Cola, whose great-grandfather had left Wexford in famine times. Keough said to him, "Where have you been all my life? I've wanted to talk to you." Keough, who became a mentor to the much younger O'Dowd, told him people wanted to connect with others with similar backgrounds and with their own family history. Keough urged O'Dowd to keep reaching out to remind people they are Irish American and show them how to celebrate it.

"Everybody wants a touchstone. Everybody wants to be grounded," O'Dowd said. "Here's a guy with every success in the world, and what he most wanted was to feel part of something that's unique. And the Irish heritage is pretty unique."

Keough, who died in 2015, became so involved that he even brought two of the richest men in the world, Warren Buffett and Bill Gates, to Ireland to try to spur economic development there.

In addition to his newspaper and magazine (and later his website, IrishCentral.com), in 1987 O'Dowd started an innovation for which he would also become well known: lists of prominent and influential Irish Americans.

He started with the "Business 100," a list of the top one hundred

Irish American business leaders in America. It was simple to find them: at the time, he said, almost a third of the Fortune 500 CEOs had some Irish roots. What was harder to find was a sense among many of them that their Irish heritage mattered.

"What I was trying to do was forge this sense of Irish identity, in different groups," he said.

> I took it into the realm of Wall Street, business, places where Irish identity wasn't previously celebrated. I just said, "Here's your culture. Here's your history."
>
> A lot of people have said to me that business people, particularly on Wall Street, don't care about their heritage. In fact, I found it quite the opposite, and they were very chuffed and very into it when I approached them about their heritage. You know, when you start an interview with the question, "Tell me about your parents," or "Tell me about your father," it has a profound impact on the person.

Robert J. McCann, chairman of UBS Americas, who has been honored on O'Dowd's lists, including the "Irish America Hall of Fame," said O'Dowd caused him to reflect on his own background and spurred him to a new activism in Irish causes. McCann grew up in Pittsburgh, the son of Irish immigrants who raised their children to focus on their life going forward in America. They didn't talk much about being Irish or the country they had left. When, for instance, McCann was invited to attend the American Ireland Fund's annual dinner in the late 1980s, he went because it was good for business, not because of any particular affection for Ireland.

But his perspective changed as he got to know O'Dowd and other influential Irish American leaders, including Pittsburgh native Dan Rooney, who was chairman of the Pittsburgh Steelers and would become the U.S. ambassador to Ireland. "It made me think differently about what it means to be Irish," McCann said. "I want to be involved in things now."

McCann said O'Dowd's first impression can be misleading.

> He always kind of looks like an unmade bed. He's normally 15 minutes late. He talks in that almost whisper of his, and words run together. It took me a couple of years to kind of figure it out, but then I realized: Niall makes all of us who are Irish American better informed, more aware, more sensitive to what is going on actually in Ireland. He's an incredibly easy person to underestimate. But anybody that does is really making a mistake and missing out.
>
> The impact of what he knows and how he conveys it to you, it makes you want to be better. It makes you want to represent Ireland and your efforts for Ireland better. There's nothing wrong with a good parade. There's nothing wrong with a good party. But we Irish are so much more than that. And we tend to underestimate ourselves or not speak boldly about what we are.

McCann eventually became involved with the American Ireland Fund, and he is now a member of its executive committee. He is a driver behind a new Irish Arts Center being built in New York (as well as supporting the Abbey Theatre in Dublin) and a key backer of Narrative 4, a foundation founded by Irish writer Colum McCann. Rather than passively showing up at a few dinners and donating some money, he's now actively working on projects that channel the talent of Irish America.

And all that started with one of O'Dowd's lists.

"At first, I didn't think the lists were that important. But what I've come to realize is, everybody likes recognition," McCann explains. "And there are a lot of people, if you give them an opportunity to become more aware of Ireland and things Irish, they're happy to take up that opportunity. But you need something to trigger that. People are busy. I've seen Niall use these lists to get people involved, and I think it's a very clever way to do it."

Maureen Mitchell, president of global sales and marketing for the asset management arm of General Electric, met O'Dowd through his lists: she has been on the "Business 100," and in 2016 she was named to the magazine's inaugural "Top 50 Power Women." She and Irish ambassador Anne Anderson were the keynote speakers at the luncheon celebrating the power women list. "There is this connective tissue that binds us," Mitchell said. "So many people have Irish surnames and they think about that on occasion. I think what Niall has done through the magazine, the website, the lists, is that he's given a very disparate community a voice and a sense of self."

Mitchell's parents were immigrants from Ireland, and she grew up in an Irish American enclave in Manhattan. She said her family was more focused on America than Ireland, in contrast to some of her neighbors—second or third generation Irish—who did focus on their Irish roots, but in a sort of "holiday Irish" way.

"What Niall has done is bring me back to that Irish community," Mitchell said. "Absolutely I see my Irishness differently. I'm once more intrigued with it and its impact on me. I will make sure that my children and my new grandchild will have a sense of that as well."

And this was the goal. Harty—who still edits *Irish America* despite splitting from O'Dowd after four years of marriage—says that starting the magazine was a way to create a bridge between the two nations and that remains true. So many people she'd met in America called themselves Irish but had never been to Ireland. "For them Ireland was this mythical place," she said. "I started to realize that you don't have to be born on the island of Ireland to be Irish. It's the same plant, just different soil."

THE IRISH CONNECTOR is also a crusader. O'Dowd uses his publications and stature to advance key causes. For decades one of his top priorities—along with peace in Northern Ireland—was working to help get legal status for undocumented Irish.

In the 1980s, O'Dowd campaigned in his editorials to pressure Congress to create "Donnelly visas," named after Representative Brian Donnelly of Massachusetts, which would go on to give many Irish immigrants legal status—including O'Dowd. Later, as the number of undocumented Irish was rising in New York and many U.S cities, due to the fact that Ireland's economic fortunes were falling, O'Dowd raised the profile of his crusade and became what Bruce Morrison, a former U.S. congressman from Connecticut, called "the trumpet, the mouthpiece," for the Irish immigration reform movement.

While in office Morrison pushed through an immigration reform bill that led to forty-eight thousand people getting visas—known as "Morrison visas"—in the early 1990s. While he used to say he could get a free drink in any Irish pub in America because of all the undocumented workers who benefited from his help, Morrison also said that O'Dowd played a key role in promoting his bill. In addition to writing about immigration constantly in his newspaper, the *Irish Voice*, O'Dowd personally lobbied members of Congress, including Senator Kennedy.

The *Irish Voice* explained the political fight, gave legal advice to the undocumented, listed resources available to them, and editorialized about the need for elected officials to help. The undocumented could pick up a copy of the paper in bars and Irish centers across America. A popular column called the Green Card, written by Debbie McGoldrick, was a must-read for thousands.

McGoldrick, the daughter of Irish immigrants who grew up on Long Island, had gotten her first job out of college at the *Irish Echo*. She remembered thinking that O'Dowd's startup newspaper would be a flash in the pan, "a rag that might last three months." But in 1991, the *Irish Voice* had only gotten stronger, and she joined. She was passionate about the issues the paper covered and never tired of reporting on them. (In 1996, she married O'Dowd, and three years later they had a daughter, named Alana.)

In December 2005, O'Dowd created the Irish Lobby for Immigration Reform, an organization that now has twenty-eight chapters across the country. He wanted to stop hiding the fact that there were so many undocumented and put it front and center. He organized hundreds of Irish people from across the country to descend on Capitol Hill, knocking on doors and demanding action from Congress. But the mood of the country was turning, and it was getting harder to push any immigration reform law through Congress.

O'Dowd mobilized Irish Americans behind an immigration reform bill sponsored by Kennedy and Arizona Republican senator John McCain. In 2007, hundreds of people swarmed Capitol Hill wearing "Legalize the Irish" T-shirts. O'Dowd's publications pushed hard. But in the end, the Kennedy-McCain immigration bill of 2007 faltered. It would mark the beginning of a far more hostile and divisive atmosphere in Washington toward immigrants.

"Once you've walked in the shoes of being undocumented, you never forget it," O'Dowd said on CNN in 2007. "I feel I have had my chance at the American dream, and it is very important to me to allow other Irish people to experience the greatest country in the world and live their version of the dream."

O'Dowd has done that for a diverse array of Irish immigrants. Brendan Fay is one of the many Irish immigrants who legally settled in America after learning about Morrison visas via the *Irish Voice*. But O'Dowd had touched Fay's life even before that. Fay said he will never forget a story O'Dowd wrote in the early 1980s about gay Irish people in San Francisco. Fay was living in Ireland at the time and recalls reading O'Dowd's portrayal of gay Irish people in America and the thrill of thinking, "We belong!" He had not seen anyone else writing about them at the time—it was as though people like him didn't exist. Fay wound up moving to the United States and later founded the Lavender and Green Alliance, which advocated for gays to openly march in New York's St. Patrick's Day parade.

Many Irish in America were socially conservative and had been brought up in strict Irish Catholic homes. But O'Dowd frequently confronted them with topics that others avoided, including the toll of the AIDS epidemic on the Irish community. He once called a public meeting through his newspaper to discuss the issue, and to his surprise a couple of hundred people turned out. "No one else was writing about the deaths, the desperation at that time," recalled Fay. "The *Irish Voice* was the place we got to tell our story and to hear our story being told for the first time." When Fay married his partner in 2003, O'Dowd featured the wedding prominently on the newspaper's front page.

O'Dowd drew the ire of many of the more conservative members of the established Irish community in New York, including the head of the Ancient Order of Hibernians, when he pressed for gays to be included in the biggest celebration of St. Patrick's Day in the world—the New York St. Patrick's Day parade. O'Dowd didn't flinch. He fought hard for the right of openly gay and lesbian groups to march, and after years of resistance, it finally happened in 2016.

To O'Dowd, it proved the promise of America, a land where even an Irish schoolteacher's son can stand up and make a difference.

"I believe in this country," O'Dowd said. "Even coming to America, pretty penniless, everything worked out for me, and it's to the credit of this country, period. I know a lot of people born in America don't understand this. But people have a tremendous opportunity to get things done when they come to America. I never forget that."

ABOVE EVERYTHING ELSE, though, O'Dowd was consumed with the issue of peace in Northern Ireland. And when a young Arkansas governor named Bill Clinton appeared on the U.S. political scene, the journalist saw an opening.

O'Dowd had been making the case for U.S. involvement to members of Clinton's campaign for months. He told them Clinton had a chance to make history, to make peace, and to shine on the international stage. And he pointed out that there could be a huge political bonanza for the candidate, since more than forty million people in the United States claim Irish roots.

When O'Dowd finally met Clinton in January 1992 in New York, they spoke briefly, and Clinton signaled his interest. "Niall, tell your friends Ireland is on my radar screen," Clinton told him. "I think we can do something."

O'Dowd sensed a historic opportunity. Irish leaders all the way back to Éamon de Valera in the 1920s had been trying to get a U.S. president to inject America into the Northern Irish debate, but none had ever seriously taken it on—not even John F. Kennedy, the first Irish American president. The bond between Washington and the UK government was just too strong.

O'Dowd could see that Clinton was not as reflexively aligned with Great Britain. Although he had studied at Oxford University on a Rhodes Scholarship in 1968–69, his time in the UK coincided with some of the most traumatic times in the Northern Ireland Troubles. He was well steeped in the civil rights issues raised by the conflict, which was at the top of UK news every evening. It also helped that the British Conservative Party under Prime Minister John Major made no secret of its support in the 1992 election for President George H. W. Bush. Perhaps most important, Clinton was well aware of the voting power of millions of Irish Americans.

"If there had been five Irish Americans in the United States it probably wouldn't have gotten the same attention" from Clinton, said former U.S. congressman Bruce Morrison, also a key player in the peace process.

With Clinton focused on the issue, O'Dowd felt "we had one hand on the Holy Grail."

To get the other hand there, O'Dowd believed he needed to get prominent Irish Americans involved. In the past many had been skittish about being politically active in the north, finding it too controversial. There were Irish American backers of the Northern

Irish Aid Committee (Noraid), which supplied money to the IRA, but as the bombings continued, Noraid's support was waning. Noraid had leveraged nostalgia and Irish patriotism to raise money among immigrants, but no high-level official in the United States, Ireland, or Britain viewed the organization as a serious player in any potential peace process.

Washington couldn't solve the Northern Ireland issue on its own, but O'Dowd hoped that the United States could be an effective outside force to help the Brits and the Irish find a way to stop shooting each other.

O'Dowd's plan was to assemble a prominent group of Irish Americans, people who had close ties to Clinton, and to use them to push for peace in Northern Ireland. They would act as unofficial intermediaries between Washington, DC, and Northern Ireland and its warring parties, most notably Sinn Féin and the IRA. Through O'Dowd's connections, the group would have the blessing of both the White House and the IRA—but both sides could still officially deny that they were talking to each other.

O'Dowd's first stop was Chuck Feeney, the self-made Irish American billionaire who had cofounded duty-free shops all around the world. Feeney was one of America's most prolific philanthropists and was in the process of giving away most of his vast fortune. O'Dowd knew that Feeney, while not particularly political, was concerned about the Northern Irish Troubles—he was born in New Jersey, but his roots were in County Fermanagh in Northern Ireland. He also knew that Feeney was reclusive and avoided any public exposure.

Over dinner at P. J. Clarke's, an Irish bar in Manhattan, O'Dowd made his pitch to Feeney. He argued that the group had a chance to make history, to be honest brokers who could help defuse one of the most intractable conflicts in the world. Or they could fail miserably and publicly. Feeney didn't hesitate. O'Dowd had his first recruit, then quickly signed up Bill Flynn, who ran Mutual of America Insurance Company in New York and was well respected in the worlds of business and politics.

Most important, O'Dowd needed a trusted, well-known figure to be the effort's spokesman. O'Dowd felt that for the group to be seen as legitimate in Ireland, the leader ought to be an American with an American accent. O'Dowd immediately thought of Bruce Morrison, who already had won credibility for his Morrison visas and who had also attended Yale with Hillary Clinton and was a close friend of the first couple.

O'Dowd and Morrison had been talking about Northern Ireland for months, and Morrison had been impressed by both O'Dowd's passion and his connections. As Penn Rhodeen recounts in his 2016 book about Morrison, *Peacerunner*, Morrison was looking for a way to do something constructive in Northern Ireland. The answer, Morrison said, "was Niall thinking very big thoughts about what we could do."

Morrison later said O'Dowd's idea to make Northern Ireland an international issue on the agenda of a U.S. president "was a radical notion at the time." And his idea of creating an unorthodox group of unofficial peace envoys was equally inspired and outside-the-box. "Niall was the convener," Morrison said. "If Niall had not been there, the group wouldn't have formed."

With his group in place, O'Dowd next needed to be sure that the IRA was truly willing to get involved. He met with Ciaran Staunton, another Irishman living in the United States, who had

deep IRA and Noraid ties. Staunton said O'Dowd's plan was ambitious, but he came to believe that it could work. "When all is said
and done, there's usually a lot more said than done," Staunton said.
"Niall's not like that. He gets things done."

Staunton helped O'Dowd create his quiet channels into Sinn
Féin and the IRA itself. He helped arrange the Dublin meeting with
Ted (O'Dowd later learned his full name was Ted Howell) where
O'Dowd made his initial pitch, and Ted relayed O'Dowd's message
to Adams and top IRA leadership.

O'Dowd had first met Gerry Adams in 1983 when he interviewed him at Sinn Féin's heavily fortified headquarters on the
Falls Road in Belfast. At age thirty, O'Dowd was an eager young
journalist profiling Adams for his start-up newspaper in San Francisco, the *Irishman*. Back then, by order of the British and Irish
governments, the media was banned from even broadcasting Adams's voice. But O'Dowd thought that silencing Adams was not
smart; it offended many around the world who valued free speech.
He especially admired the United States for its commitment to free
speech and often said, "I love the First Amendment."

A few years after their first meeting, in the mid-1980s, O'Dowd
offered Adams a monthly column in his *Irish Voice*, giving the Sinn
Féin leader a way to get his message out in America. O'Dowd felt
a better-informed public was the more effective way to get past the
decades of deadlock. O'Dowd and Adams stayed in touch through
Adams's columns in the *Irish Voice*, and both men have said that
trust grew between them over the years. O'Dowd's wife, Debbie
McGoldrick, the *Voice* editor, would sometimes type up the columns Adams dictated over the phone.

By the early 1990s, O'Dowd had come to believe that Adams was sincere about trying to persuade the IRA to "give up the gun" and press for nationalist causes through peaceful means. Adams, eager to create new international pressure to find peace, saw in O'Dowd a man he could trust. "If we gave Niall a message, it would get to the appropriate people in the White House," Adams said. "I didn't have any doubt of it." O'Dowd kept Sinn Féin apprised of his progress. As an added security measure, they usually communicated in Gaelic; O'Dowd and his Sinn Féin contacts were both fluent.

Word came back to O'Dowd that they needed a current elected official as part of the group to give it more gravitas and attract more attention. So O'Dowd enlisted Boston mayor Ray Flynn, a prominent Irish American and close Clinton ally.

Now, in early 1993, with Clinton fresh in office, O'Dowd needed something from the IRA. He sent a letter via courier to Belfast explaining that his group was ready to publicly come over to Ireland and engage with Sinn Féin. But in return, they needed a sign of good faith: the IRA had to impose a weeklong cease-fire during the group's visit. Nancy Soderberg, Clinton's Deputy National Security Advisor, told O'Dowd she needed concrete evidence that the IRA was serious about working on peace.

"If we go over, and I get a cease-fire, will you take me seriously and deal with us?" he asked her.

"Prove it. Do the cease-fire, and we'll start believing you," she replied.

A week after O'Dowd sent his letter to Belfast, a man showed up at O'Dowd's New York office, handed him an envelope, and left without saying a word. The IRA had agreed: there would be a seven-day cease-fire starting on May 4, 1993.

O'Dowd put down the paper, thrilled. This was a breakthrough.

He notified the group, and they started making arrangements. O'Dowd alerted Senator Kennedy's office, which passed the news to the White House. But then, just a few days before the start of the trip, Ray Flynn, the mayor of Boston, got cold feet about the politically risky endeavor and abruptly dropped out. The plan quickly unraveled without its high-profile political face. O'Dowd thought he looked like an amateur and an idiot to the White House. His contacts in the IRA were furious, and they summoned him to Belfast to explain himself.

A week later, O'Dowd found himself sitting in the living room of an unremarkable and secret West Belfast home, facing Gerry Adams, Ted Howell, and several men he recognized as top leaders of the IRA. Adams explained that getting the IRA to agree to a cease-fire had been a monumental feat. Having the American delegation cancel was a blow that would give ammunition to factions in the IRA that opposed any peace deal.

For the next two hours, O'Dowd explained the situation as honestly as he could to the IRA men, who were clearly skeptical. "I'm sitting there with these characters, and they said, 'Are you misleading us? Are you a spy?'" O'Dowd said. "I said, 'No. I screwed up. I picked the wrong guy.'" He thought Ray Flynn had been a mistake.

In the end, Adams accepted his explanation and asked him to reschedule the trip.

In September 1993, O'Dowd had another letter from the IRA secretly pledging another weeklong cease fire. He and his core group—Feeney, the billionaire entrepreneur; Morrison, the former congressman; and Bill Flynn, the insurance executive—arrived in Dublin and met with Irish Prime Minister Albert Reynolds and U.S. Ambassador Jean Kennedy Smith, then moved on the next day to Belfast, keeping the White House quietly updated through Senator Kennedy's office.

In Belfast, the group did two things that marked a major departure: they met with Protestant Loyalist political and paramilitary groups and Sinn Féin. While O'Dowd's heart was with Sinn Féin, he also knew that any peace plan needed the blessing of the Protestant Loyalists. He knew their voices had to be heard too, so he reached out to them. He also recruited Gary McMichael, the son of a key Loyalist figure, to write articles for his newspaper. O'Dowd would later write the foreword to McMichael's book *The Ulster Voice.*

At the Sinn Féin headquarters on the Falls Road, the group attended a public meeting to hear the stories of residents of the working-class Catholic neighborhoods that made up the core Sinn Féin constituency. People told them they had faith that American involvement could finally win them some better treatment and respect. One woman spoke of how her son had been shot by the British Army, and when she was finished, she took O'Dowd by the hand and said, "Thank you for not treating us like animals."

The group then met privately with Adams and other Sinn Féin leaders and emerged feeling that the IRA was committed to seeking peace. At the end of their eight-day visit, news broke in the local press about the IRA's specific cease-fire for the American delegation. The cease-fire, the first since the 1970s, was a clear signal that IRA leaders were serious about working with the Clinton team. Though unannounced, the cease-fire was also accompanied by a specific written statement that the White House had demanded.

At first, Nancy Soderberg didn't trust O'Dowd. She wouldn't even talk directly to him. But eventually she became his primary contact in the White House during his secret peace negotiations. She came to realize that he wasn't just a messenger but the interpreter of the message—especially the signals of Gerry Adams. "One of the frustrating things about working with Adams at the time was that the language was so cautious and twisted and contorted, it often just looked like gobbledygook to me," she said. "And Niall helped peel that onion back so that you could sort of read between the layers and understand what was going on."

Soderberg came to admire O'Dowd and appreciate that he could interpret what Adams was saying, observe what was happening on the ground, and predict what was ahead. "He was absolutely correct every single time, so I got to trust him. Nothing ever leaked, so I became really quite dependent on his analysis and interpretative skills and his discretion. And it is very unusual to have an outsider play that role."

Over the next months, O'Dowd, Morrison, and their group urged the White House to have Clinton grant Adams a long-denied visa to visit the United States. There was fierce opposition from British officials and many in the United States, including most of Clinton's own national security team, who considered Adams a terrorist. O'Dowd argued that the IRA had shown good faith by agreeing to the cease-fire, and now the White House needed to offer them something. In the end, Clinton agreed to the visa, and Adams made a high-profile visit starting on February 1, 1994.

Throughout the spring and summer of 1994, O'Dowd and his group remained in close contact with Sinn Féin. They traveled to the party's annual conference in Letterkenny in the spring and met behind closed doors with Adams and other leaders. The goal was a complete, public, unequivocal cease-fire, but O'Dowd and his group knew that trying to rush the IRA into that was a waste of time. The IRA was deeply divided and supremely cautious. The tide appeared to be moving in the right direction, but it was happening slowly.

On August 10, O'Dowd received a letter from the IRA, delivered by a Sinn Féin contact, stating that the group had an "urgent need" for details of what the Americans would give the IRA in return for a cease-fire. That letter, produced on an old-fashioned printer, is the only document from the process that O'Dowd has kept for history. It included one potentially disastrous demand, a possible deal-breaker: the IRA was demanding $1 million to open a Sinn Féin office in Washington and fund its operation for the first three years.

O'Dowd panicked. He knew that visibility and legitimacy in the United States was critically important for Sinn Féin --it had to be included in the deal. So now he had forty-eight hours to come up with a million dollars.

He knew only one man who could make that happen: Chuck Feeney.

Feeney's response was what it had been every time O'Dowd asked for his help.

"Of course," he said.

O'Dowd, Morrison, and the others, in indirect collaboration with Soderberg and her White House team, drew up a document that promised U.S. business investment in Northern Ireland, regular visas for Sinn Féin leaders, and limits on the deportation of people with ties to the IRA. It also promised to permit Sinn Féin to open a U.S. office. And while Feeney didn't pay the IRA or Sinn Féin directly, he did cover the bills for their office for the next three years. O'Dowd's wife, McGoldrick, then faxed the letter off to a secret contact in Ireland.

The contact, following agreed-upon instructions, took the letter and stood on Dublin's O'Connell Bridge on a damp night. A woman eventually appeared out of the fog. "Do you think Dublin will win the game on Sunday?" That was the signal, and the courier handed over the letter without a word.

O'Dowd quickly received a written response that seemed positive: the group should be prepared to return to Belfast. The timing was unclear, so he made a phone call. "When should I take my holidays?" O'Dowd asked, a coded inquiry about when they needed to be in Belfast. "Why don't you try the last week in August," was the reply.

On August 25, the original four—O'Dowd, Morrison, Flynn, and Feeney—arrived back in Ireland, this time joined by labor union executives Joe Jamison and Bill Lenihan. The group's presence at what seemed likely to be a historic moment was reassuring to IRA leaders, who wanted to know (and wanted the world to know) that Irish America was behind them. "It reinforced the American dimension to those in the IRA army council who were about to make what was to them a momentous decision to call off their war," wrote Conor O'Clery, an *Irish Times* journalist and author of *Daring Diplomacy: Clinton's Secret Search for Peace in Ireland.*

They met Irish prime minister Reynolds, who was adamant that anything less than a permanent IRA cease-fire would be unacceptable. The group moved to Belfast and met with Adams and other top Sinn Féin leaders, expecting some sort of last-minute complications. That fear disappeared when a relaxed looking

Adams breezed into the room and said, "The army is going to call a complete cessation."

O'Dowd was jubilant but knew that until the IRA said that publicly, the deal could still fall apart. But just before noon on August 31, 1994, as O'Dowd listened to the radio while exercising in a Dublin hotel, a young woman's voice made the IRA announcement. As of midnight, "there will be a complete cessation of military operations."

O'Dowd stepped off the treadmill and broke down in tears.

"I had had just a huge amount of personal involvement," he said. "I had completely dedicated my life to this. I lost the relationship I was in at the time, and there were just an awful lot of things I put to one side for the best part of four years. It was a huge moment."

A few minutes later, O'Dowd was called to the hotel phone. It was Senator Kennedy. "Ted was like a five year old; he was so happy." Later that day, as O'Dowd waited at a television station to give an interview, Reynolds "literally bounded in and squeeze my hand so hard I thought he was going to fracture it."

The following year, Clinton made a triumphant visit to Ireland. O'Dowd trailed the president's plane on Air Force Two, with the other members of his group and Irish American leaders from across the country. Clinton spoke to more than two hundred thousand people, the crowd chanting his name at Belfast's Christmas tree lighting ceremony. He received an equally rapturous reception at an outdoor speech in Dublin. Clinton called it the "two best days of my presidency."

The euphoria did not hold. Nor did the peace. Mistrust and missteps continued, and seventeen months later the IRA resumed bombing, this time at London's Canary Wharf in 1996. More negotiations and more cease-fires followed and persistent peace talks led by former U.S. senator George Mitchell finally, in April 1998, led to the Good Friday Agreement. That deal created a peace that has held to this day, built largely on a foundation laid by Niall O'Dowd.

Adams, who in 2016 was still the president of Sinn Féin, as well as a member of the Irish Parliament, said O'Dowd's journalism, and the secret channels that he created to help kick-start the peace process, provided just the right pressure at just the right time. "I have a huge affection for him," Adams said. "He would be able to feel the pulse of what was happening in the States, and the pulse of what was happening here [in Ireland]. I cannot stress enough the very central role that he played. There probably would have been a peace process, but there certainly wouldn't have been a peace process at that time, if Niall hadn't been so centrally involved." Adams continued:

> Sometimes, and I believe this truly, one person can make a difference. It's the difference between having a good idea, and doing it. You may have a very good idea, and you may be very genuine—as genuine as Niall O'Dowd is about Ireland—but you're busy and you have responsibilities, and so on. And you might think, "Who am I? How can I do this?" It's the difference between being a dreamer and being a visionary. The visionaries deliver.

> O'Dowd, he said, delivered for Ireland.

Acknowledgments

———◆———

THIS BOOK WAS BROUGHT TO life by a great many different people to whom I am indebted.

I want to thank the following family, friends, and colleagues who, in one way or another, helped me along in this journey: Sascha Alper, Ed Beason, Veronica Brady, Joe Conason, Dan Dibble, Karen Duffy, Eamon Harrington, Shannon and Drew Hayden, Taylor Johns, Steven Johnson, Douglas Kennedy, Robert Kennedy Jr., Sheila and Chris Kennedy, Vicki Kennedy, Edward Klaris, John Lambros, Kasey Madden, Jonathan Mahler, Domenic Mastrippolito, Bridget McCarthy, Michael McDonnell, Joe McDougall, Jeanne Pepler, Robin Pogrebin, Ed Saxon, Rosie Schaap, Jeanine Shriver, Ambassador Jean Kennedy Smith, Terry Ward, and Larry Weissman.

I also want to thank:

My brother-in-law Max Kennedy for his encouragement and support, especially in the early days—when it mattered most. My former editor, now friend, Andra Miller, who was there for me too. Emma Taylor, essential in organizing Tom Hayden's work, and Tom Deignan, essential to its completion. Barbara Williams, an incredibly loving wife and friend to Tom Hayden—thank you for your trust, kindness, and direction.

My researchers, dedicated and thorough: Barbara Clark, Kathleen Geier, Michelle Hovanetz, and Alex Singal. My consulting

editors, for the invaluable advice, collaboration, and feedback: Ja-
nette Barber, Neil A. Grauer, and Jeff Swimmer. My terrific agent,
David McCormick of McCormick Literary; David always knows
just what to do. And Ed Hemingway, my friend and partner on my
last three books, for so readily offering up his beautiful illustrations. I know Ed did it for me—as well as for his mother, Valerie,
who came here from Dublin.

I want to thank Elisabeth Scharlatt, the publisher of Algonquin
Books, the remarkable leader of what is a remarkable team. This
includes Jackie Burke, Algonquin's amazing publicity manager,
along with the whole publicity and marketing group. And in particular, Betsy Gleick, my editor, whose sure hands guided this effort. Not just smart, she is at once persistent and a pleasure—a rare
combination. Thank you, Betsy, for getting us here.

My extraordinary contributors, without whom there would
simply be no book: Pierce Brosnan, Terry Golway, Tom Hayden,
Kathleen Hill, Mary Jordan and Kevin Sullivan, Jill McDonough,
Michael Moore, Rosie O'Donnell, and Mark K. Shriver. This was
hard work, and your commitment to the project and your patience
with me, especially given your own busy lives, was very moving.
You brought compassion, talent, intelligence, and courage. I hope,
holding this book in your hands, you feel it was worth all the
trouble.

On a personal note: My mother, Madelyne, my father, Ed, and
my brother, Paul, the nearest branches on my family tree, the ones
who taught me the very meaning of family. And Ethel Kennedy
and my Kennedy in-laws, who came here from Counties Cavan,
Cork, Limerick, and Wexford, for showing me, in word and deed,
what service means.

And to my wife Rory: I am lucky to have a partner whom I love so much and whom, after all these years side by side in both life and work, I so admire. To our children, Georgia, Bridget, and Zachary: when it's more fully your turn, here in America, I know that you'll do your best—and undoubtedly better than we.

Bibliography

THE REVOLUTIONARY: THOMAS ADDIS EMMET

Books

Anbinder, Tyler. *City of Dreams: The 400-Year Epic History of Immigrant New York*. Boston: Houghton Mifflin Harcourt, 2016.

Bayor, Ronald H., and Timothy J. Meagher. *The New York Irish*. Baltimore: Johns Hopkins University Press, 1997.

Bourke, Richard, and Ian McBride. *The Princeton History of Modern Ireland*. Lawrenceville: Princeton University Press, 2016.

Brundage, David T. *Irish Nationalists in America: The Politics of Exile, 1798–1998*. New York: Oxford University Press, 2016.

Burrows, Edwin G., and Mike Wallace. *Gotham: A History of New York City to 1898*. New York: Oxford University Press, 2006.

Campbell, Malcolm. *Ireland's New Worlds: Immigrants, Politics, and Society in the United States and Australia, 1815–1922*. Madison: University of Wisconsin Press, 2008

Elliott, Marianne. *Wolfe Tone*. Liverpool: Liverpool University Press, 2012.

Emmet, Thomas Addis. *Incidents of My Life: Thomas Addis Emmet*. New York: G. P. Putnam's Sons, 1911.

———. *Memoir of Thomas Addis and Robert Emmet: With Their Ancestors and Immediate Family*. New York: Emmet Press, 1915.

Flanagan, Thomas. *The Year of the French*. New York: New York Review Books Classics, 2004.

Ford, Clyde W. *The Hero with an African Face: Mythic Wisdom of Traditional Africa*. New York: Bantam, 2000.

Foster, Robert F. *Modern Ireland: 1600–1972*. London: Penguin Books, 1990.

Geoghegan, Patrick M. *Robert Emmet: A Life*. Montreal: McGill-Queen's University Press, 2002.

Glazier, Michael. *The Encyclopedia of the Irish in America*. Notre Dame, IN: University of Notre Dame Press, 1999.

Golway, Terry. *For the Cause of Liberty: A Thousand Years of Ireland's Heroes*. New York: Simon & Schuster, 2001.

———. *Irish Rebel: John Devoy and America's Fight for Ireland's Freedom*. New York: St. Martin's Press, 1998.

Haines, Charles G. *Memoir of Thomas Addis Emmet*. New York: G. & C. & H. Carvill, 1829.

Hayden, Tom. *Irish on the Inside: In Search of the Soul of Irish America*. London: Verso, 2003.

Kinealy, Christine. *New History of Ireland*. Stroud: History Press, 2008.

King, Rufus, and Charles R. King. *The Life and Correspondence of Rufus King*. New York: Putnam, 1894.

Lecky, William E. H. *A History of Ireland in the Eighteenth Century*. Cambridge,UK: Cambridge University Press, 2011.

Madden, Richard Robert. *The Life and Times of Robert Emmet*. New York: P. M. Haverty, 1857.

———. *The United Irishmen, Their Lives and Times*. London: J. Madden, 1842.

Stephen, Small. *Political Thought in Ireland 1776–1798: Republicanism, Patriotism, and Radicalism*. Oxford: Oxford University Press, 2002.

Tone, Theobald W., and William T. W. Tone. *The Life of Theobald Wolfe Tone*. London: Whittaker, Treacher, and Arnot, 1831.

Wilson, David A. *United Irishmen, United States: Immigrant Radicals in the Early Republic*. Ithaca, NY: Cornell University Press, 1998.

Yanoso, Nicole A. *The Irish and the American Presidency*. New Brunswick, NJ: Transaction Publishers, 2016.

Magazines

Schlesinger, Arthur, Jr. "The United Irishmen and their American Legacy." *Irish America*, February/March 2016.

Websites

Trinity College Dublin. "Ireland in Rebellion: 1782-1916." YouTube .https://www.youtube.com/playlist?list=PL55XqDjybyL _Hta7QSfyoljqYL3iR7YGS.

THE CARETAKER: MARGERT HAUGHERY

Books

Margaret of New Orleans. Edited and compiled by a Friend of the Family. New Orleans: 1913.

Martinez, Raymond J. *The Immortal Margaret Haughery*. New Orleans: Hope Publications, 1956.

Strousse, Flora. *Margaret Haughery: Bread Woman of New Orleans*. New York: P. J. Kenedy, 1961.

Whyte, Robert. *The Ocean Plague: Or, a Voyage to Quebec in an Irish Emigrant Vessel: Embracing a Quarantine at Grosse Isle in 1847: with Notes Illustrative of the Ship-pestilence of that Fatal Year*. Boston: Coolidge and Wiley, 1848.

Widmer, Mary L. *Margaret, Friend of Orphans*. Gretna, LA: Pelican Publishing Company, 1996.

Newspapers

Daily Picuyune. "Margaret." Feb. 10, 1882.

Theses

Luck, Katharine A. "Finding Margaret Haughery: The Forgotten and Remembered Lives of New Orleans's "Bread Woman" In the

Nineteenth and Twentieth Centuries." Dissertation, University of
New Orleans, 2014.

Websites

Carrigallen.com. "Margaret Gaffney: The Bread Woman of New Orleans." http://www.carrigallen.com/margaretgaffney.htm.
Kelley, Laura D. "Margaret Haughery." KnowLouisiana.org. http://www
.knowlouisiana.org/entry/margaret-haughery.
Langan, Sheila. "Ireland, New Orleans, the Famine and 200 years of history." IrishCentral.com. http://www.irishcentral.com/culture/ireland
-and-new-orleans-to-celebrate-200-years-of-shared-history-photos.
Margaret of New Orleans Birthplace. "Margaret's Life." http://margarets
birthplace.com/Margaret.html.
Villarrubia, Eleonore. "An Indomitable Woman: Margaret Haughery,
The Breadwoman of New Orleans." Catholicism.org. http://catholicism
.org/an-indomitable-woman-margaret-haughery-the-breadwoman
-of-new-orleans-2.html.

THE ORGANIZER: MARY "MOTHER" JONES

Books

Atkinson, Linda. *Mother Jones, the Most Dangerous Woman in America*.
New York: Crown Publishers, 1978.
Donnelly, James S., and Samuel Clark. *Irish Peasants: Violence and
Political Unrest, 1780–1914*. Madison: University of Wisconsin Press,
2003.
Foner, Philip S. *Mother Jones Speaks: Speeches and Writings of a Work-
ing-Class Fighter*. New York: Pathfinder, 1983.
Gorn, Elliott J. *Mother Jones: The Most Dangerous Woman in America*.
New York: Hill and Wang, 2001.
Jones, Mary Harris. *Autobiography of Mother Jones*. Chicago: C. H. Kerr
& Company, 1925.

Macintyre, Angus D. *The Liberator: Daniel O'Connell and the Irish Party, 1830–1847*. London: Hamilton, 1965.

Newspapers

New York Times. "Haywood Comes Out against Socialism; Tells Industrial Commission It Is Wholly Incapable of Bettering the Labor World; Mother Jones Heard, Too." May 13, 1915.
———. "Mother Jones Asks Aid for Labor Men." May 15, 1915.
———. "Mother Jones Commends Soviets." Jan. 10, 1921.
———. "Mother Jones Dies; Led Mine Workers." Dec. 1, 1930.

THE SOLDIER: ALBERT D. J. CASHIER

Books

Blanton, DeAnne, and Lauren M. Cook. *They Fought Like Demons: Women Soldiers in the American Civil War*. Stroud: Sutton, 2005.
Groom, Winston. *Vicksburg, 1863*. New York: Alfred A. Knopf, 2009.
Tóibín, Colm, and Diarmaid Ferriter. *The Irish Famine: A Documentary*. London: Profile Books, 2001.
Wood, Wales W. *A History of the Ninety-Fifth Regiment, Illinois Infantry Volunteers*. Belvidere, IL: Boone County Historical Society, 1993.

Correspondence

Breuer, Jan, and Jackie Rever. Correspondence with author. March–April 2016.
Hodgers, Don. Correspondence with author. March–April 2016.
O'Donnell, Cheryl. Correspondence with author. March–April 2016.

Journals

Clausius, Gerhard P. "The Little Soldier of the 95th: Albert D.J. Cashier." *Journal of the Illinois State Historical Society* 51, no. 4 (1958).

Davis, Rodney O. "Private Albert Cashier As Regarded by His/Her Comrades." *Illinois Historical Journal* 82, no. 2 (1989).

Faulkner, Pádraig. "A County Louth Farm on the Eve of and During the Famine: Burren Farm Accounts' Book, 1839 to 1848." *Journal of the County Louth Archaeological and Historical Society* 23, no. 4 (1996).

Kessel, Reuben A., and Armen A. Alchian. "Real Wages in the North During the Civil War: Mitchell's Data Reinterpreted." *The Journal of Law and Economics* 2 (1959).

Petterchak, Janice. "A Conversation on History." *Dispatch from the Illinois State Historical Society* 4, no. 13 (1991).

Newspapers

Chicago Tribune. "Find Old Soldier Is Just a Woman." May 4, 1913.

Conklin, Mike. "Jennie Came Marching Home: Downstate Women Battle to Preserve the Memory of a Civil War Soldier Who Spent Most of Her Life Posing as a Man." *Chicago Tribune*, Sept. 5, 2001.

National Tribune. "Served as a Man." Nov. 25, 1915.

Omaha World-Herald. "Ives Identifies the Woman Veteran of the War." May 20, 1913.

———. "Omahan Tells of Girl Who Fought as a Man." May 28, 1921.

Theses

Lannon, Mary C., and Lucy L. Tasher. "Albert D.J. Cashier and the Ninety-Fifth Illinois Infantry (1844–1915)." Dissertation, Illinois State University, 1969.

Archives

AGO, carded medical records, 95th Illinois, cards for Cashier, Albert, RG 94. National Archives and Records Administration, Washington, DC.

AGO, CMSR, 95th Illinois Infantry, Cashier, Albert D. J., RG 94. National Archives and Records Administration, Washington, DC.

THE MUCKRAKER: SAMUEL S. MCCLURE

Books

Lyon, Peter. *Success Story: The Life and Times of S.S. McClure*. New York: Scribner, 1963.

McClure, S. S., and Willa Cather. *The Autobiography of S. S. McClure*. Lincoln: University of Nebraska Press, 1997.

Archives

McClure Publishing Company Archives. Special Collections, University of Delaware Library, Newark, DE.

Websites

Encyclopedia.com. "Samuel Sidney McClure." http://www.encyclopedia .com/people/literature-and-arts/journalism-and-publishing -biographies/samuel-sidney-mcclure.

Spartacus-educational.com. "Samuel McClure." http://spartacus -educational.com/USAmcclure.htm.

THE FATHER: FATHER EDWARD J. FLANAGAN

Books

Curtis, James. *Spencer Tracy: A Biography*. New York: Knopf, 2011.

Ivey, James R. *Boys Town: The Constant Spirit*. Chicago: Arcadia Publishing, 2000.

Lonnborg, Barbara, and Thomas J. Lynch. *Father Flanagan's Legacy: Hope and Healing for Children*. Boys Town, NE: Boys Town Press, 2003.

Oursler, Fulton, and Will Oursler. *Father Flanagan of Boys Town*. Garden City, NY: Doubleday, 1949.

Reilly, Hugh J., and Kevin Warneke. *Father Flanagan of Boys Town: A Man of Vision*. Boys Town, NE: Boys Town Press, 2008.

Stevens, Clifford. *I Remember Father Flanagan*. Bloomington, IN: iUniverse, 2013.

Magazines

Doherty, Edward. "The Boy Who Shot His Father." *Liberty*, Oct. 9, 1937.

Levy, Henry W. "Henry Monsky: 1890-1947." *American Jewish Yearbook* 49 (1948).

Lewis, Frederick. "Spencer Tracy Conquers Himself." *Liberty*, Oct. 9, 1937.

Review of *Suffer the Little Children: The Inside Story of Ireland's Industrial Schools. Publishers Weekly*, Apr. 2, 2001.

Newspapers

Biga, Leo Adam. "Flanagan-Monsky Example of Social Justice and Interfaith Harmony Still Shows the Way 60 Years Later." *Jewish Press*, Feb. 15, 2008.

Kelly, Jacques. "A brief meeting with mentor of Babe Ruth." *Baltimore Sun*, Feb. 6, 1995.

Websites

Adomites, Paul, and Saul Wisnia. "Babe Ruth Enters St. Mary's Industrial School for Boys." Howstuffworks.com. http://entertainment .howstuffworks.com/babe-ruth2.htm.

Biography.com. "Babe Ruth." http://www.biography.com/people/babe -ruth-9468009.

Boys Town. "Hall of History." http://www.boystown.org/about/visit -the-village/tours/hall-of-history.

———. "Helping Children & Families Across America." http://www .boystown.org/locations.

Father Flanagan League. "Father Flanagan's Story." http://www.father flanagan.org/biography.php.

German American Society. "Our History." http://www.germanamerican society.org/about-us/our-history/.

History.com. "Japanese American Relocation." http://www.history.com /topics/world-war-ii/japanese-american-relocation.

Social Welfare History Project. "Father Edward J. Flanagan (1886–1948): Catholic Priest and Founder of Boys Town, Omaha, NE." http://socialwelfare.library.vcu.edu//people/flanagan-father-edward-j/.

St. Joseph Seminary, Dunwoodie. Home page. http://www.dunwoodie.edu/.

Speeches

Flanagan, Edward. "To Cure, Not to Punish." Presented at the National Conference of Catholic Charities.

THE DIRECTOR: REX INGRAM

Books

O'Leary, Liam. *Rex Ingram: Master of the Silent Cinema*. New York: Barnes & Noble Imports, 1980.

Barton, Ruth. *Rex Ingram: Visionary Director of the Silent Screen*. Lexington: University Press of Kentucky, 2014.

Magazines

Askari, Kevah. "Art School Cinema: Rex Ingram and the Lessons of the Studio." *Film History* 26, no. 2 (2014).

Grantham, Bill. "The Silent Master: Rex Ingram." *Irish America*, Aug./Sept. 2012.

Websites

Trinity College Department of Film Studies. "Rex Ingram: 1893–1950." https://www.tcd.ie/film/rexingram/.

THE AUTHOR: MAEVE BRENNAN

Books

Bourke, Angela. *Maeve Brennan: Homesick at The New Yorker*. Berkeley: Counterpoint Press, 2016.

Brennan, Maeve. *The Long-Winded Lady: Notes from The New Yorker.* Dublin: Stinging Fly Press, 2017.

———. *The Rose Garden: Short Stories.* Washington, DC: Counterpoint, 2001.

———. *The Springs of Affection.* Dublin: Stinging Fly Press, 2016.

———. *The Visitor.* London: Atlantic Books, 2002.

Enright, Anne. Introduction to *The Springs of Affection,* by Maeve Brennan. Dublin: Stinging Fly Press, 2016.

McKeon, Belinda. Introduction to *The Long-Winded Lady: Notes from The New Yorker,* by Maeve Brennan. Dublin: Stinging Fly Press, 2017.

Moylan, Clare. Introduction. *The Visitor,* by Maeve Brennan, London: Atlantic Books, 2002.

Magazines

Hawthorne, Mary. "A Traveller in Residence." *London Review of Books* 19, no. 22 (Nov. 13, 1997).

THE PEACEMAKER: NIALL O'DOWD

Books

O'Clery, Conor. *Daring Diplomacy: Clinton's Secret Search for Peace in Ireland.* Boulder, CO: Roberts Rinehart Publishers, 1997.

O'Dowd, Niall. *An Irish Voice.* Dublin: O'Brien, 2010.

Rhodeen, Penn. *Peacerunner.* Dallas: BenBella Books, 2016.

Contributors

———◆———

PIERCE BROSNAN is an actor, film producer, artist, environmentalist, and two-time Golden Globe Award nominee. Irish born, Brosnan moved to Los Angeles in 1982 to star in the popular NBC television series *Remington Steele*. In the 1990s, he reinvigorated the popularity of the Bond franchise in box-office blockbusters *Goldeneye, Tomorrow Never Dies, The World Is Not Enough*, and *Die Another Day*. Brosnan's production company, Irish DreamTime, has produced eleven films to date, including *The November Man, The Matador, Evelyn,* and *The Thomas Crown Affair*. An avid painter, Brosnan will exhibit his work in 2018. He was born in County Meath.

TERRY GOLWAY is a senior editor at *Politico* and the author of several books, including *Washington's General, For the Cause of Liberty*, and, most recently, *Machine Made: Tammany Hall and the Creation of Modern American Politics*. A journalist for more than forty years, Golway is a former member of the editorial board of the *New York Times* and former city editor of the *New York Observer*. He has taught at the New School, New York University, and Kean University. Golway traces his roots back to County Donegal.

TOM HAYDEN was an activist, writer, and politician. A legend of the sixties, having drafted *The Port Huron Statement* at age twenty-one, he was a founder of Students for a Democratic Society, a Freedom Rider, a community organizer in Newark, a leader in the Vietnam antiwar movement, and eventually a state senator and assemblyman in the California

State Legislature for eighteen years. The author and editor of over twenty books, including the recently published *Hell No: The Forgotten Power of the Vietnam Peace Movement,* Hayden was on the editorial board and a columnist for the *Nation* magazine and was regularly published in the *New York Times,* the *Guardian,* the *Los Angeles Times,* the *San Francisco Chronicle,* the *Boston Globe,* and weekly alternatives. He was a leading voice in social movements for over fifty years. Hayden's family came from Counties Armagh, Cavan, Louth, and Monaghan.

KATHLEEN HILL is a novelist and teaches in the MFA program at Sarah Lawrence College. Hill's novel *Still Waters in Niger* was nominated for the International IMPAC Dublin Literary Award and named a Notable Book of the Year by the *New York Times,* the *Los Angeles Times,* and the *Chicago Tribune.* The French translation, *Eaux Tranquilles,* was shortlisted for the Prix Femina Etranger. *Who Occupies This House,* a second novel, was named an Editors' Choice at the *New York Times.* Hill's work has appeared in *Best American Short Stories, Best Spiritual Writing, Pushcart Prize XXV,* and *The Pushcart Book of Short Stories.* A memoir, *She Read to Us in the Late Afternoons: A Life in Novels,* was published in 2017. Hill's family emigrated from Counties Clare and Roscommon.

MARY JORDAN and KEVIN SULLIVAN are *Washington Post* journalists who have traveled the world as the *Post*'s bureau chiefs in Tokyo, Mexico City, and London. They won the 2003 Pulitzer Prize for International Reporting for coverage of the Mexican criminal justice system—one of only two married couples ever to win a journalism Pulitzer. They have also written two books: *The Prison Angel* and the *New York Times* #1 bestseller *Hope: A Memoir of Survival in Cleveland.* They were contributing writers on *Trump Revealed,* a 2016 *Washington Post* biography of Donald Trump. Jordan's parents emigrated from County Mayo. Sullivan's family comes from County Cork.

JILL MCDONOUGH is a poet and professor in the MFA program at UMass Boston. The author of three collections, *Habeas Corpus* (2008), *Oh, James!* (2012), and *Where You Live* (2012), McDonough is the winner of a 2014 Lannan Literary Fellowship and three Pushcart prizes and the recipient of fellowships from the National Endowment for the Arts, the Fine Arts Work Center, and the New York Public Library. Her work has appeared in *Poetry*, *Slate*, the *Nation*, the *Threepenny Review*, and *Best American Poetry*. McDonough's fourth and fifth poetry collections, *Reaper* and *Here All Night*, are forthcoming. McDonough's family comes from County Cork.

MICHAEL MOORE is an Academy Award–winning American filmmaker, bestselling author, and renowned political commentator and activist. He is the director and producer of numerous documentaries, including *Roger & Me*, *Bowling for Columbine*, *Fahrenheit 9/11*, *Sicko*, *Capitalism: A Love Story*, *Where to Invade Next*, and *Michael Moore in TrumpLand*. Moore has also produced and starred in the TV series *TV Nation* and *The Awful Truth*. His bestselling books include *Stupid White Men*, *Downsize This*, *Dude, Where's My Country*, and *Here Comes Trouble*. Moore's family hails from Counties Cork, Tipperary, and Waterford.

ROSIE O'DONNELL is a comedian, actress, author, and television personality. As host of NBC's variety daytime television show *The Rosie O'Donnell Show*, Rosie won numerous Emmy awards and left a mark on American television. She joined the cast of ABC's *The View* in 2006 and a year later went on to write her second memoir, *Celebrity Detox*. In 2009, O'Donnell shook the airwaves with her radio show, *Rosie Radio*. In addition to her work in entertainment, she launched the nonprofit Rosie's Theater Kids, formerly known as Rosie's Broadway Kids, which helps children realize their potential through the arts. Rosie's family is from County Tyrone.

MARK K. SHRIVER is senior vice president of U.S. programs and advocacy at Save the Children and president of the organization's political advocacy arm, Save the Children Action Network. Shriver created the Choice Program and is a former Maryland state legislator. His latest book, *Pilgrimage: My Search for the Real Pope Francis*, was published in November 2016. His *New York Times* and *Washington Post* bestselling memoir, *A Good Man: Rediscovering My Father, Sargent Shriver*, was published in June 2012 and received a 2013 Christopher Award. Shriver's family is from Counties Cork, Cavan, Limerick, and Wexford.

ADDITIONAL

TOM DEIGNAN is the author of *Coming to America: Irish Americans* and served as a contributing writer for the book *Irish American Chronicle*. He is a columnist for the *Irish Voice* newspaper and *Irish America* magazine. His writing has appeared in newspapers such as the *New York Times*, the *Washington Post*, and the *Sunday Business Post* (Ireland), as well as magazines such as *Commonweal*, *America*, and *Publishers Weekly*. Deignan has taught history, cinema, and English at CUNY, St. John's University, and Bowling Green State University. His family comes from Counties Cork and Roscommon.

ILLUSTRATOR

EDWARD HEMINGWAY has written and illustrated several children's books, including *Bad Apple: A Tale of Friendship*, *Field Guide to the Grumpasaurus,* and *Tough Cookie*. He is the illustrator of the books *Hemingway & Bailey's Bartending Guide to Great American Writers*, *Of All the Gin Joints: Stumbling through Hollywood History*, and the children's book *Tiny Pie*, all three written by Mark Bailey. Hemingway's mother emigrated from Dublin.